HOW TO EAT IN THE WOODS

HOW TO EAT IN THE WOODS

A complete guide to foraging, trapping, fishing, and finding sustenance in the wild

BRADFORD ANGIER

with Christopher Nyerges, Gregory J. Davenport,
Jon Young, and Tiffany Morgan

Black Dog & Leventhal Publishers
Hachette Book Group
1290 Avenue of the Americas
New York, NY 10104

www.hachettebookgroup.com
www.blackdogandleventhal.com

First Edition: March 2016

Black Dog & Leventhal Publishers is an imprint of Hachette Books, a division of Hachette Book Group.
The Black Dog & Leventhal Publishers name and logo are trademarks of Hachette Book Group, Inc.

The Hachette Speakers Bureau provides a wide range of authors for speaking events. To find out more, go to www.HachetteSpeakersBureau.com or call (866) 376-6591.

The publisher is not responsible for websites (or their content) that are not owned by the publisher.

Cover and interior design by Red Herring Design

Library of Congress Cataloging-in-Publication Data

Names: Angier, Bradford, author.
Title: How to eat in the woods : a complete guide to foraging, trapping, fishing, and finding sustenance in the wild / by Bradford Angier, Christopher Nyerges, Gregory J. Davenport, Jon Young, and Tiffany Morgan.
Description: First edition. | New York, NY : Black Dog & Leventhal, 2016.
Identifiers: LCCN 2015045594| ISBN 9781631910128 (hardback) | ISBN 9780316353557 (ebook)
Subjects: LCSH: Cooking (Wild foods) | Wild plants, Edible. | Hunting. | Wilderness survival. | Outdoor life. | BISAC: SPORTS & RECREATION / Outdoor Skills. | SPORTS & RECREATION / Hunting. | NATURE / Reference.
Classification: LCC TX823 .A485 2016 | DDC 641.3/03—dc23 LC record available at http://lccn.loc.gov/2015045594

ISBN: 978-1-631-91012-8

Printed in United States of America

LSC-C

10 9 8 7 6 5 4 3

Introduction
The Need for Food

THERE ARE MANY REASONS FOR WANTING TO understand how to eat in the woods. Some readers may wish to take advantage of the bounty all around them and want to enter a nearby forest with the intent of finding their next meal. Others may want to understand what to do should they become lost or stranded in the woods. Thousands of North America's millions of annually licensed fishermen and hunters do become lost each year, many fatally. Yet almost invariably, where such individuals suffer and all too often succumb to starvation or exposure, wild food is free for the picking, meat is free for the taking, and fire may be made.

You may be in an automobile that is stalled by mishap or storm in an unsettled area, a not uncommon occurrence that frequently results in unnecessary hardship and tragedy. Perhaps you'll be a passenger in an aircraft that has to make a forced landing. Perhaps you'll be shipwrecked.

It may even happen that you and yours will one day be compelled to seek sanctuary in the wilderness because of threats to civilization itself—an atom bomb catastrophe or the even more terrible microscopic foes of germ warfare.

"Man's capacities have never been measured; nor are we to judge what we can do by any precedents, so little has been tried," Thoreau pointed out. "What people say you can not do, you try and find you can."

It is the task of another book to explore how to survive such disaster. The intent of this volume is to use the ways of living off the land discussed herein as a foundation for ingenuity and common sense. This will allow anybody who suddenly finds themselves dependent upon their own resources to stay alive. The wilderness is too big to fight. Yet for those of us who can take advantage of what it freely offers, nature will furnish every necessity. The following pages focus on the necessities of food and water.

WILD FOODS Some of the best foods in the world are free. Long before we thought of raising them in our gardens and on our farms and ranches, all our commonest fruits and vegetables were growing wild.

Wild foods have always been important in this young country. The Pilgrims during their first desperate winter derived considerable nourishment from groundnuts, which are similar to small potatoes. California's forty-niners, plagued by scurvy because of the scarcity of food in some of the gold camps, were introduced to miner's lettuce by American Indians and the Spanish. Farther north, scurvy grass performed a similar function, both preventing and curing the vitamin-deficiency disease among early frontiersmen. When regular rations on the Lewis and Clark expedition had to be reduced to one biscuit a day, it was the sweet yellow fruit of the papaw that kept the explorers going.

Even today, in this age of space flight and split atoms, sustenance tasty enough to satisfy us in times of plenty and nourishing enough to keep us healthy if survival ever becomes a problem grows free for the taking in yards, vacant lots, and fields, along roadsides and seashores, on mesas, stream banks, and lake edges, and within marshes and sequestered woodlands— ready and waiting for those who recognize the bounties they hold.

It's easy to avoid picking any of the limited number of poisonous wild plants in North America just by positively identifying everything before you pick it—and this book, with its detailed descriptions and drawings, not only affords ample means for doing so, but also eliminates borderline plants that might reasonably cause confusion. Start with only a few wild edibles if you want—perhaps with those you've already known for years, although maybe not as foods. Each year, add a few more.

What hobby can yield the same amount of pure and vigorous pleasure with so little outlay, and such delicious returns, as the gathering of wild foods? When you become interested in them, each excursion outdoors is transformed from a purposeless stroll to an eager, rewarding quest. Each trip becomes an opportunity for making new wild edible acquaintances and enjoying hours of stimulating exhilaration.

Readers who prepare and sample even a few of the wild delicacies discussed in this book will be well on their way not only to exciting new adventures in gourmet dining but also to accumulating knowledge that can make the difference between life and death in an unforeseen emergency.

WHEN YOU NEED FOOD

Starvation is as awful as most of us would expect. The body becomes auto-cannibalistic after a few foodless hours. The carbohydrates in the system are devoured first. The fats follow.

This might not be too disagreeable, inasmuch as diets seek to accomplish much the same result, but then proteins from muscles and tendons are consumed to maintain the dwindling strength their loss more gravely weakens.

No reasonable nourishment should therefore be scorned if one needs food. Some arctic explorers, including John Richardson, John Franklin, and members of their parties, lived for weeks and sometimes months almost entirely on the lichen known as rock tripe. Wild turnips kept up John Colter's strength when the mountain man made his notable escape from Blackfoot Indians. Beaver meat was a main item on the menu while Samuel Black explored the Finlay River of western Canada.

There is no need to explain why, if any of us are ever stranded and hungry in the wilderness, we will want to start searching for food while our strength is still near its maximum.

UNDERSTANDING YOUR OPTIONS

You can, with relatively few exceptions, eat anything that crawls, swims, walks, or flies. The first obstacle is overcoming your natural aversion to a particular food source. Historically, people in starvation situations have resorted to eating everything imaginable for nourishment. A person who ignores an otherwise healthy food source due to a personal bias, or because he feels it is unappetizing, is risking his own survival. Although it may prove difficult at first, a survivor must eat what is available to maintain his health. The salad plants and potherbs growing wild on this continent are so abundant that when one stays hungry for very long in the silent spaces it is not always with good reason.

Using our hard-earned money, we purchase from stores the food that fuels our body, never understanding where it comes from or how it is procured. What would we do if the stores no longer existed?

The first 22-day trip I took to the woods I lost 25 pounds. The head-high snow and harsh weather drained my energy and left me feeling weak. The demands of my training along with a limited food supply showed me how harsh living in Mother Nature could be. I drank pine needle tea and ate the meaty cambium found between a tree's bark and inner wood. I longed for a pizza or burger. After several days of this I realized that I controlled my destiny and if I wanted the valuable nutrients nature could provide I'd have to pay closer attention to the vegetation, bugs, and animals around me. When I finally snared a squirrel it not only provided me with a welcome meal but also lifted my spirits about my ability to survive.

—*Gregory J. Davenport*

FOOD PREJUDICES

Few will disagree, at least when the moment of decision is at hand, that there is a point where luxuries as such become relatively unimportant. One of life's luxuries that we esteem most highly is the freedom to indulge our taste buds. Our taste prejudices, a better understanding of which may one day prove beneficial, are commonly based on two factors.

First, there is a human tendency to look down upon certain foods as being beneath one's social station. Where grouse have been particularly thick in the Northeast, I've seen them scorned among backwoodsmen as a "poor man's dish." The same season in the Northwest, where there happened to be a scarcity of grouse but numerous hares, the former were esteemed while I heard habitants apologizing for having rabbits in their pots. As it is everywhere in such matters, the lower the designated station of the creature, the more prejudiced against eating it the locals are.

Second, it is natural to like the food to which we have become accustomed. We in the United States and Canada have our wheat. The Mexican has his corn, the Asian his rice. These grains we like also, but it might seem a hardship to have to eat them every day as we do wheat bread.

Our fastidiousness, too, is perhaps repelled by the idea of a Polynesian islander eating freshly caught raw flesh, although we may enjoy it in such preparations as sushi and beef carpaccio. The Inuit enjoy fish mellowed by age. Many of us regard as choice some particularly moldy, odoriferous cheeses.

A RULE FOR SURVIVAL

Although it is true that under ideal conditions the human body can sometimes fend off starvation for upward of two months by living on its own tissues, it is equally certain that such auto-cannibalism is seldom necessary anywhere in the North American wilderness.

A good rule is not to pass up any reasonable food sources if we are ever in need. There are many dead men who, through ignorance or fastidiousness, did.

FOOD AND NUTRITION

The value of food—as a source of power and warmth—is measured by its nutritional benefit. Nutrition is a somewhat imprecise science, but everyone agrees that a shortage of nutrients can cause energy slumps that bring early fatigue, lassitude, mind-numbness, and a predisposition for injury. Start every trip by planning to eat a nutritionally sound diet, balancing the best foods with what is practical to carry into the wild.

The most important element of good nutrition is water. Beyond this, there are three sources of energizing foods: carbohydrates, fats, and, to some extent, proteins. Although all foods must be digested into simple compounds before they can be burned for power, carbohydrates (sugars and starches) are digested most quickly and easily. Simple carbohydrates (simple sugars, such as granulated sugar, brown sugar, honey, and molasses) are small molecular units that break down very fast, entering the bloodstream soon after you eat them. You get an energy boost right away, but most sugars are burned so quickly that energy levels can suddenly fall below your starting point if all you eat is simple carbohydrates. Therefore, complex carbohydrates (strings of simple sugars called starches, such as pasta, grains, fruits, and starchy vegetables) need to be a major portion of your diet. Being a more complex molecular unit, starches break down more slowly, providing power for the long haul. Simple sugars, in other words, are like kindling for a fire, and starches are the big, fat logs.

Fat is so important that your body will manufacture it from carbohydrates and proteins if you run short. Fats (cheese, nuts, butter, peanut butter, meat) break down very slowly in the digestive process, so more time is required for them to provide energy. That's a good thing when you need a steady source of energy over an extended period, such as long nights in the sleeping bag. But if you're used to eating a low-fat diet, add fats slowly to allow your digestive system to adjust.

Proteins are made up of amino acids, and amino acids are the basic substance of human tissue. Proteins (meat, milk products, eggs, cheese, seeds, nuts, whole grains) are not a primary energy source, but your body will use them if nothing else is available or if you exercise for a long time. But because tissue is continually lost and replaced (and new tissue is built after you exercise), proteins are essential. All the amino acids are synthesized by your body except for eight, which have to be eaten. A "complete protein" has all eight of these amino acids.

If you eat a variety of foods from all three sources—carbohydrates, fats, and proteins—and enough of it, you'll get not only the nutrition you need but also the vitamins and minerals necessary for health and performance.

FIVE BASIC FOOD GROUPS

One of the biggest problems with long-term survival is meeting your nutritional requirements. Many backcountry enthusiasts focus on meat as their main source of food and often overlook all the other supplies Mother Nature has to provide. The ideal diet has five basic food groups:

1. **Carbohydrates:** easily digested food that provides rapid energy; most often found in fruits, vegetables, and whole grains.

2. **Fats:** slowly digested food that provides long-lasting energy that is normally utilized once the carbohydrates are gone; most often found in butter, cheese, oils, nuts, eggs, and animal fats. In cold environments it isn't uncommon for the natives to eat fats before bed, believing they will help keep them warm throughout the night.

3. **Protein:** helps with the building of body cells; most often found in fish, meat, poultry, and blood.

4.. **Vitamins:** provide no calories but aid in the body's daily function and growth. Vitamins occur in most foods and when you maintain a well-balanced diet you will rarely become depleted.

5. **Minerals:** provide no calories but aid with building and repairing the skeletal system and regulating the body's normal growth. As with vitamins these needs are met when a well-balanced diet is followed. In addition to food, minerals are often present in our water.

The five major food groups and a sixth "use sparingly group" make up your basic dietary regimen:

- **Bread, cereal, rice, and pasta group**—six to eleven servings a day.
- **Vegetable group**—three to five servings a day.
- **Fruit group**—two to four servings a day.
- **Meat, poultry, fish, dry beans, eggs, and nuts group**— two to three servings a day.
- **Milk and cheese group**—two to three servings a day.
- **Fats, oils, and sweets**—use sparingly.

No one group is more important than the other—you need them all for good health. A healthy diet begins with plenty of grains, generous amounts of vegetables and fruits, and a smaller amount of protein and dairy products.

AVOIDING SCURVY

Scurvy has gathered more explorers, pioneers, trappers, and prospectors to their fathers than can be reckoned, for it is a debilitating killer whose lethal subtleties through the centuries have too often been misinterpreted and misunderstood.

Scurvy, which is characterized in its early stages by fatigue and bleeding from gums and mucous membranes, is now known to be a deficiency disease. If you have it, taking vitamin C into your system will cure you. Eating a little vitamin C regularly will, indeed, keep you from having scurvy in the first place.

Fresh meat will both prevent and cure scurvy. So will fresh fish. So will fresh fruits and vegetables, wild or otherwise. So will lime juice and lemon juice, but, no matter how sour, only if they too are fresh. The vitamin C in all these is lessened and eventually destroyed by oxidation, by age, and, incidentally, by salt.

FREE VITAMINS

Survival Tips

If you don't have water, don't eat! It takes water to process food, and without water to replace what is lost, you'll accelerate the dehydration process.

Overcome food aversions. If you can't stomach eating a bug, cook it in a stew. In a survival setting bugs may be your only source of carbohydrates, protein, and fats.

Avoid mushrooms. Mushrooms have virtually no nutritional value, and since so many are poisonous, the risk is not worth the benefit.

Spruce tea made by steeping fresh evergreen needles in water will be as potent with the both preventative and curative ascorbic acid (vitamin C) as ordinary orange juice. You can get this vitamin even more directly by chewing the tender new needles, whose starchy green tips are particularly pleasant to eat in the spring.

HOW RABBIT STARVATION REALLY HAPPENS

A man can have all the rabbit meat he wants to eat and still perish. So-called rabbit starvation, as a matter of fact, is particularly well known in the Far North.

An exclusive diet of any lean meat, of which rabbit is a practical example, will cause digestive upset and diarrhea. Eating more and more rabbit, as one is compelled to do because of the increasing uneasiness of hunger, will only worsen the condition.

The diarrhea and general discomfort will not be relieved unless fat is added to the diet. Death will otherwise follow within a few days. One would probably be better off on just water than on rabbit and water.

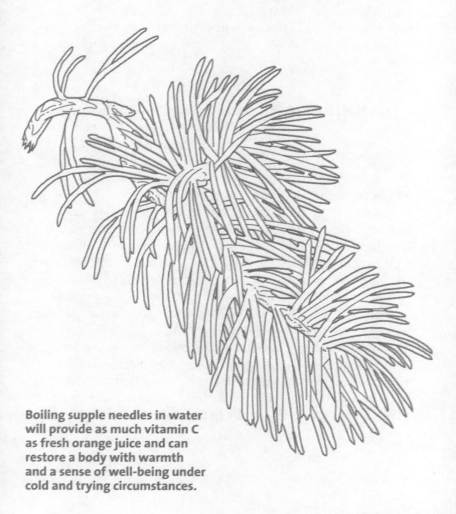

Boiling supple needles in water will provide as much vitamin C as fresh orange juice and can restore a body with warmth and a sense of well-being under cold and trying circumstances.

THE TREMENDOUS IMPORTANCE OF FAT

Why is fat so important an item in a survival diet? Part of the answer, as we have seen, lies in the fact that eating lean flesh without a sufficient amount of fat will kill us, an actuality that may seem astonishing, for in civilization we obtain numerous fats from a very great number of often unrecognized sources. These include butter, margarine, lard, milk, cheese, bacon, salad oil, mayonnaise, various sauces, candy, nuts, ice cream, and the fatty ingredients in such staples as bread.

If in an emergency we have to subsist entirely on meat, the fat of course will have to come from the meat itself. The initial consideration in a meat diet, therefore, is fat.

Yet history tells of supposedly experienced men who, although starving, have burned vital fat to give nutritiously inferior lean meat what seemed to them a more appetizing flavor—a suicidal error of which we, having learned better in an easier way, need never be guilty.

CANNIBALISM

It has always been believed, among all social levels of all peoples, that starving human beings left to their own resources will devour everything suspected of having food value, including their fellow human beings.

"It is rare, except in fiction, that men are killed to be eaten. There are cases where a member of a party becomes so unsocial in his conduct toward the rest that by agreement he is killed; but if his body then is eaten it is not logically correct to say that he was killed for food," explorer Villijalinur Stefansson says. "What does happen constantly is that those who have died of hunger, or of another cause, will be eaten. But long before cannibalism develops the party has eaten whatever else is edible."

Some scientists, who point out that objections are psychological and sociological, declare abstractly that animal proteins are desirable in direct ratio with their chemical similarity to the eating organism, and that therefore for the fullest and easiest assimilation of flesh, human meat can hardly be equaled.

WHAT TO EAT Nearly every part of North American animals is edible. (Exceptions, not found in the woods in any case, are polar bear and ringed and bearded seal liver which become so excessively rich in Vitamin A that they are poisonous to some degree at certain times and are usually as well avoided.) All freshwater fish are likewise good to eat.

All birds are good to eat. When they are molting and unable to fly, it is not difficult to corner them on foot. Large flocks may be occasionally captured by driving them into nets or traps. Roosting or nesting birds can be secured by a noose fastened to the end of a pole. Birds can also be caught in fine snares placed where they nest, feed, or congregate. Deadfall traps immobilize them, too.

Even the riper eggs, or any eggs it may be possible to secure, are nourishing. If one has continued access to a large colony at nesting time, one way to be assured of fresh eggs is to mark whatever is already in the nests, perhaps removing all but a few if conditions seem to justify it.

WINTER EATING IN THE WOODS Here are some tips for planning your cold-weather menu:

- Apart from basic nutrition, the single most important factor in cold-weather food consumption is eating food you enjoy.

- Your cold tolerance will improve if you eat a high-fat snack (about one-third of the calories from fat) every couple of hours. In fact, your blood sugar will stay sufficiently high if you eat a full breakfast and a full dinner, and snack throughout the day's activities. Food and drink every hour helps to maintain warmth and strength. Another snack just before bedtime will help keep you warm while you sleep.

- Spoilage is not a problem on winter trips, because the cold temperatures preserve the food. The biggest problem will be keeping food unfrozen. Wrap the food bag in your pack inside extra clothing for insulation. Keep snacks handy (and thawed) in a pocket near your body.

- Cut your cheese, meats, and butter into chunks before leaving home. Even if they freeze solid, you will still have manageable pieces.

- Think simple. You'll be cold and tired, so quick one-pot meals will be more appealing.

Part I

PLANTS

Chapter 1
Plants as Food

I N A SURVIVAL SITUATION YOU SHOULD ALWAYS
be on the lookout for familiar wild foods and live off the
land whenever possible.

You must not count on being able to go for days
without food, as some sources would suggest. Even in the
most static survival situation, maintaining health through a
complete and nutritious diet is essential to maintaining
strength and peace of mind.

Nature can provide you with food that will let you survive
any ordeal, if you don't eat the wrong plant. You must therefore
learn as much as possible beforehand about the flora of the region
where you will be operating. Plants can provide you with
medicines in a survival situation. Plants can supply you with
weapons and raw materials to construct shelters and build fires.
Plants can even provide you with chemicals for poisoning fish,
preserving animal hides, and for camouflaging yourself and
your equipment.

EDIBILITY OF PLANTS

Plants are valuable sources of food because they are widely available, easily procured, and, in the proper combinations, can meet all your nutritional needs.

Absolutely identify plants before using them as food. Poison hemlock has killed people who mistook it for its relatives, wild carrots and wild parsnips.

At times you may find yourself in a situation for which you could not plan. In this instance you may not have had the chance to learn the plant life of the region in which you must survive. In this case you can use the Universal Edibility Test (see page 28) to determine which plants you can eat and those to avoid.

It is important to be able to recognize both cultivated and wild edible plants in a survival situation. Most of the information in this chapter is directed toward identifying wild plants because information relating to cultivated plants is more readily available.

> ## Warning
>
> The critical factor in using plants for food is to avoid accidental poisoning. Eat only those plants you can positively identify and you know are safe to eat.

WARNING SIGNS

Remember the following when collecting wild plants for food:

- Plants growing near homes and occupied buildings or along roadsides may have been sprayed with pesticides. Wash them thoroughly. In more highly developed areas with many automobiles, avoid roadside plants, if possible, due to contamination from exhaust emissions.

- Plants growing in contaminated water or in water containing *Giardia lamblia* and other parasites are contaminated themselves. Boil or disinfect them.

- Some plants develop extremely dangerous fungal toxins. To lessen the chance of accidental poisoning, do not eat any fruit that is starting to spoil or showing signs of mildew or fungus.

- Plants of the same species may differ in their toxic or subtoxic compounds content because of genetic or environmental factors. One example of this is the foliage of the common chokecherry. Some chokecherry plants have high concentrations of deadly cyanide compounds, while others have low concentrations or none. Horses have died from eating wilted wild cherry leaves. Avoid any weeds, leaves, or seeds with an almond-like scent, a characteristic of the cyanide compounds.

- Some people are more susceptible to gastric distress from plants than others. If you are sensitive in this way, avoid unknown wild plants. If you are extremely sensitive to poison ivy, avoid products from this family, including any parts from sumacs, mangoes, and cashews.

- Some edible wild plants, such as acorns and water lily rhizomes, are bitter. These bitter substances, usually tannin compounds, make them unpalatable. Boiling them in several changes of water will usually remove these bitter properties.

- Many valuable wild plants have high concentrations of oxalate compounds, also known as oxalic acid. Oxalates produce a sharp burning sensation in your mouth and throat and damage the kidneys. Baking, roasting, or drying usually destroys these oxalate crystals. The corm (bulb) of the jack-in-the-pulpit is known as the "Indian turnip," but you can eat it only after removing these crystals by slow baking or by drying.

MUSHROOM DANGER Do not eat mushrooms in a survival situation! The only way to tell if a mushroom is edible is by positive identification. There is no room for experimentation. Symptoms of the most dangerous mushrooms affecting the central nervous system may show up after several days have passed, when it is too late to reverse their effects.

PLANT IDENTIFICATION

You identify plants, other than by memorizing particular varieties through familiarity, by using such factors as leaf shape and margin, leaf arrangements, and root structure.

The basic leaf margins are toothed, lobed, and toothless or smooth.

LEAF MARGINS

TOOTHED   **LOBED**   **TOOTHLESS**

These leaves may be lance-shaped, elliptical, egg-shaped, oblong, wedge-shaped, triangluar, long-pointed, or top-shaped.

LEAF SHAPES

LANCE-SHAPED   **ELLIPTICAL**   **EGG-SHAPED**   **OBLONG**

WEDGE-SHAPED   **TRIANGULAR**   **LONG-POINTED**   **TOP-SHAPED**

The basic types of leaf arrangements are opposite, alternate, compound, simple, and basal rosette.

LEAF ARRANGEMENTS

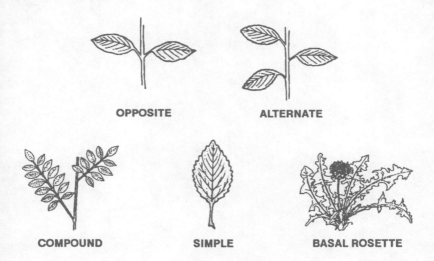

OPPOSITE ALTERNATE

COMPOUND SIMPLE BASAL ROSETTE

ROOT STRUCTURES

The basic types of root structures are the bulb, clove, taproot, tuber, rhizome, corm, and crown. Bulbs are familiar to us as onions and, when sliced in half, will show concentric rings. Clove are those bulblike structures that remind us of garlic and will separate into small pieces when broken apart. This characteristic separates wild onions from wild garlic. Taproots resemble carrots and may be single-rooted or branched, but usually only one plant stalk arises from each root. Tubers are like potatoes and daylilies, and you will find these structures either on strings or in clusters underneath the parent plants. Rhizomes are large creeping rootstocks or underground stems, and many plants arise from the "eyes" of these roots. Corms are similar to bulbs but are solid when cut rather than possessing rings. A crown is the type of root structure found on plants such as asparagus and looks much like a mop head under the soil's surface.

Learn as much as possible about plants you intend to use for food and their unique characteristics. Some plants have both edible and poisonous parts. Many are edible only at certain times of the year. Others may have poisonous relatives that look very similar to the ones you can eat or use for medicine.

Chapter 2

How to Test for Edibility

INNUMERABLE EDIBLE WILD FRUITS, BARKS, ROOTS, seeds, flowers, pods, saps, gums, herbs, nuts, leaves, greens, and tubers are both nourishing and satisfying. However, the need for extreme discretion unless one is sure of what he is eating cannot be overemphasized, as we all realize.

It has been said that more than 300,000 species of plants can be found on the earth's surface. With this in mind, it seems logical that plants can provide a major source of your diet. The best way to learn if a plant is edible is from those who are indigenous to the area, along with a good plant reference book. Still, be careful and always positively identify a plant before eating it. There are many plants throughout the world. Tasting or swallowing even a small portion of some can cause severe discomfort, extreme internal disorders, and even death. Therefore, if you have the slightest doubt about a plant's edibility, apply the Universal Edibility Test before eating any portion of it.

However, this test should only be used under the most extreme conditions when starvation seems imminent. Before testing a plant for edibility, make sure there are enough plants to make the testing worth your time and effort. Each part of a plant (roots, leaves, flowers, and so on) requires more than twenty-four hours to test. Do not waste time testing a plant that is not relatively abundant in the area.

Remember, eating large portions of plant food on an empty stomach may cause diarrhea, nausea, or cramps. Two good examples of this are such familiar foods as green apples and wild onions. Even after testing plant food and finding it safe, eat it in moderation.

You can see from the steps and time involved in testing for edibility just how important it is to be able to identify edible plants.

UNIVERSAL EDIBILITY TEST

General rules

1. Ensure there's an abundant supply of the plant.
2. Use only fresh vegetation.
3. Always wash your plants with treated water.
4. Perform the test on only one plant and plant part at a time.
5. During the test, don't consume anything else other than purified water.
6. Don't eat eight hours prior to starting the test.

Avoid plants with these characteristics (these are general guidelines; there are exceptions)

1. Mushrooms or mushroom-like appearance
2. Umbrella-shaped flower clusters (resembling Queen Anne's lace or dill)
3. Sap that is milky or turns black when exposed to the air
4. Bulbs (resembling onion or garlic)
5. Carrotlike leaves, roots, or tubers
6. Bean- and pealike appearance
7. Fungal infection (common in spoiled plants procured off the ground)
8. Shiny leaves or fine hairs

In addition, to avoid potentially poisonous plants, stay away from any wild or unknown plants that have any of the following characteristics:

- Milky or discolored sap
- Beans, bulbs, or seeds inside pods
- Bitter or soapy taste
- Spines, fine hairs, or thorns
- Dill, carrot, parsnip, or parsley-like foliage
- Almondlike scent in woody parts and leaves
- Grain heads with pink, purplish, or black spurs
- Three-leaved growth pattern

Using the criteria on the previous page as eliminators when choosing plants for the Universal Edibility Test will cause you to avoid some edible plants. More important, these criteria will often help you avoid plants that are potentially toxic to eat or touch.

TO TEST A PLANT

1. Break the plant into its basic components: leaves, stems, roots, buds, and flowers.

2. Test only one part of the potential food source at a time.

3. Smell the plant for strong or acid odors. If present, it may be best to select another plant.

4. Do not eat for eight hours before starting the test.

5. During the test period, take nothing by mouth except purified water and the plant part you are testing.

6. Select a small portion of a single part and prepare it the way you plan to eat it (raw, boiled, or baked).

7. Place a piece of the plant part being tested on the inside of your wrist for fifteen minutes. Monitor for burning, stinging, or irritation. If any of these occur, discontinue the test, select another plant or another component of the plant, and start over.

8. If you experienced no reaction, hold a small portion (a pinch) to your lips and monitor for five minutes. If any burning or irritation occurs, discontinue the test, select another plant or another component of the plant, and start over.

9. Place the plant on your tongue, holding it there for fifteen minutes. Do not swallow any of the plant juices. If any burning or irritation occurs, discontinue the test, select another plant or another component of the plant, and start over.

10. If there is no reaction, thoroughly chew a pinch and hold it in your mouth for fifteen minutes. Do not swallow. If you experience a reaction, discontinue the test, select another plant or another component of the plant, and start over. If there is no burning, stinging, or irritation, swallow the plant.

11. Wait eight hours. Monitor for cramps, nausea, vomiting, or other abdominal irritations. If any occur, induce vomiting and drink plenty of water. If you do experience a reaction,

discontinue the test, select another plant or another component of the plant, and start over.

12. If no problems are experienced, eat a quarter-cup of the plant, prepared in the same fashion as before. Wait another eight hours. If no ill effects occur, the plant part is edible when prepared in the same fashion as tested.

Caution

Test all parts of the plant you intend to use. Some plants have both edible and poisonous sections. Do not assume that a part that is edible when cooked is edible when raw, or vice versa. Always eat the plant in the same fashion in which the edibility test was performed. After the plant is determined to be edible, eat it in moderation. Although considered safe, large amounts may cause cramps and diarrhea.

THE BERRY RULE In general, the edibility of berries can be classified according to their color and composition. The following are approximate guidelines to help you determine if a berry is poisonous. In no way should the berry rule replace the edibility test. Use it as a general guide to determine whether the edibility test needs to be performed upon the berry. The only berries that should be eaten without testing are those that you can positively identify as nonpoisonous.

1. Green, yellow, and white berries are 10 percent edible.
2. Red berries are 50 percent edible.
3. Purple, blue, and black berries are 90 percent edible.
4. Aggregate berries such as thimbleberries, raspberries, and blackberries are considered 99 percent edible.

Dandelion

ALL PARTS EDIBLE

COMMON EDIBLE WILD PLANTS An entire encyclopedia of edible wild plants could be written, but space limits the number of plants presented here. Learn as much as possible about the plant life of the areas where you train regularly and where you expect to be traveling or working. Listed below and on the following pages are some of the most common edible and medicinal plants. For this book we are interested in plants found in the woods, such as those in as the following list and those noted in the Edible Vegetation Identification Guide:

Temperate Zone Food Plants
- Amaranth (*Amaranthus retroflexus* and other species)
- Arrowroot (*Sagittaria* species)
- Asparagus (*Asparagus officinalis*)
- Beechnut (*Fagus* species)
- Blackberries (*Rubus* species)
- Blueberries (*Vaccinium* species)
- Burdock (*Arctium lappa*)
- Cattail (*Typha* species)
- Chestnut (*Castanea* species)
- Chicory (*Cichorium intybus*)
- Chufa (*Cyperus esculentus*)
- Dandelion (*Taraxacum officinale*)

- Daylily (*Hemerocallis fulva*)
- Nettle (*Urtica* species)
- Oaks (*Quercus* species)
- Persimmon (*Diospyros virginiana*)
- Plantain (*Plantago* species)
- Pokeweed (*Phytolacca americana*)
- Prickly pear cactus (*Opuntia* species)
- Purslane (*Portulaca oleracea*)
- Sassafras (*Sassafras albidum*)
- Sheep sorrel (*Rumex acetosella*)
- Strawberries (*Fragaria* species)
- Thistle (*Cirsium* species)
- Water lily and lotus (*Nuphar, Nelumbo,* and other species)
- Wild onion and garlic (*Allium* species)
- Wild rose (*Rosa* species)
- Wood sorrel (*Oxalis* species)

Acacia

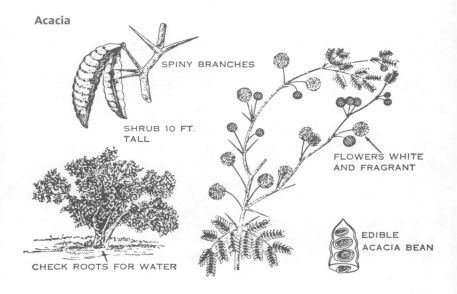

SPINY BRANCHES

SHRUB 10 FT. TALL

CHECK ROOTS FOR WATER

FLOWERS WHITE AND FRAGRANT

EDIBLE ACACIA BEAN

Chapter 3

Eating Plants

ALTHOUGH SOME PLANTS OR PLANT PARTS are edible raw, you must cook others to make them edible or palatable. Edible means that a plant or food will provide you with necessary nutrients, while palatable means that it is actually pleasing to eat. Many wild plants are edible but barely palatable. It is a good idea to learn to identify, prepare, and eat wild foods.

COOKING METHODS Methods used to improve the taste of plant food include soaking, boiling, cooking, or leaching. Leaching is done by crushing the food (for example, acorns), placing it in a strainer, and pouring boiling water through it or immersing it in running water.

Boil leaves, stems, and buds until tender, changing the water, if necessary, to remove any bitterness.

Boil, bake, or roast tubers and roots. Drying helps to remove caustic oxalates from some roots like those in the Arum family.

Leach acorns in water, if necessary, to remove the bitterness. Some nuts, such as chestnuts, are edible raw but taste better roasted.

You can eat many grains and seeds raw until they mature. When they are hard or dry, you may have to boil them, or grind them into meal or flour.

The sap from many trees, such as maples, birches, walnuts, and sycamores, contains sugar. You may boil these saps down to a syrup for sweetening. But keep in mind that it takes about 35 liters of maple sap to make one liter of maple syrup!

EDIBLE PARTS OF A PLANT

Some plants are completely edible, whereas others have both edible and poisonous parts. Unless you have performed the edibility test on the whole plant, eat only the parts that you know are edible. Plants can be broken down into several distinct components: underground; stems and leaves; flowers; fruits; nuts; seeds and grains; and gums, resins, and saps.

Eating Underground (tubers, roots and rootstalks, and bulbs)

Found underground, these plant parts have a high degree of starch and are best served baked or boiled. Some examples of these are potato (tuber), cattail (root and rootstalk), and wild onion (bulb).

Eating Stems and Leaves (shoots/stems, leaves, pith, and cambium)

Plants that produce stems and leaves are probably the most abundant source of edible vegetation in the world. Their high vitamin content makes them a valuable component of our daily diet. Shoots grow like asparagus and are best when parboiled (boiled five minutes, drained off, and boiled again until done). Some examples of these are bracken fern (to be eaten only in moderation), young bamboo, and cattail. Leaves may be eaten raw or cooked, but to achieve the highest nutritional value they are best eaten raw. Dock, plantain, amaranth, and sorrel are a few examples of edible leaves. Pith, found inside the stem of some plants, is often very high in its food value. Some examples are sago, rattan, coconut, and sugar. Cambium is the inner bark found between the bark and the wood of a tree. It can be eaten raw, cooked, or dried and then pulverized into flour.

Eating Flowers (flowers, buds, and pollens)

Flowers, buds, and pollens are high in food value and are best eaten raw or in a salad. Some examples include hibiscus (flower), rosehip (bud), and cattail (pollen).

Eating Fruits (sweet and nonsweet)

Fruits are the seed-bearing part of a plant and can be found in all areas of the world. They are best when eaten raw (when they retain all of their nutritional value) but may also be cooked. Examples of sweet fruits are apples, prickly pears, huckleberries, and wild strawberries. Examples of nonsweet fruits include tomatoes, cucumbers, plantains, and horseradish.

Eating Nuts

Nuts are high in fat and protein and can be found around the world. Most can be eaten raw, but some, like acorns, require leaching with several changes of water to remove their ...nic acid.

Eating Seeds and Grains

The seeds and grains of many plants are a valuable food resource and should not be overlooked. Some examples are grasses and millet and are best eaten when ground into flour or roasted. Purple or black grass seeds should not be eaten; they often contain a fungal contamination, which can make you very sick.

Eating Gums and Resins

Gums and resins are sap that collects on the outside of trees and plants. Their high nutritional value makes them a great supplement to any meal. Examples can be found on pine and maple trees.

Caution

If unable to identify a plant, DO NOT eat it without first performing the Universal Edibility Test.

CONDIMENTS Besides supplying vegetables for the main course, wild plants also furnish some of the best condiments known anywhere, as well as confections and beverages that top off any meal superbly or can be enjoyed between meals. Take horseradish, for instance: Everyone knows that horseradish enlivens the flavor of meat dishes, but those who haven't tried it freshly grated don't know just how good it can be.

SALAD GREENS Even those who don't like to cook will enjoy making easy-to-fix tossed and wilted salads from Nature's own salad greens in a blend of the familiar and the exotic. Many of them—like prickly lettuce, wild lettuce, and lettuce saxifrage— can be used just like the common varieties of lettuce found in supermarkets, but they are much more versatile. Once you are back in your own kitchen you will find that prickly lettuce, for instance,

can be used to make a tasty casserole. Wild lettuce makes an
excellent cream soup and an intriguing baked loaf. Lettuce
saxifrage pie is an epicurean delight.

Among other versatile greens often found growing wild are
live-forever, which makes a zippy relish as well as an uncommonly
good tossed salad, and rock cress, whose pungent flavor can do
anything for salads that radishes can do.

Best of all, these greens are all widely distributed and are free
for the picking.

FIDDLEHEADS   In the spring, bright green young
ferns begin to poke up through the
soil. As each emerges, you will see a
coil of green called a fiddlehead, or
crosier. These names refer to the coil's
shape—the first for its resemblance to the head of a violin, and the
second for a bishop's ceremonial staff also called a crosier, which is
a stylized shepherd's staff with a crook at the top.

The fiddleheads are coiled because the upper and lower surfaces
of the fronds grow at different rates. As the fern grows, the fiddlehead
unrolls and expands, revealing tiny new fronds. Sometimes the
fiddlehead has a cover of fuzzy brown scales. Some ferns have a
cover of silky hairs on the rachis (stem) when the young fiddlehead
unrolls. Before the development of synthetic materials, these hairs
from large tropical tree ferns were used for upholstery stuffing.

Ferns are easier to find than you might think. You will find
them in moist, shaded areas, along riverbanks, around ponds, and
in the woods. Locate a patch of ferns during the summer months,
and return there the following spring to observe the fiddleheads
poke through the soil, unfurl, and release their folded leaflets.
Record your observations in your field notebook. On what date do
you first notice the fiddlehead? Is it wearing a brown, tan, or white
fuzzy protective hood? How long does it take to reach its full height?
Look for different types of ferns. Do all the ferns you observe have
fiddleheads? Which ferns have them and which do not?

In the fall, you can find fiddleheads by poking around the base
of the fern. They are tightly coiled, hard, round structures that hug
the rhizomes and may be covered by a thin sheet of soil.

Some people relish fiddleheads as tasty vegetables, reminiscent
of asparagus. The fiddlehead of commerce is the ostrich fern, great
quantities of which are collected in the spring and shipped to
markets or canneries. Should you come across fiddleheads in this

manner, and not foraging the woods yourself, be sure to select fiddleheads that are newly arrived to the grocer's shelves, choosing only those that are bright green and tightly coiled. Cut off the long tails. Between your palms, rub away the fuzzy or brown, papery covering, and wash the fiddleheads well. Steam them until fork-tender, and rinse in cool water. Dry them thoroughly, then toss with a favorite salad dressing. Or, if you prefer, stir-fry them in oil with ginger to taste for about two minutes. Add 2 cloves of garlic, ¼ cup of chicken broth, and salt to taste. Cover and simmer for about five minutes.

If eating fiddleheads does not appeal to you, you can still buy a few and unfurl them to examine how the leaves are packaged.

TREES FOR SUSTENANCE

Most individuals worry that, if forced to shift for themselves in the unfrequented farther places, they would starve. Yet there are actual forests of food.

Everyone, of course, knows that trees furnish delectable fruits and nuts, but few people realize that the inner bark and sap of many trees such as the poplar and maple are not only edible but delicious to boot.

Trees offer another dividend, too. Because they provide shelter and food for so many game birds and animals, they often furnish clues to the presence of birds and animals that can supply meat for the table or sustenance during an emergency.

HOW TO EAT BARK

The inner bark of a tree—the layer next to the wood—may be eaten raw or cooked. You can even make flour from the inner bark of cottonwood, aspen, birch, willow, and pine trees by pulverizing it. Avoid the outer bark because of the presence of large amounts of tannin.

Pine bark is rich in vitamin C. Scrape away the outer bark and strip the inner bark from the trunk. Eat it fresh, dried, or cooked, or pulverize it into flour.

Chapter 4
Poisonous Plants

SUCCESSFUL USE OF PLANTS IN A SURVIVAL situation depends on positive identification. Knowing poisonous plants is as important to a survivor as knowing edible plants. Knowing the poisonous plants will help you avoid sustaining injuries from them.

LEARN ALL ABOUT PLANTS It is to your benefit to learn as much about plants as possible. Many poisonous plants look like their edible relatives or like other edible plants. For example, poison hemlock appears very similar to wild carrot. Certain plants are safe to eat in certain seasons or stages of growth and poisonous in other stages. For example, the leaves of the pokeweed are edible when it first starts to grow, but it soon becomes poisonous. You can eat some plants and their fruits only when they are ripe. For example, the ripe fruit of mayapple is edible in moderate amounts, but all other parts and the green fruit are poisonous. Some plants contain both edible and poisonous parts: Potatoes and tomatoes are common plant foods, but their green parts are poisonous.

Some plants become toxic after wilting. For example, when the black cherry starts to wilt, hydrocyanic acid develops. Specific preparation methods make some plants edible that are poisonous raw. You can eat the thinly sliced and thoroughly dried corms (drying may take a full year) of the jack-in-the-pulpit, but they are poisonous if not thoroughly dried.

Learn to identify and use plants before a survival situation arises. Some sources of information about plants are pamphlets, books, films, nature trails, botanical gardens, local markets, and local natives. Gather and cross-reference information from as many sources as possible, because many sources will not contain all the information needed.

HOW PLANTS POISON

Plants generally poison by

- Contact. When a person makes contact with a poisonous plant that causes any type of skin irritation or dermatitis.

- Absorption or inhalation. When a person either absorbs the poison through the skin or inhales it into the respiratory system.

- Ingestion. When a person eats a part of a poisonous plant.

Plant poisoning ranges from minor irritation to death. A common question asked is, "How poisonous is this plant?" It is difficult to say how poisonous plants are, because

- Some plants require contact with a large amount of the plant before any adverse reaction is noticeable, while contact with only a small amount of others will cause death.

- Every plant will vary in the amount of toxins it contains due to different growing conditions and slight variations in subspecies.

- Every person has a different level of resistance to toxic substances.

- Some people may be more sensitive to a particular plant.

Some Common misconceptions about poisonous plants are

- "Watch the animals and eat what they eat." Most of the time this statement is true, but some animals can eat plants that are poisonous to humans.

- "Boil the plant in water and any poisons will be removed." Boiling removes many poisons, but not all.

- "Plants with a red color are poisonous." Some red plants are poisonous, but not all.

The point is that there is no one rule to aid in identifying poisonous plants. You must make an effort to learn as much about them as possible.

Contact Dermatitis

Contact dermatitis from plants will usually cause the most trouble in the field. The effects may be persistent, spread by scratching, and are particularly dangerous if there is contact in or around the eyes.

The principal toxin of these plants is usually an oil that gets on the skin upon contact with the plant. The oil also can get on equipment and then infect anyone who touches the equipment. Never burn a contact-poisonous plant, because the smoke may be as harmful as the plant. There is a greater danger of being affected by skin contact with toxins when overheated and sweating. An infection may be localized, or it may spread over the body.

Symptoms may take from a few hours to several days to appear. Signs and symptoms can include burning, reddening, itching, swelling, and blisters.

When you first make contact with poisonous plants or the first symptoms appear, try to remove the plants' oil from skin by washing with soap and cold water. If water is not available, wipe your skin repeatedly with dirt or sand. Do not use dirt if blisters have developed; the dirt may break open the blisters and leave the body open to infection. After you have removed the oil, dry the area. To treat plant-caused rashes, you can wash with a tannic acid solution—which can be made from oak bark—and crush and rub jewelweed on the affected area.

Poisonous plants that cause contact dermatitis include the following:

- Cowhage
- Poison ivy
- Poison oak
- Poison sumac
- Rengas tree
- Trumpet vine

Ingestion Poisioning

Ingestion poisoning can be very serious and could lead to death very quickly. Do not eat any plant unless you have positively identified it first. Keep a log of all plants eaten.

Signs and symptoms of ingestion poisoning can include nausea, vomiting, diarrhea, abdominal cramps, depressed heartbeat and respiration, headaches, hallucinations, dry mouth, unconsciousness, coma, and death.

If you suspect plant poisoning, try to remove the poisonous material from the victim's mouth and stomach as soon as possible. Induce vomiting by tickling the back of his throat or by giving him warm saltwater, if he is conscious. Dilute the poison by administering large quantities of water or milk, if he is conscious.

The following plants can cause ingestion poisoning if eaten:

- Castor bean
- Chinaberry
- Death camas
- Lantana
- Manchineel
- Oleander
- Pangi
- Physic nut
- Poison and water hemlocks
- Rosary pea
- Strychnine tree

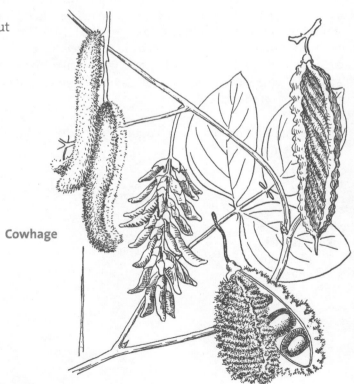

Cowhage

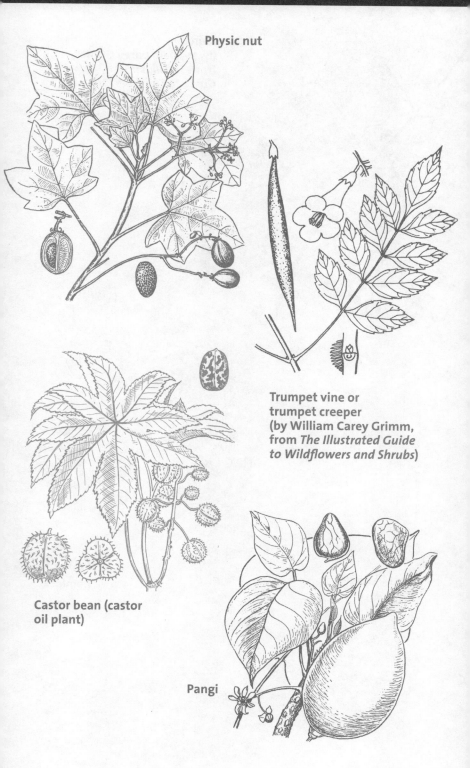

Physic nut

Trumpet vine or
trumpet creeper
(by William Carey Grimm,
from *The Illustrated Guide
to Wildflowers and Shrubs*)

Castor bean (castor
oil plant)

Pangi

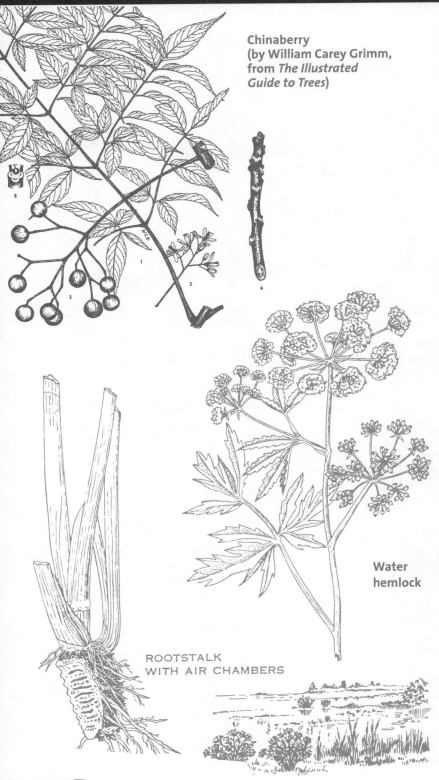

Chinaberry
(by William Carey Grimm,
from *The Illustrated
Guide to Trees*)

Water
hemlock

ROOTSTALK
WITH AIR CHAMBERS

POISON SUMAC
Toxicodendron vernix

FIELD MARKS. A shrub or small tree 4 to 15 feet high; growing in swamps, bogs, and wet places. Branchlets moderately stout, smooth, the end bud present. Leaves alternate, compound, 6 to 12 inches long; the 7 to 13 leaflets short-stalked, elliptic or egg-shaped, broadly pointed at base, pointed at tip, margin untoothed, lustrous above, paler beneath, smooth, 2 to 4 inches long; leafstalks usually reddish. Flowers small, greenish, in axillary clusters; blooming May to July. Fruits roundish, smooth, waxy white, about 3/16 inch in diameter, in loose and drooping clusters; ripening August or September and persisting.

RANGE. Southwestern Maine to Ontario and Minnesota, south to Florida and Texas.

Caution

All parts of poison sumac, poison ivy, and poison oak contain dangerous skin irritants.

Poison Sumac

POISON IVY
Toxicodendron radicans

Poison Ivy

FIELD MARKS. An erect or trailing leaf-losing shrub, or a woody vine climbing by means of aerial rootlets on the stems; growing in wooded areas, thickets, clearings, or along fence rows and roadsides. Leaves alternate, long-stalked, compound, 4 to 12 inches long; the 3 leaflets oval or egg-shaped, rounded or broadly pointed at base, pointed at tip, usually with a few coarse teeth on margin, lustrous above, paler and slightly downy beneath, 1½ to 8 inches long; the end leaflet long-stalked, the side ones almost stalk-less. Flowers small, yellowish green, in axillary clusters; blooming May to

July. Fruits roundish, waxy white, about ³/₁₆ inch in diameter; maturing August to October and persisting.

RANGE. Nova Scotia to British Columbia; south to Florida, Texas, and Arizona.

POISON OAK
Toxicodendron
pubescens

FIELD MARKS. A stiffly erect, simple or sparingly branched, leaf-losing shrub 1 to 2½ feet high; growing in dry, sandy pine and oak woods and clearings. Leaves alternate, long-stalked, compound, 3 to 8 inches long; the 3 leaflets often broadly egg-shaped, pointed at base, blunt at tip, with 3 to 7 often deep lobes, somewhat downy above, more densely so and paler beneath, 2 to 5 inches long; the end leaflet rather long-stalked, the side ones almost stalkless; leafstalks downy. Flowers and fruits similar to those of poison ivy, but usually more downy.

RANGE. Chiefly coastal plain; New Jersey and Maryland south to Florida; Tennessee to eastern Oklahoma south to Alabama and Texas.

Poison oak

RULES FOR AVOIDING POISONOUS PLANTS

Your best policy is to be able to look at a plant and identify it with absolute-certainty, and to know its uses or dangers. Many times this is not possible. If you have little or no knowledge of the local vegetation, use the rules to select plants for the Universal Edibility Test. Remember:

- Avoid all mushrooms. Mushroom identification is very difficult and must be precise, even more so than with other plants. Some mushrooms cause death very quickly. Some mushrooms have no known antidote. Two general types of mushroom poisoning are gastrointestinal and central nervous system.

- Avoid unnecessarily touching or otherwise coming into contact with plants.

Chapter 5
What About Mushrooms?

A MUSHROOM, NO MATTER ITS SHAPE OR COLOR or size, is a fruiting body of an organism known as a fungus (plural, fungi). Fungi have an entire kingdom to themselves in the taxonomic system, separate from plants. While resembling plants in their immobility, fungi lack the green pigment chlorophyll and obtain essential carbon compounds not by manufacturing them, as plants do through photosynthesis, but by gleaning them from living or dead matter. Fungi break down and consume plants: grasses, leaves, wood, fruit, and other plant parts. The fungi—which include molds, yeasts, smuts, and mildews—are key decomposers of vegetation, and without them, life on earth would be utterly different than we know it.

COLLECTING MUSHROOMS Collecting mushrooms is a popular hobby. Although some fungi are edible, others are poisonous, and there are no hard and fast rules or tests by which a poisonous type can safely be discerned, other than by correctly identifying it. My father was fond of the saying "There are old mushroom hunters and bold mushroom hunters, but there are no old, bold mushroom hunters." Fortunately, most of the poisonous species are not fatal to people who ingest them: They bring on symptoms that resemble food poisoning, including nausea, cramps, vomiting, and diarrhea, lasting one or more days. Some mushrooms cause hallucinations. In general, the faster such symptoms show up, the less severe the ultimate outcome. Some mushrooms, however, deal death.

EDIBILITY When seeking nourishment in the woods, mushrooms are often a tempting choice. About 16,000 varieties of edible fungi grow in different parts of the world. The mushrooms you eat on your steaks and the mold in the blue cheese that you spread on crackers are two forms of fungi.

Although fungi are not a good substitute for meat, they are comparable in vitamins to common leafy vegetables, and they often are available in areas where other edible plants are scarce. However, unless you are familiar with mushrooms or have a good guide with you, it is better to avoid mushrooms altogether. Remember, mushrooms have very little general food value. If you are not already an expert, the incurred risks will be far out of proportion to the possible gain.

FALLACY OF TESTING MUSHROOMS No single practical test is recognized, unfortunately, by which all poisonous mushrooms can be detected. It is untrue that if silver boiled with mushrooms does not turn black, the fungi are necessarily edible. It is a false presumption that when the skin can be peeled from the cap, the species is proved wholesome. It is not true that pink gills are evidence that the mushroom is good. It is incorrect that if salt rubbed on some part of the mushroom causes a color change, the fungus must be suitable for the table.

Another dangerous fallacy, particularly under the stress of a fight for survival, is the apparently reasonable but nevertheless wholly false presumption that any mushroom gathered by animals and birds is suitable for human consumption. Among the mushrooms ordinarily harvested and dried by squirrels are some of the poisonous amanita group for which no antidote has been discovered.

So many myths are circulated, often by those who in their own neighborhoods successfully gather one or two types of edible mushrooms year after year, that it can not be here repeated too strenuously: *No single test short of eating can distinguish between a poisonous and a safe mushroom.* As for puffballs, although it is correct that puffballs that are white throughout are edible when fresh, it is also true that some lethal mushrooms when young look like puffballs.

FATAL MUSHROOMS   Mushrooms contain several different poisons. One poisonous mushroom in an overflowing packsack of edible fungi can be enough to cause certain death, with symptoms taking so long to become evident that once they are recognized even the most immediate medical attention is often powerless. In the case of the deadly amanita, the individual may not realize anything is at all amiss until he is doubled up with cramps and vomiting, perhaps fifteen hours after eating the fatal toadstool.

Chapter 6

Edible Vegetation Identification Guide

THOUSANDS OF BUSHES, FLOWERS, MOSSES, AND TREES are edible. Here is an A-to-Z guide of some of the most common and fortifying vegetation you can use as food to survive in the woods.

Eastern White Oak

ACORNS (*Quercus* species)

There is no need for anyone to starve where acorns abound, and from 200 to 500 types of oaks (botanists differ) grow in the world. Some eighty-five of these are native to the United States. Although some of the latter species are scrubby, the genus also includes some of our biggest and most stately trees. Furthermore, except in our northern prairies, oaks are widely distributed throughout the contiguous states, thriving at various altitudes and in numerous types of soil.

Abundant and substantial, acorns are perhaps this country's most important wildlife food. The relatively tiny acorns of the willow oak, pin oak, and water oak are often obtainable near streams and ponds, where they are relished by mallards, wood ducks, pintails, and other waterfowl. Quail devour such small acorns and peck the kernels out of the larger nuts.

Pheasants, grouse, pigeons, doves, and prairie chickens enjoy the nuts as well as the buds. Wild turkeys gulp down whole acorns regardless of their size. Squirrels and chipmunks are among the smaller animals that store acorns for off-season use. Mule deer and white-tailed deer, elk, peccaries, and mountain sheep enjoy the acorns and also browse on twigs and foliage. Black bears grow fat on acorns.

Acorns probably rated the top position on the long list of wild foods depended on by American Indians. It has been stated, for example, that acorn soup, or mush, was the chief daily food of more than three-quarters of the native Californians. The eastern settlers were early introduced to acorns, too. In 1620, during their first hungry winter in Plymouth, the Pilgrims were fortunate enough to discover baskets of roasted acorns that local Indians had buried in the ground. In parts of Mexico and in Europe, the natives today still use acorns in the old ways.

All acorns are good to eat. Some are less sweet than others, that's all. But the bitterness that is prevalent in different degrees is due to tannin, the same ingredient that causes tea to be bitter. Although it is not digestible in large amounts, it is soluble in water. Therefore, even the bitterest acorns can be made edible in an emergency.

Oaks comprise the most important group of hardwood timber trees on this continent. A major proportion of our eastern forests is oak. Its dense, durable wood has many commercial uses. Furthermore, oaks are among the most popular shade trees along our streets and about our dwellings.

The oaks may be separated into two great groups: the white oaks and the red oaks. The acorns of the former are the sweet ones. They mature in one growing season. The inner surfaces of the shells are smooth. The leaves typically have rounded lobes, but they are never bristle-tipped. The bark is ordinarily grayish and is generally scaly.

Among the red oaks, the usually bitter acorns do not mature until the end of the second growing season. The inner surfaces of the shells are customarily coated with woolly hair. The leaves have distinct bristles at their tips or at the tops of their lobes. The typically dark bark is ordinarily furrowed.

For example, the Maidu, Paiute, and other western tribes—who were collectively referred to by European settlers as "Digger Indians" for their dietary reliance on acorns and roots—roasted acorns from the western white oak, *Quercus lobata*, hulled them, and ground them into a coarse meal that they formed into cakes and baked in crude ovens. In the East, the acorns of the white oak, *Quercus alba*, were also ground into meal but then often mixed with cornmeal before being shaped into cakes and baked. Roasted and ground white oak acorns provide one of the wilderness coffees.

Indians leached their bitter acorns in a number of ways. Sometimes the acorns would be buried in swamp mud for a year, after which they would be ready for roasting and eating whole. Other tribes let their shelled acorns mold in baskets, then buried them in clean freshwater sand. When they had turned black, they were sweet and ready for use.

Some tribes ground their acorns by pounding them with stone pestles and then ran water through the meal by one method or another for often the greater part of a day until it was sweet. The meal might be placed in a specially woven basket for this purpose, or it might just be buried in the sandy bed of a stream.

To make the familiar, somewhat sweetish soup or gruel of the results, all that is necessary is to heat the meal in water. The Indians generally used no seasoning. As a matter of fact, until the white man came they ordinarily had no utensils but closely woven baskets. These were flammable, of course, and the heating had to be done by putting in rocks heated in campfires. Still showing how little one can get along with, the tribe then ate from common baskets, using their fingers.

It's an easy thing to leach acorns today. Just shell your nuts and boil them whole in a kettle of water, changing the liquid every time it becomes yellowish. You can shorten the time necessary for this to as little as a couple of hours, depending of course on the particular acorns, if you keep a teakettle of water always heating on the stove while this process is continuing. The acorns can then be dried by rolling them around in a frying pan over the camp fire and either eaten as is or ground into coarse bits for use like any other nuts or into a fine meal.

APPLE
(*Malus* species)

Apple

Henry David Thoreau, an early expert on the subject of apples, averred that

The time for wild apples is the last of October and the first of November. They then get to be palatable, vivacious and inspiring, for they ripen late.

To appreciate the wild and sharp flavors of these October fruits, it is necessary that you be breathing the sharp October or November air. The outdoor air and exercise which the walker gets give a different tone to his palate, and he craves a fruit which the sedentary would call harsh and crabbed.

This noblest of fruits must be eaten in the fields, when your system is all aglow with exercise, when the frosty weather nips your fingers, the wind rattles the bare boughs or rustles the few remaining leaves, and the jay is heard screaming around. What is sour in the house a bracing walk makes sweet. Some of these apples might be labelled, "To be eaten in the wind".

Apples, natives of Asia and Europe, were not brought to
Massachusetts until some nine years after the arrival of the
Pilgrims, but they soon escaped into the wilderness. Nearly two
hundred years ago, the pioneer preacher named John Chapman,
better known as Johnny Appleseed, traveled some 100,000 miles
between Massachusetts and Missouri planting seeds and seedlings.
Apples and crab apples now grow wild in every state of the Union.

Most of these are only occasionally to be relished raw, although
they cook up all the better for that. However, as Thoreau noted
more than a century ago, "Who knows but this chance wild fruit,
planted by a cow or a bird on some remote and rocky hillside, may
be the choicest of its kind. It was thus the Porter and the Baldwin
grow. Every wild apple shrub excites our expectation thus, somewhat as every wild child it is, perhaps, a prince in disguise."

Everyone knows the apple. Even though your yellow-green
find may be little more than an inch in diameter, and hard and
sour to boot, very few wild fruits are as quickly gathered, and their
very tartness and firmness lend themselves to some of the finest
apple dishes you have ever eaten. The flowers of the apple are
perhaps the most beautiful of any tree. The scent of both the
blossoms and the later-developing fruit has a piquancy unequaled
in any costly perfume.

Deer, bears, raccoons, and foxes are among the wild animals
who seek out apples. Apple buds are a favorite winter sustenance
of the ruffed grouse. Pheasants, quail, and prairie chickens dine
well on fruit, seeds, and buds.

The Iroquois, employing wild apples and maple syrup, made an
applesauce that was all the more flavorsome because the fruit was
used unpeeled. With the help of a kitchen blender, you can do an
even smoother job of this today: Cut up the apples first, removing
the cores. Barely cover with water, bring to a simmer, and cook
with only an occasional bubble ascending to the top until the fruit
is soft. Transfer at once to a blender and process until nothing
remains of the peel but the savor and color. Add sugar to taste,
preferably stopping short of obliterating all the tartness. You
may also like what a little cinnamon and lemon juice will do for
applesauce. A bit of salt will help bring out the deliciousness, too.
Much depends on the particular wild fruit. Many like this best
when it is warm, perhaps with a splash of cream.

If you can beat the deer and other forest folk to them, you sometimes come upon wild apples plump and sweet enough for baking.

BARBERRY (*Berberis vulgaris*)

Barberry

Barberries become redolent expanses of golden blossoms in the springtime, shiny and opulent green masses during the summer, and turn bright scarlet and bronze hues in the nippy weeks of autumn. The wood, a particularly lovely yellow, is sometimes used for jewelry. This shrub grows some 8 or 9 feet tall along fences, in dusty thickets, in stony pastures, and along the rims of rocky woodlands. The berries of this particular bush-like herb are for the most part red. Oval-shaped, not unlike fairy footballs, they are rather dry, acidulous, and rich in vitamin C. You can make a pleasantly cooling drink from the berries or turn them into appetizingly tart sauces, jams, purees, and preserves. Parched hikers find chewing a few of the agreeably acid, younger leaves refreshing.

BAYBERRY
(*Myrica cerifera*)

These evergreen shrubs and small trees sometimes grow 30 feet high or more. The attractive fruit, actually a nutlet, is based on a hard stone that encloses a two-seeded kernel. On the outside of the stone are gunpowder-like grains. Over this is a dryish, pleasantly scented crust of granular, green-white wax that once smelled will never be forgotten. When bruised, the leaves, too, give off a memorable aroma. The winy evergreen leaves of the bayberry, used in moderation and removed before the dish is brought to table, have been doing wonderful things for soups, broths, stews, and steaming chowders since colonial times.

Bayberry

BEECH
(Fagus grandifolia)

O ur single native beech is one of four recognized species and is a big, handsome tree with vivid green leaves that turn coppery in the autumn. Its distinctively smooth, light gray, tight, often mottled bark invites carved initials and arrowed hearts. Wild creatures vie with man for its important nut crop, which, as Indians and early settlers well knew, is one of the most flavorful products of our northern woodlands. Beechnuts are so small and delicious that a large proportion of them are enjoyed raw, but they are good cooked, too. The inner bark of the tree, dried and pulverized for bread flour in times of need, is an emergency food to remember. Beech sawdust can also be boiled in water, roasted, and then mixed with flour for bread.

Beech

BIRCH *(Betula* species)

T wo general varieties of the trees grow across the continent: the black birch and those similar to it, and the familiar white birches whose cheerful foliage and softly gleaming bark lighten the northern forests. However, native birches with dark bark might be confused with some of the wild cherries if it were not for the following differences: The broken twigs of birches may have a strong wintergreen odor in contrast to the bitter-almond smell of cherry twigs, bud scales are fewer, the leaf stems do not have glands, and the bark of numerous birches can be separated into paperlike sheets. In fact, such thin sheets can be your woodland paper.

Black birch

The inner bark of birches is edible and in emergencies has kept many from starving. Dried and then ground into flour, this has been used by Indians and frontiersmen for bread. It is also cut into strips and boiled like noodles into stew. But you don't need to go to that much trouble; just eat it raw. You can drink the refreshing sap just as it comes from the trees in springtime or boil it down into a syrup.

The nutritious bark of the black birch is said to have probably saved the lives of scores of Confederate soldiers during Garnett's retreat over the mountains to Monterey, Virginia. For years afterward, the route the soldiers took could be followed by the peeled birch trees.

The black birch may be identified at all times of the year by its tight, reddish-brown, cherry-like bark, which has the aroma and flavor of wintergreen. Smooth in young trees, the bark darkens and separates into large, irregular sections as these birches age. The darkly dull green leaves, paler and yellower beneath, are 2 to 4 inches long, oval to oblong, short-stemmed, silky when young, smooth when mature, with double-toothed edges. They give off an odor of wintergreen when bruised. The trees have both erect and hanging catkins, on twigs that also taste and smell like wintergreen. In fact, when the commercial oil of wintergreen is not made synthetically, it is distilled from the twigs and bark of the black birch.

Black birches enhance the countryside from New England to Ontario, south to Ohio and Delaware, and along the Appalachian Mountains to Georgia and Alabama.

A piquant tea, brisk with wintergreen, is made from the young twigs, young leaves, the thick inner bark, and the bark from the larger roots. This latter reddish bark, easily stripped off in the spring and early summer, can be dried at room temperatures and stored in sealed jars in a cool place for later use. A teaspoon to a cup of boiling water, set off the heat and allowed to steep for 5 minutes, makes a tea that is delicately spicy. Milk and sugar make it even better. As a matter of fact, the leaves, twigs, and bark from any of the birches make good tea.

All the birches furnish prime emergency food. Two general varieties of the trees grow across the continent: the black birch and those similar to it, and the familiar white birches whose cheerful foliage and softly gleaming bark lighten the northern forests. Layer after layer of this latter bark can be easily stripped off in great sheets—although because of the resulting disfigurement to the tree this should only be done in an emergency—and used to start a campfire in any sort of weather.

Black walnut

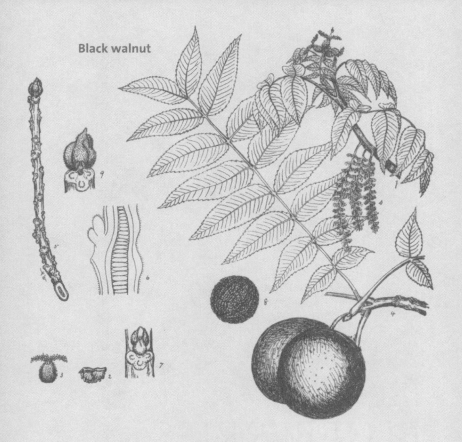

BLACK WALNUT
(*Juglans nigra*)

Growing alone and in pairs, the nuts of the black walnut tree ripen about October, soon thereafter falling from the widely spreading branches. The hardest part about gathering and using wild walnuts is getting off the husks, with their indelible brownish dye. As a youngster I didn't mind this, and, just stamping on the husks and breaking them off with bare fingers, I collected stained hands that defied parental scrubbings for weeks. A knife will remove the green hides. During the warm days of summer the nuts of the black walnut, covered with a warty and greenish husk, become 2 to 3 inches in diameter. Incidentally, although certainly unsporting and illegal, these bruised nut husks can be used to kill fish for food, something to remember if starvation is ever imminent in a survival situation.

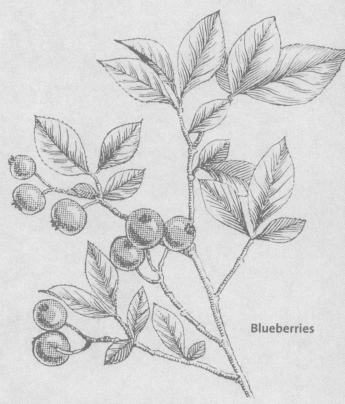

Blueberries

BLUEBERRIES *and* OTHER WILD BERRIES

There are more than a score of different species of blueberries, also known in some localities as whortleberries or huckleberries, some crowding tall bushes while others fill tiny shrubs only 3 or 4 inches from the ground.

Blueberries are historically one of the most valuable foods of Indians, who have long eaten them as is, dried, with meat, as a thickening for soups, and in numerous other ways. Frontiersmen pick them by the bushel, often with the same sort of toothed scoop used for cranberries.

Other Berries Other wild fruits
are so obviously numerous that
it is impractical to do more than
mention a few. All of us might
well make it our business to learn
what edibles abound in our favorite
woodlands and, if possible, in any
wilderness area where we may one
day travel.

The numerous gooseberries
and currants are widely popular.
Indians utilized dried currants
extensively to flavor pemmican,
which is essentially equal parts by
weight of dried meat and rendered
fat. The serviceberry is another fruit
that was included in pemmican.

Elderberries

The younger one is, the more irresistible the various wild
cherries seem to be, especially when raw. Adults prefer to gather
the more astringent of these for making jelly and for boiling with
an added sweetener for table syrup.

Many of us have savored wild grapes and wild plums. Elderberries
are well known. The dry, bland, reddish bearberry is edible although
practically tasteless. So are the equally innocuous berries of the
kinnikinnick, whose leaves have been so often used instead of
tobacco or to supplement dwindling tobacco supplies that many
other substitutes, such as the
inner bark of the flowering
dogwood, are also called
kinnikinnick.

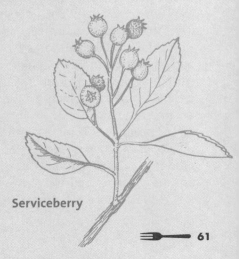

**Gooseberries
and currants**

Serviceberry

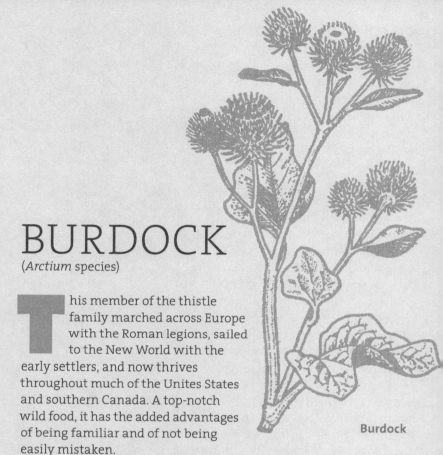

BURDOCK
(*Arctium* species)

This member of the thistle family marched across Europe with the Roman legions, sailed to the New World with the early settlers, and now thrives throughout much of the Unites States and southern Canada. A top-notch wild food, it has the added advantages of being familiar and of not being easily mistaken.

Burdock

The somewhat unpleasant associations with its name are, at the same time, a disadvantage when it comes to bringing this aggressive but delicious immigrant to the table. Muskrats are sold in some markets as swamp rabbits, while crows find buyers as rooks. But unfortunately in this country burdock is usually just burdock, despite the fact that varieties of it are specially cultivated as prized domestic vegetables in Japan and elsewhere in the Eastern Hemisphere.

Burdock is found almost everywhere it can be close to people and domestic animals—along roads, fences, and stone walls, in yards and vacant lots, and especially around old barns and stables. Its sticky burrs, which attach themselves cozily to man and beast, are familiar nuisances.

The burdock is a coarse biennial weed that, with its branches, rapidly grows to between 2 and 6 feet high. The large leaves, growing on long stems, are shaped something like oblong hearts and are rough and purplish with veins. Tiny, tubular, usually magenta flowers appear from June to November depending on the locality, in the plant's second year. These form the prickly stickers, which, of course, are actually the seed pods.

No one need stay hungry very long where the burdock grows, for this versatile edible will furnish a number of different delicacies. It is for their roots, for instance, that they are grown throughout Asia. Only the first-year roots should be used, but these are easy to distinguish as the biennials stemming from them have no flower and burr stalks. When found in hard ground, the deep, slender roots are harder to harvest, although they are worth quite a bit of effort.

The tender pith of the root, exposed by peeling, will make an unusually good potherb if sliced like parsnips and simmered for 20 minutes in water to which about ¼ teaspoon baking soda has been added. Then drain, barely cover with fresh boiling water, add a teaspoon of salt, and cook until tender. Serve with butter or margarine spreading on top.

If caught early enough, the young leaves can be boiled in two waters and served as greens. If you're hungry, the peeled young leaf stalks are good raw, especially with a little salt. These are also added to green salads and to vegetable soups and are cooked by themselves like asparagus.

It is the rapidly growing flower stalk that furnishes one of the tastier parts of the burdock. When these sprout up the second year, watch them so that you can cut them off just as the blossom heads are starting to appear in late spring or early summer. Every shred of the strong, bitter skin must be peeled off. Then cook the remaining thick, succulent interiors in two waters as you would the roots, and serve hot with butter or margarine.

The pith of the flower stalks has long been used, too, for a candy. One way to make this is by cutting the whitish cores into bite-size sections. Boil these for 15 minutes in water to which ¼ teaspoon baking soda has been added. Drain. Heat what you judge to be an approximately equal weight of sugar in enough hot water to dissolve it, and then add the juice of an orange. Put in the burdock pieces, cook slowly until the syrup is nearly evaporated, drain, and roll in granulated sugar. This never lasts for very long.

The first-year roots, dug either in the fall or in early spring, are also used back of beyond as a healing wash for burns, wounds, and skin irritations. One way to make this is by dropping 4 teaspoons of the root into a quart of boiling water and allowing this to stand until cool.

BUTTERNUT *(Juglans cinerea)*

Confederate soldiers and partisans were referred to as "butternuts" during the Civil War because of the brown homespun clothes of the military, often dyed with the green nut husks and inner bark of these familiar trees. Some of the earliest American settlers made the same use of them. As far back as the Revolutionary War, a common laxative was made of the inner bark: a spoonful of finely cut pieces to a cup of boiling water, cooled and drunk cold. Indians preceded the colonists in boiling down the sap of this tree, as well as that of the black walnut, to make syrup and sugar, sometimes mixing the former with maple syrup.

The butternut thrives in chillier climates than does the black walnut, ranging higher in the mountains and farther north. Otherwise this tree, also known as white walnut or oilnut, closely resembles its cousin except for being smaller and lighter colored. Its wood is comparatively soft, weak, and light, although still close-grained. The larger trees, furthermore, are nearly always unsound.

Butternut

Butternuts grow from Canada's Maritime Provinces south to the northern mountainous regions of Georgia and Alabama, and west to Ontario, the Dakotas, Kansas, and Arkansas. They are medium-size trees, ordinarily from about 30 to 50 feet high, with a trunk diameter of up to 3 feet. Some trees, though, tower up to 90 feet or more. The furrowed and broadly ridged bark is gray.

The alternate compound leaves are from 15 to 30 inches long. Each one is made up of eleven to seventeen lance-shaped, nearly stemless leaflets, 2 to 6 inches long and about half as broad, with sharply pointed tips, sawtooth edges, and unequally rounded bases. Yellowish green on top, these are paler and softly downy underneath. The catkins and the shorter flower spikes appear in the spring when the leaves are about half grown.

The nuts are oblong rather than round, blunt, about 2 to 2½ inches long and a bit more than half as thick. Thin husks, notably sticky and coated with matted rusty hairs, enclose the nuts, whose bony shells are roughly ridged, deeply furrowed, and hard. Frequently growing in small clusters of two to five, these ripen in October and soon drop from the branches.

The young nuts, when they have nearly reached their full size, can be picked green and used for pickles that bring out the flavor of meat like few other things and really attract notice as hors d'oeuvres. If you can still easily shove a large needle through the nuts, it is not too late to pickle them, husks and all, after they have been scalded and the outer fuzz rubbed off.

To pickle butternuts, put them in a strong brine for a week, changing the water every other day and keeping them tightly covered. Then drain and wipe them. Pierce each nut all the way through several times with a large needle. Then put them in glass jars with a sprinkling of powdered ginger, nutmeg, mace, and cloves between each layer. Bring some good cider vinegar to a boil, immediately fill each jar, and seal. You can start enjoying this unusual delicacy in two weeks.

Noteworthy desserts can also be made with butternuts when you are home.

CATTAIL (*Typhaceae* family)

Who does not know these tall strap-leaved plants with their brown sausage-like heads, which, growing in large groups from 2 to 9 feet high, are exclamation points in wet places throughout the temperate and tropical countries of the world?

Although now relatively unused in the United States, where four species thrive, cattails are deliciously edible both raw and cooked, from their starchy roots to their cornlike spikes, making them prime emergency foods. Furthermore, the long, slender basal leaves, dried and then soaked to make them pliable, provide rush seating for chairs as well as tough material for mats. As for the fluff of light-colored seeds, which enliven many a winter wind, these will softly fill pillows and provide warm stuffing for comforters.

Cattails are also known in some places as rushes, cossack asparagus, bulrushes, cat-o'-nine-tails, and flags. Sure signs of fresh or brackish water, they are tall, stout-stemmed perennials with thin, stiff, sword-like green leaves up to 6 feet long. These have well-developed round rims at the sheathing bases.

The branched rootstocks creep in crossing tangles a few inches below the usually muddy surface. The flowers grow densely at the tops of the plants in spikes that, first plumply green and finally a shriveling yellow, resemble long bottle brushes and eventually produce millions of tiny, wind-wafted seeds.

These seeds, it so happens, are too small and hairy to be very attractive to birds except to a few like the teal. It is the starchy underground stems that attract such wildlife as muskrat and geese. Too, I've seen moose dipping their huge, ungainly heads where cattails grow.

Cattail
LEFT: **leaves, head, and flower spike.** RIGHT: **basal leaves and root.**

Another name for this prolific wild edible should be wild corn. Put on boots and have the fun of collecting a few dozen of the greenish yellow flower spikes before they start to become tawny with pollen, while they are still succulent. Husk off the thin sheaths and, just as you would with the garden vegetable, put into rapidly boiling water for a few minutes until tender. Have plenty of butter or margarine by each plate, as these will probably be somewhat roughly dry, and keep each hot stalk liberally swabbed as you feast on it just as you would on corn. You'll end up with a stack of wiry cobs, feeling deliciously satisfied.

These flower spikes later become profusely golden with thick yellow pollen, which, quickly rubbed or shaken into pails or onto a cloth, is also very much edible. A common way to take advantage of this gilded substance, which can be easily cleaned by passing it through a sieve, is by mixing it with an equal amount of regular flour for use in breadstuffs.

It is the tender white inner flesh of about the first 1 or 1½ feet of the peeled young cattail stems that, eaten either raw or cooked, lends this worldwide delicacy its name of cossack asparagus. These highly edible aquatic herbs can thus be an important survival food in the spring.

Later on, in the fall and winter, quantities of the nutritiously starchy roots can be dug and washed, peeled white still wet, dried, and then ground into a meal, which can be sifted to get out any fibers. Too, there is a pithy little tidbit where the new stems sprout out of the rootstocks that can be roasted or boiled like young potatoes. All in all, is it any wonder that the picturesque cattails, now too often neglected except by nesting birds, were once an important Indian food?

CHOKECHERRY
(Prunus species)

Perhaps the most widely distributed tree on this continent, the chokecherry grows from the Arctic Circle to Mexico and from ocean to ocean. Despite their puckery quality, one handful of the small ripe berries seems to call for another when you're hot and thirsty. The fruit, which can be red or black, also makes an enjoyable tart jelly.

Often merely a large shrub, the chokecherry also becomes a small tree up to 25 feet tall with a trunk about 8 inches in diameter. It is found in open woods, but is more often seen on stream banks, in thickets in the corners of fields, and along roadsides and fences. Although the wood is similar to that of the rum cherry, it has no commercial value because of its smallness.

Chokecherry leaves, from 2 to 4 inches long and about half as wide, are oval or inversely ovate, with abrupt points. They are thin and smooth, dull dark green above and paler below. The edges are finely indented with narrowly pointed teeth. The short stems, less than an inch in length, have a pair of glands at their tops. The long clusters of flowers blossom when the leaves are nearly grown.

Chokecherry
LEFT: **flowering branch.**
CENTER: **branch with leaves and fruit.** RIGHT: **winter twig**

The red to black fruits, the size of peas, are frequently so abundant that the limbs bend under their weight. The pits, like those of the domestic peach, should be avoided because of their cyanogenetic content. The leaves are also poisonous, especially in spring and early summer.

CHUFA (*Cyperus* species)

Chufa was so valued as a nutriment during early centuries that as long as 4,000 years ago the Egyptians were including it among the choice foods placed in their tombs. Wildlife was enjoying it long before that. Both the edible tubers and the seeds of this plant, also known as earth almond and as nut grass, are sought by waterfowl, upland game birds, and other wildlife. Often abundant in mudflats that glisten with water in the late fall and early winter, the nutritious tubers are readily accessible to ducks. Where chufa occurs as a robust weed in other places, especially in sandy soil and loam, upland game birds and rodents are seen vigorously digging for the tubers.

Abounding from Mexico to Alaska and from one coast to the other, this edible sedge also grows in Europe, Asia, and Africa, being cultivated in some localities for its tubers. Sweet, nutty, and milky with juice, these are clustered about the base of the plant, particularly when it grows in sandy or loose soil where a few tugs will give a hungry man his dinner. In hard dirt, the nuts are widely scattered as well as being difficult to excavate.

Except for several smaller leaves at the top of the stalk supporting the flower clusters, all the light green, grass-like leaves of the chufa grow from the roots. These latter are comprised of long runners, terminating in little nutlike tubers. The numerous flowers grow in little, flat, yellowish spikes.

Chufa furnishes one of the wild coffees: Just separate the little tubers from their roots, wash them, and spread them out to dry. Then roast them in a slow (250°F) oven with the door ajar until they are a rich brown throughout, grind them as in the blender, and brew and serve like the store-bought beverage. Prepared this way, chufa tastes more like a cereal "coffee" than like the regular brew. But it is wholesome, pleasant, and contains none of the sleep-retarding ingredients of the commercial grinds.

Chufa

The Spanish make a refreshing cold drink from the chufa, enjoyed both as is and as a base for stronger concoctions. The Spanish recipe calls for soaking ½ pound of the well-washed tubers for two days. Drain them and either mash them or put them through the blender along with 4 cups of water and ⅓ cup sugar. Strain the white, milky results, and you're in business. A popular alcoholic drink is made by partially freezing this beverage in the refrigerator, then adding an equal volume of light rum to make a sort of wild frozen Daiquiri.

CLOVER
(*Trifolium* species)

E veryone who as a youngster has sucked honey from the tiny tubular florets of its purple and reddish blossoms, or who has searched among its green beds for the elusive four-leaf combinations, knows the clover. Some seventy-five species of clover grow in this country, about twenty of them thriving in the East.

Clover

Clovers, which are avidly pollinated by bees, grow from an inch or so to 2 feet high in the fields, pastures, meadows, open woods, and along roadsides of the continent. Incidentally, when introduced into Australia, it failed to reproduce itself until bumblebees were also imported.

The stemmed foliage is usually composed of three small leaflets with toothed edges, although some of the western species boast as many as six or seven leaflets. This sweet-scented member of the pea family provides esteemed livestock forage. Red clover is Vermont's state flower. White clover is all the more familiar for being grown in lawns. Quail are among the birds eating the small, hard seeds, while deer, mountain sheep, antelope, rabbit, and other animals browse on the plants.

Bread made from the seeds and dried blossoms of clover has the reputation of being very wholesome and nutritious, and of sometimes being a mainstay in times of famine. Being so widely known and plentiful, clover is certainly a potential survival food that can be invaluable in an emergency.

The young leaves and flowers are good raw. Some Indians, eating them in quantity, used to dip these first in salted water. The young leaves and blossoms can also be successfully boiled, and they can be steamed as the Indians used to do before drying them for winter use.

If you're steaming greens for four people, melt 4 tablespoons of butter or margarine in a large, heavy frying pan over high heat. Stir in 6 loosely packed cups of greens and blossoms, along with 6 tablespoons of water. Cover, except when stirring periodically, and cook for several minutes until the clover is wilted. Salt, pepper, and eat.

The sweetish roots may also be appreciated on occasion, some people liking them best when they have been dipped in oil or in meat drippings.

Clover tea is something you may very well enjoy. Gather the full-grown flowers at a time when they are dry. Then further dry them indoors at ordinary house temperatures, afterward rubbing them into small particles and sealing them in bottles or jars to hold in the flavor. Use 1 teaspoon of these to each cup of boiling water, brewing either in a teapot or in individual cups.

COMMON CHICKWEED
(Stellaria media)

The deceivingly meek little member of the pink or carnation family is a seemingly feeble but really vigorous weed that thrives in green, ground-covering masses. In lawns and in gardens, it is regarded as troublesome by those who have not relished its edibility. The leaves, which are smoothly oval and somewhat sharply pointed, grow in opposite pairs on numerous slim branches. Each of the small white flowers has five minute petals which are deeply cleft, almost into two parts. Closed nights and overcast days, they open to bright sunshine. Good in salads when young, chickweed makes a particularly wholesome and nutritious potherb. More tender than most wild greens, it can be enjoyed either raw or cooked very slightly.

Common chickweed

COWSLIP *(Caltha palustris)*

The glossy yellow flowers of the cowslip, also known as marsh marigold and by over two dozen other common names, are among the first to gleam in the spring along stream banks and in marshy cool spots from Alaska to Newfoundland and as far south as Tennessee and South Carolina. This wild edible is also eagerly awaited in Europe.

Cowslip

One reason this member of the crowfoot family gained its name of cowslip is that you often see it growing in wet barnyards and meadows and in the trampled soggy ground where cattle drink. Few wild blossoms are more familiar or beautiful, and New Englanders find few wild greens that boil up so delicately so soon after the long, white winters.

The bright golden blossoms, which grow up to 1½ inches broad and which somewhat resemble large buttercups, have from five to nine petal-like divisions that do not last long, falling off and being replaced by clusters of seed-crammed pods. These flowers grow, singly and in groups, on slippery stems that lift hollowly among the leaves.

Cowslips, growing up to 1 and 2 feet tall, have crisp, shiny, heart-shaped lower leaves, some 3 to 7 inches broad. These grow on long, fleshy stems. On the other hand, the upper leaves appear almost directly from the smooth stalks themselves. The leaf edges, sometimes wavy, are frequently divided into rounded segments.

There are two things to watch out for if you are going to enjoy the succulent cowslip. First, this plant must be served as a potherb, as the raw leaves contain the poison helleborin, which is destroyed by cooking. It is, therefore, a good idea to gather cowslips by themselves to avoid the mistake of mixing them with salad greens. Second, ordinary care must be taken not to include any of the easily differentiated poisonous hellebore or water hemlocks that sometimes grow in the same places.

The two poisonous plants are entirely different in appearance from the distinctive cowslip. The water hemlock plant superficially resembles the domestic carrot plant but has coarser leaves and a taller, thicker stem. The white hellebore, which can be mistaken for a loose-leaved cabbage, is a leafy plant that somewhat resembles skunk cabbage—one reason why that not altogether agreeable edible has been omitted from these pages.

The dark green leaves and thick, fleshy stems of the cowslip are at their tastiest before the plant flowers. The way many know them best is boiled for an hour in two changes of salted water, then lifted out in liberal forkfuls and topped with quickly spreading pads of butter.

The leaves and stems aren't the only deliciously edible portions of this bright little harbinger of spring. You can make pickles from the buds, soaking them first for several hours in salted water, draining, and then simmering them in spiced vinegar, whereupon they take on the flavor of capers.

CRANBERRY (*Oxycoccus* species)

The firm red cranberry, which grows on thin vines that creep over innumerable acres of marsh and moist woodland, is a familiar sight on fruit counters, particularly around the Thanksgiving and Christmas holidays. The cranberry's only drawback as an emergency food is its unpalatable bitterness. Stewed with an added sweet such as the blueberries that are often growing nearby, the cranberry's rightfully deserved popularity is easier to recognize.

Frontiersmen still gather the wild fruit by the bushels, many whittling flat-bottom scoops with a series of long V-shaped teeth so as to strip the vines more easily. It then becomes a pleasant evening occupation to help empty pails onto a stretched, slanted blanket. Leaves, stems, and other debris are thus caught and are later shaken away, while the ripe cranberries roll and bound into containers for later use in a variety of dishes ranging from pies to bannock.

Cranberry

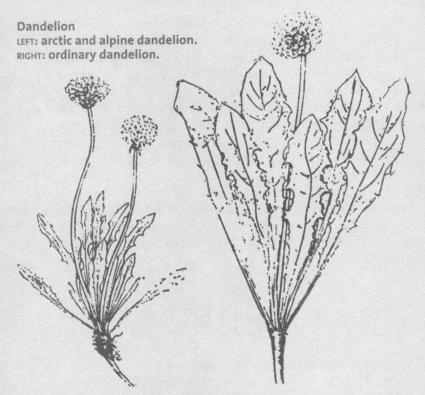

Dandelion
LEFT: arctic and alpine dandelion.
RIGHT: ordinary dandelion.

DANDELIONS
(*Taraxacum* species)

Gathering wild greens is a happy way to sharpen a satisfactory hunger, even if you go no farther than to collect a bagful of common dandelions. Actually, this familiar vegetable, all too well known because of the way it dots many a lawn, is among the best of the wild greens.

The well-known dandelion of flowerbeds, lawns, pastures, meadows, roadsides, and other moist, open places boasts some three species in this country and about twenty-five in the civilized world, over which it is widespread. The green leaves are long and narrow, spreading in a rosette at the bottom. Their coarse edges, irregularly lobed and toothed, give this wild edible its name, which means "lion's tooth."

The flowers are yellow, maturing into full white ovals of plume-tailed seeds that later scatter in the wind to make dandelions plentiful and persistent. The hollow and leafless flower stems discharge a bitterish milky juice when bruised or severed, as do the roots when the greens are cut free. These roots are generally thick and deep. Such wildlife as white-tailed and mule deer relish the green foliage, while grouse and pheasants find the seeds delectable.

The tender young leaves, available in the early spring, are among the first wild edibles I gather while bear hunting, trout fishing, or just plain hiking or horseback riding through the greening wilderness. At first they are excellent in salads. Later, when the plants begin blossoming, they develop a toughness and bitterness. Changing the boiling water once during cooking will remove much of this bitter taste if you want, but I find it clean and zestful. Incidentally, when you can, include as many buds as possible, as they liven both the color and the flavor.

Although they contain a laxative, taraxacum, the roots when young are often peeled and sliced, like carrots or parsnips, for boiling as a vegetable. To remove the characteristic tinge of bitterness, you may choose to change the salted water once. Serve with melting butter or margarine. Being particularly nourishing, these roots are a famous emergency food, having saved people from starving during famines.

Although the woods afford a multitude of teas, they are short on coffees. The dandelion will provide one of the latter. Roast the roots slowly in an open oven all afternoon until, shriveling, they resemble miniature dragons and will snap crisply when broken, revealing insides as brown as coffee beans.

Grind these roots and keep tightly covered for use either as regular coffee or for mixing to extend your normal supplies. Dandelion roots may be used the year around for this purpose. Because I generally roast my grind shortly before freeze-up in the fall, when the roots are near their strongest, I find I only have to use a level tablespoon of this homemade mixture per cup, whereas I prefer a heaping tablespoon of store coffee.

Dandelion wine is famous. If you'd like to make your own, pick a gallon of the flowers early on a dry morning, making sure that no parts of the bitterish stems are included. Press these into a 2-gallon crock. Pour a gallon of boiling water over them and leave for 3 days. Then strain through a cloth, squeezing all the liquid from the blossoms.

Add the juice, thinly sliced rind, and pulp of 3 oranges and 3 lemons. Stir in 3 pounds sugar. Add 1 ounce yeast. Cover the crock with a cloth and let it stand, out of the way, for 3 weeks while the mixture ferments. Then strain, bottle, and cork or cap tightly.

DOCKS (*Rumex* species)

Dock

Docks are stylishly stout plants, bulky with mainly basal leaves, rich in vitamins C and A. They flower in tall, baton-like, whorled clusters of tiny green blossoms that sometimes take on a regally purplish cast. With a delicately bitter, lemonish flavor, young dock is great in salads. A delicious puree can be made from the young leaves, although it depends on your particular palate. To some, all dock is too bitter for enjoying without cooking. Some species of dock are more bitter than others, especially when older. However, in many areas dock continues to put up new leaves despite frosts and can often be gathered, young and tender, throughout warm spells during the winter.

EVENING PRIMROSE
(*Oenothera* species)

Evening primrose

These fragrant blossoms are known to many because of their habit of opening after dusk. They carry on their reproductive functions in the dimness, when their scent and light-colored hues lure the night-hovering moths upon whom they rely for fertilization. Although some of these brief-lived blooms remain open in daylight, many of them shut their four broad petals toward dawn, wilt more and more, and then drop off. It is mainly the nutritious, tasty, somewhat nutlike roots that are eaten by Americans, Canadians, and some Europeans. These are generally boiled by themselves or in stews.

FIREWEED
(Chamerion angustifolium)

Fireweed is another herb difficult to mistake, especially when the single multi-leaved stalks brighten with purplish flowers. Thousands of acres of burnt lands turn to magenta, so thickly does fireweed bloom there when frost leaves the ground. The young stems when they first appear are tender enough to cook like asparagus. More mature stalks are peeled and their sweetish interiors eaten raw. The young leaves make passable greens.

Dried fireweed leaves, like those of plantain and many other eatables, find their way into boiling kettles from which, after the water has been infused, are poured beverages that are drunk as tea.

Fireweed

FRITILLARY
(Fritillaria species)

It is the bulbs of these plants that are edible. While these are more or less similar, the tops differ markedly, especially in color, from large bell-like flowers in a dark winelike hue, to single golden blossoms, to solitary, nodding flowers that are deep purple and mottled with a greenish-yellow color. Tasting something like potatoes when raw, more like rice when cooked, the starch-rich bulbs are nourishing and delicious, as are the tender, young green seed pods.

Fritillary

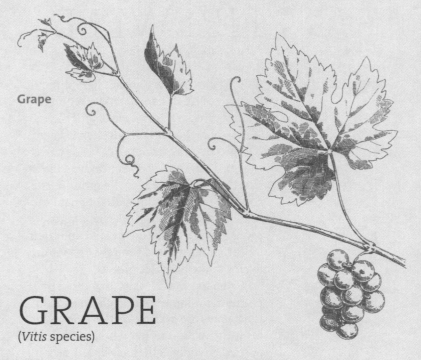

Grape

GRAPE
(*Vitis* species)

The various species of broad-leaved, tendril-clinging, high-climbing, or trailing wild grapes, one of the survival foods of the Lewis and Clark expedition and long an Indian mainstay throughout much of the continent, include the large fox grape, the aromatic muscadine, the pleasant pigeon grape, and the notable scuppernong. All are too familiar to require description.

At least half the world's wild grapes are native to this country, some two dozen or so species being widely distributed over the United States. Favoring moist, fertile ground, they frequently twine toward sunlight along stream banks, beaches, fences, stone walls, and near the edges of woods. Birds find the dense foliage excellent sanctuary and even use the bark for some of their nests.

Fruit, leaves, and young shoots are all edible. Among the game making use of them are deer, black bear, opossum, rabbit, squirrel, dove, wood duck, ruffed grouse, ring-necked pheasant, bobwhite, prairie chicken, and wild turkey. Even when clusters of fruit dry like raisins on the vines, they are sought by birds and animals during all seasons.

GROUND CHERRY
(*Physalis* species)

Ground cherries, close relations to the tomato but not even distant cousins of the cherry family, grow in all parts of the country except Alaska. Also known as strawberry tomatoes and husk tomatoes, they have long found their way into occasional markets, being raised commercially in some localities. They are also found in fields, waste places, and in open country, but particularly in recently cleared and cultivated ground, where they ripen from July through September.

This rapidly growing annual takes up a lot of room, its single or forked branches many times sprawling over several feet of ground, but it seldom grows more than a foot high. The pointed leaves have broadly and roundly indented edges. The decorative flowers—which make one hardy perennial of the family, the Chinese lantern plant or winter cherry, a flower garden favorite—resemble tiny yellow funnels. Their five petals later greatly expand, completely enclosing the round yellow berry in a tiny papery husk.

These large yellowish coverings so protect the single golden fruits that when, as often happens, they fall early, they still ripen on the ground. If you store the encased berries dry, they will continue to become more sugary for several weeks. But in some areas you have to beat the game birds and some of the game and fur animals to them.

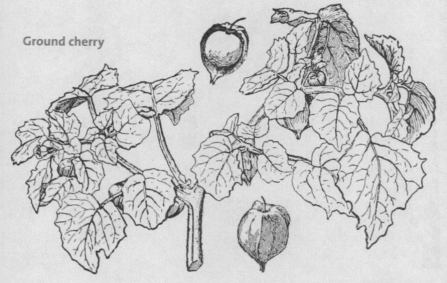

Ground cherry

Ground cherries are very easily put up: Just make a syrup by boiling 6 cups water, 3 cups sugar, and the juice of 3 lemons for 5 minutes. Spoon in enough ground cherries to come to the top of the syrup. Simmer until the fruit is tender and clear, pour into hot sterilized jars, and seal.

The raw berries, which are very refreshing when you're out for the day, make a pleasant dessert with sugar and milk. Or try them with vanilla ice cream sometime. They're good with this, too, after they've been blended as for pie and stewed.

The jam, too, is really scrumptious. Crush 4 cups of fully ripe fruit, a layer at a time, so that each berry is reduced to pulp. Add 4 tablespoons lemon juice and a package of pectin. Bring the mixture quickly to a boil, stirring occasionally. Then put in 4 cups sugar. Bring back to a hard boil for 1 minute, continuing to stir. Remove from the heat and skim off any foam. Let cool for 5 minutes, stirring occasionally, for better consistency. Then pour into hot sterilized glasses and seal at once as usual.

GROUNDNUT
(*Arachis hypogaea*)

Asa Gray, the noted botanist, once opined that if civilization had started in the New World rather than the Old, the little groundnut would have been the first tuber to have been cultivated as a food. Many trying it for the first time do like it better than the modern potato. The Pilgrims, introduced to the groundnut by the friendly Massachusetts Indians, depended on them to a large extent during their first rugged winter in Plymouth. Thus they became familiar to early European settlers, many of whom found the tubers very acceptable substitutes for bread. The beanlike seeds, better known as peanuts, are also edible.

Groundnut

HAWTHORN
(*Crataegus* species)

I t is fortunate that it's easy to distinguish the hawthorn from other shrubs and small trees. Even the professionals find it difficult to identify the separate species, the number of which in the United States is estimated to run all the way from about 100 to as many as 1,200. They grow from one coast to the other, making them valuable when survival is a problem. Taste varies considerably, and the only way to determine the edibility of hawthorn you've come across is by sampling. The better of them are delicious raw, and when turned into jelly require very little sugar.

These cousins of the domestic apple are also known as thorn apples, thorn plums, thorns, mayhaws, red haws, scarlet haws, haws, cockspur thorn, etc. Wood ducks eat the fruit. Pheasants, grouse, pigeons, and turkeys relish both buds and fruit. Black bears, rabbits, beavers, raccoons, and squirrels include both fruit and bark in their diets. Deer browse on the foliage and the apple-like pomes. In addition to all this, hawthorns provide almost impregnable nesting places.

Hawthorn

You can readily identify a hawthorn even in winter, particularly as the long, sharp, usually straight, occasionally slightly curved thorns, ranging in length up to about 5 inches, are not shared by any of our other native trees and shrubs.

Showy when blossoming in the spring and attractive when colorful with fruit, especially against the snow, hawthorns thrive in sunny locales in clearings, pastures, and abandoned fields, and along roads and fences. The white and occasionally pinkish flowers, which have five petals, grow in terminal clusters. The fruit, which is usually red but sometimes greenish or yellowish, looks like tiny apples. Each contains one to five bony, one-seeded nutlets.

HAZELNUT
(*Corylus* species)

The three native varieties of this multibranched shrub are much alike, although the nuts vary some. The so-called American hazelnut is a shrub with wide heart-shaped leaves with double teeth. The brown nuts, which are ½ to ¾ inch long and enwrapped in a downy whorl of two leaf-like bracts whose edges are fringed, are usually sweet and ripe in August and, if not bothered—which is unlikely—cling to the shrubs until late in the autumn. Hazelnuts, treats by themselves, go well with cookies, candies, and other delicately flavored delights.

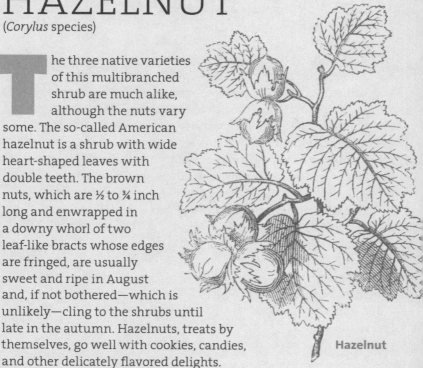

Hazelnut

HEMLOCK
(*Tsuga* species)

Hemlock tea is famous in northern New England and Canada. Drunk hot and black, its taste is reminiscent of the way a Christmas tree smells. More important for trappers, prospectors, and other outdoorsmen, this tea contains the vital vitamin C.

Of the seven to nine species of hemlocks recognized in the world, four are native to North America. These tall, straight evergreens are typical of cool, damp slopes, ravines, and swamps, generally in northern regions and in the higher mountains. They also spring up after tree-cutting operations, their low dense foliage affording fine winter cover for grouse, turkey, deer, and other wildlife.

The needles grow in spirals, although they often seem to be attached in two ranks. The hanging cones have thin segments that hide a pair of tiny winged seeds, which are important food for birds and red squirrels. Hemlocks in New England and the Maritimes are often killed by porcupines eating the bark.

Incidentally, these conifers are no relation whatsoever to the poison hemlock from which Socrates and other ancients brewed their deadly draughts. Those entirely different plants are members of the parsley family.

It doesn't really make too much difference if you mistake one of the other conifers for hemlock. All these members of the pine family provide aromatic and beneficial tea. The bright green young tips, when they appear in the springtime, are best. These are tender and starchy at this time and can also be enjoyed raw. Older green needles will do, too. I just put a handful in a receptacle, cover them with boiling water, and let them steep until the tea tastes strong enough. If you prefer this black, as I do, there's no need of any straining. Just narrow your lips on the rim and quaff it down.

The hemlocks and other members of the great pine family, which includes the numerous pines themselves, as well as spruces, firs, balsams, and others, have another feature that, if one is ever lost or stranded, can mean the difference between life and death: The inner bark can be cut off and eaten, either raw or boiled, to provide strength and nourishment.

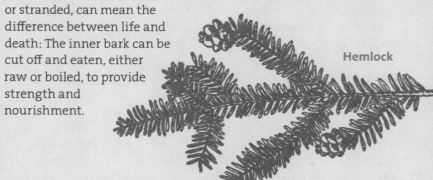

Hemlock

HICKORY *(Carya* species)

Hickories are probably our most important native nuts. The Indians used them in great quantities for food, and the settlers soon followed suit, even tapping the sweet sap in the spring for syrup and sugar. Today the nuts are familiar in the stores of this country.

The shellbark hickory, also called the shagbark, is the leader of the clan, although there are twenty to twenty-two other species, depending upon the botanist. All are edible, although the taste of

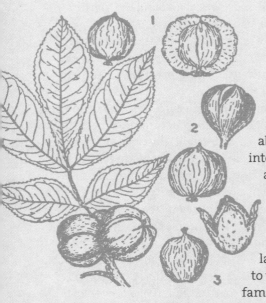

Hickory
1. Shagbark;
2. Pignut;
3. Bitternut.

some is not appealing. There are the sweet hickories, including the above, in which the husk splits into four parts when the nuts are ripe. There are the pignuts, often bitter but sometimes delicious, in which the thin husk splits only above the middle, or, sometimes late in the season, all the way to the base. There are also the familiar pecans.

The stout twigs and the gray bark, which loosens in shaggy narrow strips attached at the middle, distinguishes the shellbark and the shagbark, actually two different species, from all other trees. The leaves, from 7 to 14 inches long, are composed of usually five but sometimes seven leaflets. Dark yellowish green above, these are lighter and often downy beneath, with fine sharp teeth marking the edges.

Hickories grow slowly, and the shellbark does not produce nuts until it is about eighty years old. It becomes a large stately tree, reaching a height of up to 180 or more feet and a trunk diameter of 1 to 3 feet. Its wood is used for such things as bows, skis, and ax handles, while hickory-smoked hams and bacon are famous. Wood duck, ring-necked pheasant, bobwhite, and wild turkey compete with man for the nuts. Black bear, raccoon, squirrel, and rabbit eat both nuts and bark, while the white-tailed deer relishes these as well as the younger twigs.

The shellbark, which leafs out later than most other trees and sheds its bronze foliage earlier, ranges from Maine and Quebec west to the Great Lakes and Minnesota, and south to northern Florida and eastern Texas. The fruits, varying a great deal in size, are on the average from 1 to 2 inches in diameter, nearly round or somewhat oblong, and depressed at the top. The husks, which are about ¼ inch thick, split into four pieces at maturity. The familiar white or tawny nuts are a bit flattened with four ridges, an easily cracked thin shell, and large sweet kernels.

HORSERADISH
(*Armoracia rusticana*)

There is little comparison between store-bought horseradish and the freshly grated version you can prepare yourself using the wild roots and lemon juice instead of the commonly employed wine vinegar. Mouth-tickling horseradish, popular the world over, has been used as a food seasoning for centuries.

The perennial horseradish, regrowing in the same places for dozens of years and spreading where there is sufficient moisture, came to the New World from England. Originally planted around the cabins and other buildings of the northeastern United States and southern Canada, it has thrived and dispersed until it now grows wild throughout much of the same general area. The nose-stinging, eye-watering white roots, so good when used in moderation with less tasty foods, are edible the year around.

The small white flowers of the horseradish, like those of all other members of the mustard family, have just four petals. They grow in short-stemmed, loosely branched clusters. Although seeds are seldom produced, there are the occasional round pods, each of which is divided into two cells with perhaps four to six seeds in each.

Numerous large leaves grow from the root on strong, long stalks. These leaves, often 6 inches wide and nearly twice as long, have wavy, scalloped edges. The much smaller, stemless leaves that grow directly from a smooth, round, erect, central spike, often several feet long, are oblong and serrated.

The leaves when tender in the spring make greens that are tastier than most when dropped into a small amount of boiling salted water, cooked uncovered only until

Horseradish

85

tender, and then served immediately with a crowning pat of butter or margarine.

But it is for its heartily peppery roots that horseradish has been famous for thousands of years. These fleshy roots, sometimes as long as a foot and as thick as 1 or 2 inches, are tapering, conical at the top, and many times abruptly branched near the end. They are white both within and without. When bruised or scraped, they give off a strongly pungent odor. When a particle is transferred to the tongue, it is immediately hot and biting.

The simplest way to prepare this masterful condiment for the table is by scraping some of the scrubbed root into a small dish, then stirring in fresh lemon juice or wine vinegar to taste.

Then there are innumerable refinements, the easiest of which is to add a small amount of sugar to the original mixture, again by taste. In any event, for the most pleasing results make only small amounts of the sauce at a time—an easy thing to do, as horseradish roots can be freshly gathered year-round.

Besides enjoying horseradish roots and leaves, pioneers used to apply the freshly scraped roots externally as they would mustard plasters. Horseradish was also used as an internal medicine, a teaspoon of the scraped root to a cup of boiling water. This was allowed to cool. One or two cupfuls were then drunk throughout the day, several sips at a time, as a stimulant to the stomach.

JACK-IN-THE-PULPIT (*Arisaema* species)

Many Indians relied on the dried and powdered roots of the familiar jack-in-the-pulpit for flour. Today, however, this edible has its principal value as an emergency food, especially for people stranded in one place for a long time. Widely known and easily recognizable, it can then be a lifesaver.

Indian turnip, wake-robin, and dragonroot are among the local names for this North and South American member of the great Arum family, used for food by people the world over. Both the leaves and the bright red fruit are eaten by the ring-necked pheasant and the wild turkey.

In the moist, sequestered woodlands of April and May, the jack-in-the-pulpit preaches his silent sermon to a congregation of wild violets and other spring neighbors. Unmistakable, the brown, green, and purplish "pulpit" is a striped 2- to 4-inch spathe terminating with a hood over the top. The "preacher" is a club-like spadix, 2 or 3 inches long, with small greenish yellow flowers, occasionally varying greatly in hues and in brightness, near its base.

Jack-in-the-pulpit

The plant, growing in rich woods from the Maritime Provinces south to Florida, and west to Minnesota and Louisiana, grows 1 to 3 feet high. The two leaves, growing on long stems, are each composed of three egg-shaped, sometimes lobed, pointed leaflets. Green clusters of berries become handsome scarlet masses that brighten the dark woods in late August.

All parts of the plant, especially the round roots, will burn the mouth like liquid fire if eaten raw. Many youngsters used to have a standard ceremony for initiating newcomers to town, and perhaps still do. This consisted of offering the tenderfoot the tiniest morsel of what they claimed was the finest delicacy their woods had to offer. At first contact, this innocent-looking tidbit was palatable enough. But then the taste became as bitingly hot as a teaspoon of red pepper. This burning sensation, which was followed by inflammation and tenderness, seemed to permeate every part of tongue, mouth, and throat and to linger for hours, although cold milk did appear to allay it some.

The wonder is that aborigines the world over have learned to rid Arum roots of this corrosive acridness and thus capitalize upon their nutritious, delicate, white starchiness. Boiling won't do it! Drying will. The fastest way to do this is by roasting. The simplest method is just to cut the fresh roots into very thin slices, then set these aside in a dry place for at least three months. They then provide pleasant snacks, either as is or with a dip. Or you can crumble the crisp slices into flour and use it in regular recipes, preferably half and half with wheat flour.

Once the fire had been taken out of them, jack-in-the-pulpit roots were also held to be medicinally valuable. One prescription for spasms of asthma consisted of a handful of the dried and chipped roots, aged for three days in a quart of whisky. Even then, the dosage was conservative: It was a single tablespoon twice a day.

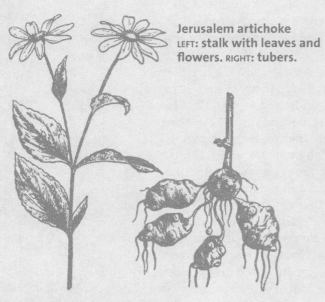

Jerusalem artichoke
LEFT: **stalk with leaves and flowers.** RIGHT: **tubers.**

JERUSALEM ARTICHOKE (*Helianthus* species)

Jerusalem artichokes, the distinctively flavored tubers of a native wild sunflower, were cultivated by Indians and much used by early settlers. Besides still growing wild, they are also raised for today's markets and commonly known as "sunchokes," all of which indicates how well worth finding they are.

They have no connection with the Holy City. Soon introduced into Europe following Columbus's voyages to the New World, they became popular along the Mediterranean and were called *girasole* in Italian and *girasol* in Spanish. These words, denoting "sunflower," became corrupted in English to Jerusalem. The artichoke part of the name stems from the fact that even centuries ago the flower buds of some of the edible sunflowers were boiled and eaten with butter like that vegetable.

About ninety species of sunflowers occur in the world. Some two-thirds of these grow in the United States, among them these tall perennials whose roots are such a delicacy. You have to like them, of course. I've learned to prepare them so that I do.

Wild Jerusalem artichokes, which should be harvested no sooner than fall, are native to the central parts of the United States and Canada. Their popularity among Indians and arriving Europeans, plus their cultivation in different parts of the country, helps explain why this native has long since escaped its original bounds and is now often found in abundance elsewhere—such as east of the Appalachians, where it has moved to usually moist soil along ditches, streams, roadways, fence rows, and in vacant fields and lots.

These perennial sunflowers grow with thin stalks commonly 5 to 10 feet tall. The rough leaves, whose tops are hairy, develop sharp points from oblong or egg-shaped bodies that are broadest near their bases. The frequently numerous flowers are yellow. From 2 to 3 inches broad, and maturing on slender stems that rise from where the higher leaves meet the stalk, these blossoms lack the purplish and brownish centers of those sunflowers that yield edible, oil-rich seeds. But the tubers, which are attached to the thickly creeping roots, more than make up for this deficiency.

History is all in favor of these delicacies whose somewhat sweetish juiciness, however, may take a bit of getting accustomed to. On the other hand, Jerusalem artichokes are nutritious and easily digestible enough to be regarded as a favored food for invalids. Here are a couple of hints that may help along your enjoyment: Dig them late in the year, even in winter if the ground is not too frozen, previously noting their whereabouts when they are conspicuously in bloom. Secondly, take care that they are not cooked too long nor at too high temperatures, as either will toughen them.

Your cooking efforts may be as simple or as elaborate as you want them to be. The long, somewhat flat tubers are good just scrubbed, simmered in their skins in enough water to cover until just tender, and then peeled and served like potatoes, either with salt and butter or margarine or with a cream sauce. They then afford a by-product, too. When cold, the water in which they were boiled becomes jellylike, providing a flavorful and substantial foundation for soup.

Juniper

JUNIPER (*Juniperus* species)

Black bear, quail, and band-tailed pigeon are among the game dining on the fruit of the juniper. These evergreen shrubs and shrubby trees with their compact branches, thin shreddy bark, and scale-like leaves pressed closely to the twigs grow from Alaska to Labrador and as far south as New Mexico and California. The usually sprawling juniper prefers exposed dry slopes and rocky ridges, and many a hunter has lounged in one to glass the country or to watch a game trail. The not unpleasant sharpness of some of their short needles makes one feel warmer on a brisk day.

The fruit, whose flavor and aroma is familiar to anyone who has had contact with gin, is dark blue and has a bloom to it. Growing in large numbers on the shoots of the female shrubs, these berries are to be found year-round. They are the size of peas. The flesh surrounding the large seed is sweetish and resinously aromatic.

American Indians used to dry and grind juniper berries and use them for cakes and for mush. The principal individual use today is as a nibble and as a woodsy seasoning. A few will take the edge off hunger. Too many, though, are irritating to the kidneys. In fact, a diuretic is made of the berries: a teaspoon of berries to a cup of boiling water, drunk cold, a large mouthful at a time, one or two cups a day.

Juniper tea, quaffed in small amounts, is one of the decidedly pleasant evergreen beverages. Add about a dozen young berryless sprigs to a quart of cold water. Bring this to a boil, cover, reduce the heat, and allow to simmer for 10 minutes. Strain and serve like regular tea.

KENTUCKY COFFEE TREE
(Gymnocladus dioicus)

Roasted and ground, the seeds of the Kentucky coffee tree were used by early settlers in the New World as a substitute for coffee. Some Indian tribes roasted them and ate them like nuts. The trees, often planted today for shade and for landscaping, range from New York to southern Minnesota and south to Tennessee and Oklahoma.

Usually a medium-size tree, reaching a height of 40 to 90 feet and a trunk diameter from 1 to 3 feet, the Kentucky coffee tree ordinarily branches a few feet above the ground into three or four limbs that climb almost vertically to form a narrow crown.

The dark green leaves, which remain on for only about half of the year, are sometimes almost 3 feet long and 2 feet wide. They are composed of up to forty or more short-stemmed leaflets. Long clusters of greenish-white flowers appear in June. These develop into reddish-brown pods from 4 to 10 inches long and from 1 to 2 inches wide. Each contains six to nine large, oval, flat, hard brownish seeds encased in a dark sweetish pulp.

You can roast these seeds slowly in the oven, grind them, and brew them like coffee. They have none of the caffeine of regular coffee, and the resulting beverage agrees with some people better.

Kentucky coffee tree

KNOTWEED *(Polygonum* species)

Some thirty or so species of knotweed occur in practically every part of the United States. Grouse, mourning doves, pheasants, quail, prairie chickens, woodcocks, and partridges devour the rather large, dark seeds. Antelope and deer eat the plants.

Man has long dined on knotweed, using various members of the family as vegetable, fruit, and even as nut. The fleshy and starchy rootstocks of the *Polygonum bistorta* in British Columbia and the Yukon are cooked and eaten as a substitute for nuts because of their almond-like taste, and from the Arctic south to New England and Colorado, the raw roots of the *Polygonum bistorta* are enjoyed for the same nutlike characteristic.

It is the Japanese knotweed, *Polygonum cuspidatum*, with which many are most familiar. This is well known, although not always by name, from North Carolina to Missouri, north to southern Canada, growing in large, coarse stands from about 3 to 8 feet high. The enlarged joints of the stalks are encased with thin, papery sheaths. When these hollow stalks die, they form bamboo-like thickets that clack and rattle in the wind and serve to identify the young, edible sprouts when, somewhat resembling asparagus in shape although not in taste, these shoot up lustily in the spring.

The stemmed green leaves of this knotweed are roundly egg-shaped, being broad at their bases but rather abruptly pointed at their tips. The whitish-green flowers, each with its five outer lobes, grow profusely in branching clusters that appear in the angles between leaves and stalk.

Knotweed shoots, before the leaves start to unfurl, are delicately delicious when some 12 to 15 inches high. They cook up much more rapidly than asparagus; 3 or 4 minutes in boiling salted water will do the

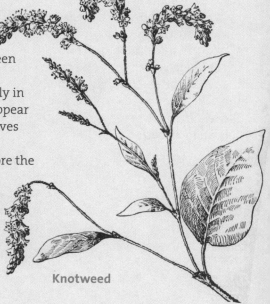

Knotweed

job. Their toothsome acidity is then brought out with melted butter or margarine. The shoots also taste good cold with mayonnaise. Either way, they go well with hot buttered toast.

LAMB'S QUARTER

(*Chenopodium* species)

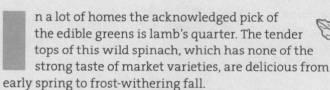

Lamb's quarter

I n a lot of homes the acknowledged pick of the edible greens is lamb's quarter. The tender tops of this wild spinach, which has none of the strong taste of market varieties, are delicious from early spring to frost-withering fall.

The entire young plant is good from the ground up. Even from older ones tender leaves can usually be stripped. However, the pale green leaves with their mealy-appearing undersides and the slim stalks are not the only taste-tempting components, also widely known as pigweed and goosefoot.

Indians long used the ripe seeds—75,000 of which have been counted on a single plant—for cereal and for grinding into meal. These tiny gleaming discs, which develop from elongated dense clusters of small green flowers, are also handy for giving a pumpernickel complexion to biscuits and breads.

Some twenty of the sixty or more species in this genus, which belongs to the same family as beets and spinach, grow in nearly every part of the United States. Lamb's quarter is a very common annual that grows from 2 to 7 feet tall. By searching, you can usually find plenty of young plants up to about 12 inches high, and these are best for the table. These young plants have a mealy whiteness to them, but they do not require parboiling. Later, the tender tips alone are excellent. The alternate leaves, which are fleshy and tasty, have long stems and angular margins.

Along with other of the more tender leafy greens, lamb's quarter can be given a bit more taste on occasion with the help of a vinegar sauce. The addition of a flavorful acid also tends to preserve vitamins C and A in such vegetables. Alkalis, on the other hand, such as the commonly but inadvisably used baking soda, destroy an unnecessary proportion of these food values.

LIVE-FOREVER
(*Sempervivum* species)

This is the wild edible that youngsters sometimes call "frog plant" because of the way one of its fleshy green leaves, after being loosened as by holding it between the warm tongue and the roof of the mouth, can be blown up like an inflated frog's throat. Our pioneer predecessors went one step further and used the insides of these leaves, once they had been blown or cut apart, to apply to warts. The fresh leaves also have a cooling quality and have long been used to soothe burns, insect bites, bruises, and other such irritations. Further, both the plant tops and the roots are deliciously edible, making them pleasant table companions as well as prime survival foods.

Live-forever

MAPLE
(*Acer* species)

Maple seeds are edible for humans; some Indians would hull the larger of them and then boil them. The sugar-rich young leaves are also edible. The inner bark of the maple is one of the more appetizing sap layers and is eaten in times of need, either raw or cooked. But it is for the sap that the tree has long been famous.

Maple

You can purchase the necessary supplies and pails for sap gathering, but unless you plan on going in for sugaring in a big way, you can do very well on your own. Drill a 2-inch-deep hole with a little gimlet, or brace and bit, and close this with a peg. For the spout, just make a single bend in a can top cut off by a smooth-cutting can opener. Don't try to suspend the can or pail from this, however. Instead, drive a small nail into the tree for this purpose. Then it's just a matter of boiling the sap and spooning off the characteristic scum as it rises, until some 35 parts or so of water evaporate, leaving a clear amber syrup. Delectable!

MAYAPPLE
(*Podophyllum peltatum*)

In springtime these attractive plants poke up like miniature forests of little opening umbrellas, preferring moist, rich woods and banks. Their creamy-white flowers in later spring are familiar from southeastern Canada to Florida and west to Minnesota and Texas. These produce sweetly scented, lemon-yellow fruits, which, when delectably ripe, are relished by many.

This native perennial, a member of the barberry family, is also known as mandrake, wild lemon, and raccoon berry. Only the fruit is edible. The root, which Indians collected soon after the fruit had ripened and used in small quantities as a cathartic, is poisonous. So are the leaves and stems.

Each spring the long horizontal roots, which stay alive year after year, shoot up single-stemmed plants 12 to 18 inches high. These roots, incidentally, are dark brown, jointed, and very fibrous. Internally yellow, they are mostly about half the size of a finger.

The solitary stems bear either one or two large leaves, which open like tiny parasols. These produce single flowers, which nod on short stems that rise from the fork of the leaves. About 2 inches wide, these oddly scented blossoms have from six to nine waxy white petals and twice that number of golden stamens.

The sweet yellow fruit, the size and shape of small eggs, ripens from July to September depending on the climate, generally when

Mayapple
LEFT: **stem with flower and leaves.**
RIGHT: **fruit.**

the dying plants have dropped to the ground. Despite numerous seeds and a tough skin, it is very enjoyable in moderation raw, although there are those who, as in the case of serviceberries, prefer the mayapple cooked.

The raw juice, however, really touches up sweet lemonade and other fruit drinks, while in some regions there are those who add it, along with sugar, to wine.

MILKWEED (*Asclepias* species)

Although milkweed grows from coast to coast and was long used by the Indians, it is the common milkweed, *Asclepias syriaca*, with which many are most familiar. This native perennial, thriving from the Maritimes west to Saskatchewan and south to Kansas and the Carolinas, has stout stems reaching from 2 to 5 feet high.

This milkweed is abundant in meadows, old fields, marshes, and along roadsides, where in the fall its seeds with their familiar parachutes waft away by the thousands into the wind. These, plus a milky juice—latex, the subject of numerous experiments seeking a native rubber—are the plant's two predominant characteristics. However, these edibles should never be identified by this milky sap alone.

The leaves of this branchless edible grow in opposite pairs. Their short stems, like the stalks, are stout and sturdy. From 4 to 9 inches long and about half as wide, these oblong to ovate leaves taper at both top and bottom. They have wide central ribs.

The clusters of numerous tiny flowers have a memorable fragrance. They vary in color from greenish lilac to almost white. Each of the components of the delicate blossoms, which are deadly traps to many of the insects that seek their nectar, is divided into five parts. They eventually produce large green pods 3 to 5 inches long. The warty coverings of these finally split, exposing silk-tufted seeds.

Young milkweed sprouts up to about 8 inches tall are excellent asparagus substitutes, especially when cooked with a small piece of salt pork—if "substitute" is the right word, since milkweed sprouts are so regally satisfying in their own right. Then the young leaves provide cooking greens. The flower buds are a delicacy. Running the sprouts a close second—and even surpassing them in some estimations—are the firm, young pods. If they are at all

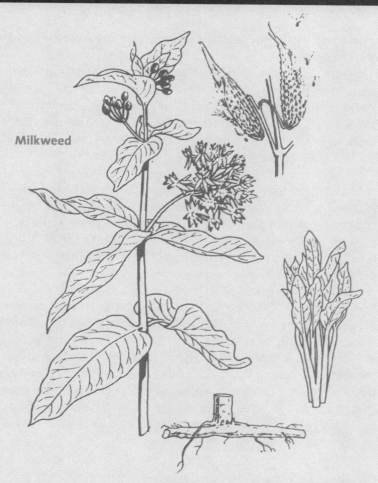

Milkweed

elastic in your fingers, however, the silken wings of the seeds have developed too far to make for good eating.

There is one caution to keep in mind: All parts of the plant are bitter with the pervasive latex. However, this is readily soluble in water. Put your milkweed—whether sprouts, young leaves, flower buds, or seedpods—all ready for cooking, in a saucepan. Cover with boiling water, bring again to a boil over high heat, and pour the water off. Do this at least once again and maybe more times, depending on your palate. To some, a slight bitterish tinge is invigorating. In any event, finally cover again with boiling water, add a bit of salt, and simmer until tender. This may require a bit longer than expected, as milkweed takes more cooking than most other greens. Serve with margarine or butter melting on top.

I've also used the similar *Asclepias speciosa* with its purplish flowers on the western side of the continent, from British Columbia to California. The tough fibers of the mature stalks of this milkweed were employed by the Indians for making string and rope and for coarse weaving. The milky juice was applied to warts and to ringworm infections, as well as to ordinary sores and cuts. The exquisitely packed ripe seeds were gathered just before soaring and skittering over the landscape, their hairy protuberances burned off, and the remainder ground into a salve for sores. These seeds were also boiled in a minimum of water and the concentrated liquid applied to draw the poison out of rattlesnake bites.

Besides serving as a cough medicine, a hot beverage made by steeping the roots was taken to bring out the rash in measles. Externally, it was supposed to help rheumatism. The root, mashed with water, was applied as a poultice to reduce swelling.

Once the shoots are more than 8 inches tall and too old to eat, the bottom leaves can no longer be used, but the young top leaves are still tender and tasty before the green flowers. These are fine mixed with young dandelion leaves, although they are good by themselves, too. Then there are the buds themselves, prepared and cooked the same way. Finally, the young pods are fine served on the side with roast or steak, or you may like what they can do for a stew.

Getting back to the blossoms, Indians supposedly have used them for sweetening on summer mornings, shaking the dew-laden nectar onto their foods before this dampness evaporated in the heat of the day. This has never worked for me, however, perhaps because I've become too lazy too soon.

MINER'S LETTUCE
(Claytonia perfoliata)

Miner's lettuce

This salad plant, whose crisp leaves and stems may also be boiled as greens, is notably easy to distinguish. Anyone who does not know it already only has to look for a small green plant with flower stems growing from a short mass of leaves at ground level. The clinching feature is that partway up each stem a pair of leaves grow together so as to form a sort of cup through whose middle the stalk continues. The plant got its name because of a deserved popularity during gold rush days in California, when it was one of the fresh vegetables eaten to cure and avert scurvy. I've enjoyed it here in the spring, gathering it in damp locations beneath the coastal pines.

MOUNTAIN SORREL (*Oxyria* species)

Mountain sorrel is a green I've enjoyed in such diverse places as New Mexico, British Columbia, and the green-sloped White Mountains of New Hampshire. This member of the buckwheat family, which grows from Alaska and Greenland to Southern California, is also widely enjoyed in Europe and Asia. It is known in different parts of this country as sourgrass, scurvy grass, and Alpine sorrel.

Mountain sorrel

The perennial mountain sorrel springs from a few inches to 2 feet high from a large, thick, deep, fleshy root. The small leaves, growing one or two on stems that for the most part rise directly from the rootstock, are smooth and either round or broadly kidney-shaped. Scarcely noticeable greenish or crimson flowers grow in rising clusters on long, full stems that extend above the mostly basal leaves. These blossoms turn into tiny reddish capsules.

The juicy leaves, which are at their best before the plant flowers, have a pleasantly acid taste that somewhat resembles rhubarb. In fact, mountain sorrel looks to some like miniature rhubarb, although it so happens that the leaves of domestic rhubarb, whether raw or cooked, are poisonous. Those of mountain sorrel, on the other hand, are delicious for salads, potherbs, and purees. Where this wild edible grows in the Arctic, the Inuit and Yupik peoples of America and Asia ferment some of it as a sauerkraut. The tender young leaves will also give a zip to sandwiches.

Mountain sorrel leaves can be turned into a puree by simmering them for 20 minutes, then pressing them through a colander or mashing them, and adding butter or margarine, salt, and pepper. You'll save vitamins, flavor, and time, though, if you use a meat grinder or kitchen blender on these juicy greens, then quickly cook and add them to a piping hot base.

MUSTARD
(*Brassica* species)

Mustard, which flourishes wild over most of the globe, is universally recognizable because of its brilliant yellow flowers that become almost solid gold across many a field and hillside. Five species are widely distributed over the United States. Most important of these is black mustard, an immigrant from Europe and Asia, which has become so much at home on this continent that it now grows over most of the United States and southern Canada.

This annual ordinarily grows from 2 to 6 feet tall, although in California I have seen it as tall as a telephone pole. A relative of cabbages, turnips, cauliflowers, radishes, brussels sprouts, and similar cultivated vegetables, black mustard grows erect with widely spreading branches. The leaves on the young plants, which are the ones to pick, are rather fuzzy and feel stiffly hairy. The finely toothed lower leaves are deeply indented at the bases of the stalks and less indented as they ascend. These lobes do not appear on the upper, small, extremely bitter leaves that grow, nearly stemless, from the flower stalks.

The sunny yellow flowers are small but numerous. Typically for mustard, each has four petals and six little upright stamens, four

Mustard

long and two shorter. The blossoms mature during the summer into small, short pods. These are filled with dark, minute, zestfully pungent seeds.

Mustard, whether used in soup or elsewhere, is most agreeable when it first appears. The young stalks are not hard to identify, particularly as older mustard is often standing in the same patch. The slightly peppery young leaves are enjoyable raw. So are the young flowers with their then-subtle pungency. The entire young plant goes well cooked with fish and meat.

Later on, the profusion of golden flowers can be capitalized upon to make a broccoli-like dish. When you pick the flowers over, it is best to eliminate any of the small upper leaves because of their bitterness. The blossoms boil up quickly in salted water. Bring them to a rapid boil, then let them stand away from the heat, tightly covered, for 5 minutes. Drain, spread with melting butter or margarine, and sprinkle with a little vinegar. Besides being colorful and delicious, this repast is full of vitamins and protein.

The easily gathered seeds of wild mustard, even after the plant has grown old and tough, are hard to equal for garnishing salads, adding to pickles and such for that extra seasoning, giving a final authority to barbecue sauces, and lending a wisp of zip and zest to stews. Mustard's very name comes from its seeds, being a corruption of "must seeds," which harks back to ancient Roman-occupied Britain, where mustard seeds were processed by saturating them in a solution of grape juice, or must, as it was sometimes called.

Table mustard can be made by finely grinding wild mustard seeds between two stones if you're in camp, or in the family food processor if you're at home, and adding enough water or vinegar to make a paste. After that, it's up to you. Commercially prepared condiments often contain such additional ingredients as flour, salt, turmeric, and other spices. If you choose to modify your raw mustard with up to an equal volume of flour, brown the flour slowly and lightly in an oven first to take away the starchy taste. The vinegar may be diluted, depending on its strength, up to half and half with water. Occasionally, the blender likes the added flavor of horseradish. This white-flowered member of the mustard family, with pungent white roots, likewise grows wild.

NETTLES (*Urtica* species)

Don't overcook your wild vegetables. Even with such a formidable green as young nettles—which, like prickly pears, are best gathered with leather gloves and a knife—once the salted water has reached the boiling point and the dark green nettles have been dropped in, they'll be tender almost immediately and ready for that crowning pat of butter or margarine as soon as they are cool enough to eat.

Nettles, which re-grow in the same places year after year across Canada and the United States, are for the most part erect, single-stemmed greens that sometimes grow up to 7 feet tall. The opposite leaves are coarsely veined; egg-shaped to oblong, with heart-like bases; and roughly and sharply toothed. Both stem and leaf surfaces bristle with a fuzz of numerous fine prickles containing irritating formic acid. Very small green flowers, which, like those of plantain, are easy to overlook, appear in multibranched clusters between leaves and stalk.

Nettle leaves may be gathered in the spring and early summer. These unlikely but delectable edibles are among the first wild vegetables available near our log cabin when greenery begins thrusting up like spring fire, but even so, early in the season the presence of stinging bristles makes it necessary to wear gloves while harvesting them. If the skin should be irritated, maybe at the wrists, alcohol can be administered. The Indians of southeastern Alaska, several hundred miles west of our homesite, relieve the stinging by rubbing the

Nettles

irritated skin with the dryish, rusty, feltlike material that covers young ferns or fiddleheads.

When young, nettle leaves and the entire small plants quickly lose their stinging properties when boiled. They have such a delicate flavor that they are good by themselves. Topped with butter or margarine, they are far more subtly delicious than spinach and are excellent sources of vitamins A and C and some of the minerals.

Because they are so easily and positively identified, nettles may be an important emergency food. In a pinch, the stems of the older plants will yield a strong fiber, useful for fishing lines.

PASTURE BRAKE

(*Pteridium* species)

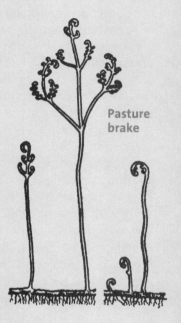

Pasture brake

When I attended college in Maine, I used to see fiddleheads regularly displayed for sale in the spring in the Lewiston markets. Later, I used to feast on them while spring bear hunting in New Brunswick. I have relished them many times in the West and Far North. They are the young, uncoiled fronds of the fern family's brakes, so called because in this emerging state they resemble the tuning ends of violins. They are also known in many localities as crosiers or croziers because of their resemblance to the shepherd's crook-like staffs of bishops, abbots, and abbesses.

Although some other similar fronds are edible, it is the fiddleheads from the widely distributed and familiar pasture brake, *Pteridium aquilinum*, that are most commonly enjoyed. These grow, often luxuriantly, throughout the Northern Hemisphere, in Europe and Asia as well as in North America. They are found, sometimes in waving acres that brush your knees as you ride through on horseback, from Alaska across Canada to Newfoundland, and south to California and Mexico.

These are edible, however, only while still fiddleheads and therefore young. They are then good both raw and cooked. Later, the full-grown fronds toughen and become poisonous to cattle as well as humans. While still in the uncurled state, on the other hand, they are found very acceptable by some wildlife, including the mountain beaver.

Pasture brake is variously known as just plain brake, bracken, hog brake, bracken fern, eagle fern, brake fern, and Western bracken. It often decorates shady roadsides, dry open woods, pastures, and clearings, and may be seen adding welcome green to recently burned forests.

Brake is a coarse perennial fern, with a blackish root so favored by the Japanese for thickening and flavoring soups that laws had to be passed there to prevent the fern's extinction. Early in the spring, the roots send up scattered fiddleheads. These later uncoil and stretch into long, erect stalks with typically fernlike leaflets, whose greenness takes on a straw to purplish-brown color with maturity. The widely triangular fronds, which may be from 1 to 3 feet across, are distinctively separated into three usually broadly spreading branches.

The fiddleheads, too, are noticeably three-forked. They are easily recognized, also, because of the fact that they are often found near the tangled previous year's bracken, perhaps flattened by snows. They are best when not more than 5 to 8 inches high, while still rusty with a woolly coating. Break them off with the fingers as low as they will snap easily, remove the loose brown coatings by rubbing them between the hands, and they're ready for eating. If you like mucilaginous vegetables such as okra, you'll probably enjoy a few of these raw.

The rather pleasant ropy consistency of this delicately glutinous juice is changed to a certain extent by cooking, but the sweetish fiddleheads are still reminiscent of okra. One way to enjoy fiddleheads is simmered in a little salted water until tender, then salted and peppered to taste, and eaten hot with plenty of melting butter or margarine.

PAPAW (*Asimina* species)

Τhis fruit so relished by raccoons and possums, sometimes called false banana because of its appearance, is also widely known as custard apple in deference to both its deliciousness and its family. Like the highbush cranberry, papaws are usually an acquired taste. But once you come to like their creamy sweetness, they can become one of your favorite fruits. They are sometimes found in city markets, but they are at their best harvested when ripe, which in the North may mean after the first frost.

This hardy cousin of similar tropical fruits is native from New York southward to Florida and west to Nebraska and Texas. Preferring ground that is moist and fertile, it is most often seen in stream valleys and on the lower adjoining hills. It grows, too, in small clearings and along shaded roadsides. Papaws planted during landscaping often turn out to be doubly valued for their decorativeness as well as for their fruit.

A big shrub or a small tree, the papaw occasionally grows some 40 feet high in the South, with a trunk perhaps as much as a foot in diameter. Northward, however, even the taller trees are often 15 to 20 feet high, with trunks only a few inches thick. The papaw's large and often drooping leaves, which give it a tropical appearance, are from 6 to 12 inches long and, growing on short stems, are dark green above and paler beneath.

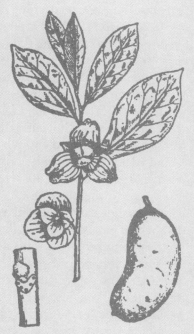

In early spring, just as these first leaves are starting to open, it blossoms with greenish flowers that later turn to a brownish or reddish purple. Growing from where the branches are met by the stems of the previous year's leaves, these are unusual in that they have six petals in two sets of three. The inner trio bunch together in a little chalice around which the outer

Papaw
LEFT: **bud and leaf scar.**
CENTER: **branch with flowers and leaves.** RIGHT: **fruit.**

three are outstretched like a saucer. About 1½ inches wide, these produce slender fruits that look like short bananas, up to about 5 inches long, with smooth, greenish-yellow hides that become brown a day or two after the papaws are plucked.

Despite the nuisance of several large dark seeds, the papaw has a wealth of bright yellow pulp whose mellow sweetness makes it really something to feast on outdoors, as the hungry members of the Lewis and Clark expedition discovered on their homeward journey. They are quickly gathered, often from the ground. You can also pull them slightly green and put them out of the way in a dark and dry place to ripen.

PIÑON (*Pinus* species)

The soft little nuts from the pinecones of millions of low-spreading conifers in the western United States and Mexico are not only pleasantly sweet by themselves, but they also afford prime flavoring for salads of the edible greens often seen flourishing nearby.

Toast the piñons first, after shelling them with the help of pliers or hammer, by spreading them in a single layer in a pan and placing the pan for 5 minutes in a moderate (350°F) oven. Shake the pan several times during the toasting process.

Coarsely chop ½ cup of the toasted piñons. Mix with ⅛ teaspoon cinnamon and ¼ teaspoon each of grated lemon peel, tarragon, and salt. Shake well with ½ cup salad oil and ¼ cup vinegar. This salad dressing can be stored, tightly covered, in the refrigerator. Use only about 1½ teaspoons for every cup of greens. As exciting as a honking wedge of geese undulating across the blue evening sky, it will make everything taste new.

Piñon pines have needlelike leaves in clusters of from two to five which persist for two, three, or more years. The flowers appear in the spring, producing an abundance of yellow, sulphur-like pollen that enlivens the wind. Once the pollen fertilizes the pistillate flowers, which are scattered among the new shoots, the familiar cones develop, taking two or occasionally three years to reach maturity and disperse their winged seeds on the breezes. It is only on the innumerable small, low-growing pines in the vast drier mountainous regions of the West that these seeds become large enough to bother with. They are regularly available in stores.

However, if the cones' seeds, no matter how greatly relished by squirrels, turn out to be small, at least there will be nothing

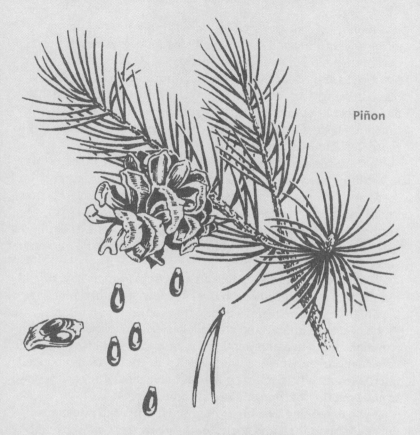

Piñon

unwholesome about them. Romanian cooks grind entire young pinecones and use them to flavor game sauces. Some Indians used to roast the soft centers of green cones by the fringes of their campfires and feast on the syrupy results.

The settlers learned early to gather the inner bark of the pines in the spring, dry it throughout the summer, and then grind it and mix it with regular flour. Next to devouring it raw, though, the easiest way to eat this sweet cambium is to first cut it into thin strips, then cook it like spaghetti. The bland flavor goes well with meat simmered at the same time.

Even pine needles, when they are new and starchy, are pleasantly nutritious to chew on. Some Indians boiled the still firm, spikelike flower clusters, in which the petalless blossoms grow in circular rows on slender stalks, to flavor their meats.

The piñons have also long been important medicinally. Hot pine tea, made by steeping the needles or by boiling gum or pitch, was one of the earliest cold remedies. Chewing the gum was considered soothing to sore throats. Too, the resin was dried, powdered, and applied to sore throats by swabs.

Piñon resin was also used by various Indians, and later by white adventurers and settlers, as a cure for everything from rheumatism and flu to indigestion. Heated, it was applied as a poultice to draw out splinters and to bring boils to a head. This hot resin dressing was also smeared on cuts, burns, sores, abrasions, and insect bites. Applied liberally to a hot cloth, it was used like mustard plasters in treating pneumonia, neuralgia, and general muscular soreness and stiffness.

The pines as a whole hold a position near the peak in importance to wildlife, partly because many birds and mammals feast on the seeds and to some extent because of the year-round cover the trees afford game birds, fur bearers, and both large and small game animals. Grouse, pigeons, doves, quail, prairie chickens, and turkeys eat the needles as well as the seeds. Deer, elk, moose, and mountain sheep browse on the foliage.

When the early frontiersmen learned from Indians how to obtain nuts from the piñons and related low-spreading pines, they began an adventure in good eating that continues to this day. Piñon cakes are unique and are delicious both hot and cold. You can make them in camp, perhaps where you're gathering the nuts, or at home. In either event, the shelled nuts first must be chopped or crushed, as with a rolling pin, to a coarse meal. The easiest way to go about this, of course, is in the home blender.

If you're cooking over an open fire, just mix 1 cup piñon meal with ¼ teaspoon salt and about ⅓ cup lukewarm water to make a stiff batter. Get 1 tablespoon shortening warming in a large, preferably heavy frying pan until it is just short of smoking. Drop the batter from a tablespoon, flattening it into cakes with a spatula. Reduce the heat and tan the cakes slowly on one side before turning them to brown the other side.

If you are at home, you can make a slightly less primitive cake by stirring 1 cup piñon meal, then ¼ cup all-purpose flour, into a well-beaten egg. Drop on a greased baking tin with a teaspoon. Bake in a moderate (375°F) oven about 10 minutes, until lightly browned. The flavor of these is even more delicate.

PLANTAIN
(*Plantago* species)

Plantain is almost as good as lamb's quarter. Furthermore, plantain is as well known to most of us as are the similarly prepared and eaten dandelions, although not usually by name.

It is a short, stemless potherb whose broadly elliptic green leaves rise directly from the root around a straight central spike. This singular spike blossoms, although possibly you've never noticed it, with minute greenish flowers that later turn into seeds. At any rate, plantain is found all over the world, even growing through sidewalks in New York, San Francisco, and Boston.

Some nineteen kinds of plantain thrive in the United States. One of the more widely distributed of these is the seaside plantain, also known as goose-tongue, which grows along such widely separated coasts as those of

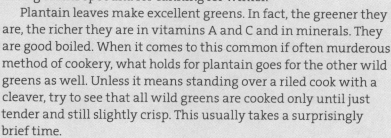

Plantain

Quebec, Nova Scotia, New England, Alaska, British Columbia, and California. The natives in Alaska boil goosetongue fresh both for eating on the spot and for canning for winter.

Plantain leaves make excellent greens. In fact, the greener they are, the richer they are in vitamins A and C and in minerals. They are good boiled. When it comes to this common if often murderous method of cookery, what holds for plantain goes for the other wild greens as well. Unless it means standing over a riled cook with a cleaver, try to see that all wild greens are cooked only until just tender and still slightly crisp. This usually takes a surprisingly brief time.

The simple gimmick with these wild vegetables is to start them in a minimum amount of boiling water and to cook them, covered, as rapidly and briefly as possible. Young plantain and such can be lifted directly from the rinse to the saucepan and cooked without added water.

POKEWEED (*Phytolacca* species)

The first wild greens of the spring in many a happy household, pokeweed flourishes in the eastern half of the country (except along the Canadian border), west to Texas, and south to the tropics. The Indians found it delicious, and some of the first European adventurers on these shores were in such agreement that they took the seeds back to France and southern Europe, where the vegetable became popular. Today pokeweed finds its way into many of our stores as a springtime delicacy. Some devotees like it so well that they even grow it in their cellars.

Also known as pokeberry, poke, scoke, pigeonberry, garget, coakum, and inkberry, this wild vegetable has a huge perennial root often as large as a man's forearm. Fibrous and covered with a thin tannish bark, this can be easily broken to size and planted in garden soil in a deep, flat box. Best are the medium-size roots, 3 or 4 inches in diameter, broken or cut into 6-inch lengths, dug and replanted indoors after the first heavy freeze of fall. Kept in a dark, warm cellar and regularly watered, these will regularly send up shoots for months. For a family of three, you'll want about a dozen such roots.

The fat young sprouts, especially when they are about 6 to 8 inches high, are the only part of pokeweed that is good to eat. The bitter roots—cathartic, emetic, and somewhat narcotic—are poisonous. So are the mature stalks when they take on a purplish cast. You may have seen birds get tipsy on the berries.

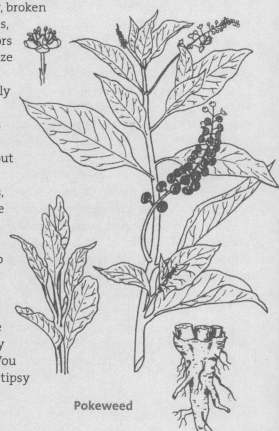

Pokeweed

You'll want to be able to recognize the full-grown plants, however, as in the spring it is near their dried remains that the tender young shoots will arrow upward. These annuals grow into round stalks, about an inch in diameter, which reach and branch upward from 4 to 9 feet. The leaves, which are shaped like rounded lances, have stems on one end and points on the other. Scattered, smooth on both sides, and wavy-margined, they are up to about 10 inches long.

Both flowers and fruit grow in long clusters on short stems. The numerous, small flowers are a greenish white. The round, ripe berries are a deep purple and are an important source of food for the mourning dove. Their reddish-purple juice, as boys sometimes used to confirm in the fall when school classes were first resuming, will serve as an ink for fountain pens.

Gather your small, tender pokeweed shoots when they are no more than about 8 inches tall. Remove skin and leaves, saving the latter for greens. Simmer the whole stems in a small amount of lightly salted water for 10 minutes or until tender. Serve on hot buttered toast, steaming with sauce.

POPLAR (*Populus* species)

The poplar's sweetish, starchy sap layer is edible both raw and cooked. This lies between the wood of trunks, branches, and twigs and the outside bark, the latter being intensely bitter with salicin, which for some reason is relished by moose, beaver, and rabbit and is an ingredient in some tonics concocted for the benefit of mankind.

All three animals chaw poplar bark, and poplar trunks and branches are common in beaver dams and houses. Deer, elk, and mountain sheep browse on the twigs and foliage. Grouse, prairie chickens, and quail are among the game birds relying on poplar buds, catkins, and seeds.

One of the most common trees on the continent, the life-giving poplar grows about as far north as any other on the great barrens of Canada. Cottonwoods as well as aspens are poplars. On the other hand, the so-called yellow poplar of the Southeast is not a poplar at all. In numerous northern areas, poplars quickly spring up in burns and clearings.

The poplars, members of the great willow family that has saved more than one man from starving, have alternate leaves with

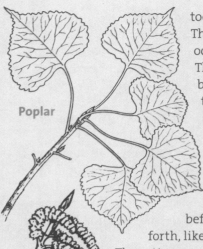

Poplar

toothed and sometimes lobed edges. The stems are long and slender, occasionally being definitely flattened. The branches are characteristically brittle and, breaking easily from trunks and big limbs, make excellent firewood for lone campfires, burning with a clean, medicinal odor.

Pollen fills the wind when the flowers, growing in drooping spikelike clusters, appear in the first warm weather of spring before the light-green leaves blaze forth, like pale green fire crowning the forest. The cottony aspect of the later splitting capsules of seeds, each with its long, fibrous hairs, has given the name "cottonwood" to some species.

The soft formative tissue between wood and bark can be scraped off and eaten on the spot. One of the modern ways of obtaining such nourishment is in tea. It can also be cut into strips or chunks and cooked like noodles in soups and stews. Dried and powdered, it is a flour additive and substitute. No matter how it is eaten, however, it can by itself keep you going for weeks.

PRAIRIE TURNIP

(*Psoralea esculenta*)

3/5

Prairie turnip

When John Colter, a mountain man once with the Lewis and Clark expedition, escaped from the Indians and came back safely with his incredible story of what now is Yellowstone National Park, he lived for a week largely on prairie turnips. This famous vegetable of the plains and the West, a mainstay of such Indians as the Sioux, is also known as the prairie apple,

Indian breadroot, wild potato, *pomme blanche*, *pomme de prairie*, and wild turnip. Early plainsmen, frontiersmen, settlers, trappers, traders, and explorers soon came to relish its starchy, sweetish, and somewhat turnip-like taste.

The prairie turnip is a member of the pea family. It is a perennial whose large root, or sometimes group of roots, resembling sweet potato roots, lies entirely beneath the ground. The generally branched stalks, characterized by soft, whitish bristles, are erect and about 6 to 18 inches tall. Five inversely ovate leaflets, narrowest at their bases, comprise each leaf. These leaflets are about ½ to 1 inch wide and twice as long. The plant blooms with dense spikes of small, bluish, pealike flowers, which eventually become tiny pods.

The tops of the prairie turnips mature early, breaking off in the unfettered winds and bounding over the plains like tumbleweed, which incidentally is also edible when gathered very young and simmered until tender. The roots, thus, are left unmarked. To find them, the Indians had to harvest them in the early summer. They were then peeled and hung up in long strings to dry for winter use.

Prairie turnips, edible peeled and raw, were even better liked by the early settlers when boiled or roasted in small lone campfires.

PURSLANE (*Portulaca oleracea*)

Purslane, although commonly unnoticed except as a weed, is sometimes the tastiest crop in the home gardens where it widely occurs. This annual also frequently becomes troublesome in fields and waste places throughout the contiguous forty-eight states, in the warmer parts of Canada, and even in Mexico, where it is sold in the markets.

The reason for this distribution, which is worldwide, is its tremendous production of seeds, relished by birds and rodents. Although purslane does not become large, 52,300 seeds have been counted on a single plant. Indians in the American Southwest used these for making bread and mush.

The trailing, juicy plant, which is familiar to almost everyone who has ever weeded a yard, is native to India and Persia, where it has been a food for more than 2,000 years. An early mover to Europe, it has been eaten there for centuries. Introduced to the New World back in colonial days, it has spread into almost every American city and town.

"I learned that a man may use as simple a diet as the animals, and yet retain health and strength. I have made a satisfactory

Purslane

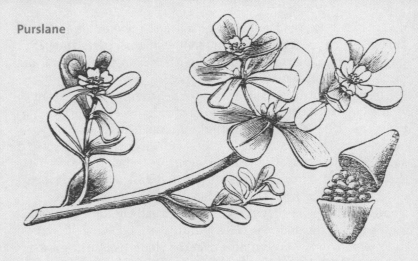

dinner off a dish of purslane which I gathered and boiled," Henry Thoreau noted in Massachusetts over a century ago. "Yet men have come to such a pass that they frequently starve, not for want of necessaries but for want of luxuries."

The semisucculent purslane, also sometimes called pusley, prefers fertile sandy ground, over which it trails and crawls, sometimes forming mats. It seldom reaches more than an inch or so into the air, although it often spreads broadly. The jointed stems, purplish or greenish with a reddish tinge, are fleshy and forking. The narrow, thick leaves, scattered in nearly opposite positions, grow up to about 2 inches long.

Unfolding their six or seven petals and some eleven stamens only on bright mornings, the small yellow flowers peek out from stems lifting from the forkings of the stalk. They produce tiny round seed vessels whose tops, when ripe, lift uniquely off like lids.

There's a trick, incidentally, to gathering purslane for the table. If you'll just nip off the tender leafy tips, they'll rapidly sprout again. This way just a few plants will furnish you with greens from late June until frost.

Purslane makes excellent salads. However, after its usual grittiness is removed by washing, it has most frequently been enjoyed as a potherb wherever I've lived. Just drop it into salted boiling water, simmer for about 5 minutes or until tender, and serve with melted butter or margarine. A little purslane goes surprisingly far, as it loses little bulk in cooking.

Raspberry and blackberry

RASPBERRY *(Rubus idaeus)*
and BLACKBERRY
(Rubus villosus)

The most valuable wild fruit on this continent both in terms of money and of importance as a summer wildlife food, the raspberry–blackberry genus includes between fifty and four hundred species in the United States alone. Although there are differences in taste, all are good to eat, with the so-called black raspberry being of one of the more delicious of the tribe. The fresh fruit is an extremely rich source of vitamin C. The tender young peeled sprouts and twigs are also pleasant and nutritious to eat when you're outdoors and hungry.

ROCK TRIPE
(Umbilicaria species)

Rock tripe

Perhaps the most widely known of the wild foods of the Far North is the lichen called rock tripe, whose growth reaches into the southern states. Rock tripe resembles a leathery dark lettuce leaf, up to about 3 inches wide and attached at its center to a rocky surface. Unless the day is wet, rock tripe is apt to be rather dry. It can be eaten raw, but much of the time you'll probably prefer it boiled to thicken soups and stews.

ROSE
(*Rosa* species)

Delicious wild foods grow everywhere. For example, there is this familiar berry that, although you may never have sampled it, has the flavor of fresh apples. More important, its juice is from six to twenty-four times richer in vitamin C than even orange juice. Throughout much of the continent you can pick all you want the greater part of the year, even when temperatures fall a booming sixty degrees below zero. As for recognizing the fruit, no one with a respect for brambles and a modicum of outdoor knowledge is going to get the wrong thing by mistake. It is the rose hip, the ordinary seed pod of roses everywhere.

Some thirty-five or more varieties of wild roses thrive throughout the United States, especially along streams, roadsides, fences, open woods, and in meadows, often forming briary thickets. The hips or haws, somewhat roundly smooth and contracted to a neck on top, grow from characteristically fragrant flowers, usually pink, white, or red. Remaining on the shrubs throughout the winter and into the following spring, they are available for food in the North when other sources of nourishment are covered with snow.

These rose hips have a delicate flavor that's delectable. They're free. They're strong medicine, to boot. Studies in Idaho found that the scurvy-preventing vitamin in the raw pulp runs from 4,000 to nearly 7,000 milligrams a pound. Daily human requirements, estimated to be 60 to 75 milligrams, provide a yardstick for this astonishing abundance.

Three rose hips, the food experts say, have as much vitamin C as an orange. We don't pay much attention to these gratuitous vitamins in the United States and Canada. But in England during World War II, some five million pounds

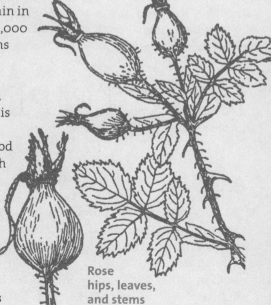

Rose hips, leaves, and stems

of rose hips were gathered from the roadsides and put up to take the place of then-scarce citrus fruits. Dried and powdered, rose hips are sold in Scandinavian countries for use in soups, for mixing with milk or water to make hot and cold drinks, for sprinkling over cereals, and so on, all of which they do admirably.

This cousin of the apple, one of the many members of the rose family, is nutritious whether eaten off the bushes, cut up in salad, baked in cake or bread, or boiled into jam or jelly. As a matter of fact, plain dried rose hips are well worth carrying in a pocket for lunching on like raisins. To prepare them for this latter use, just cut each in half. Remove the central core of seeds. Dry the remaining shell-like skin and pulp quickly in a cool oven or in a kettle suspended above the fringes of a small campfire.

With rose hips up to sixty times richer in vitamin C than lemon juice—and richer in iron, calcium, and phosphorus than oranges—you might as well get the most good out of them while ensuring maximum flavor. The best way to do this is to use the rose hips the day they are picked and to gather them while they are red but slightly underripe on a dry, sunny day.

But even after frost or later in the winter when they are shriveled and dry, rose hips are still worth picking. Earlier in the season, the petals themselves, varying in flavor like different species of apples, are delicious if you discard the bitterish green or white bases. Dark red roses are strong-tasting, the flavors becoming progressively more delicate as colors become subdued through the light pinks.

Even the seeds in rose hips are valuable, being rich in vitamin E. Some backwoods wives grind them, boil them in a small amount of water, and strain through a cloth. The resulting vitamin-rich fluid is used in place of the water called for in recipes for syrups, jams, and jellies.

The flowers make a rather tasty tea if each heaping teaspoon of dried petals, or twice that amount of fresh petals, is covered with a cup of boiling water, then steeped for 5 minutes. A little honey or sugar helps bring out the fragrance. Rose leaves, roots, and the rose hips themselves are also occasionally used for tea.

ROSEROOT *(Sedum* species)

Roseroot is another of the wild greens that is known as scurvy grass because of the often life-saving amounts of vitamin C it has provided for explorers, trappers, prospectors, sailors, and other venturers on this continent's frontiers. It is also sometimes known as stonecrop and rosewort. Seen in rocky ground, on cliff walls and ledges, in damply rich mountain soil, and on the vast northern tundras, it may be found from Alaska and British Columbia across Canada to Labrador and Newfoundland, and south to North Carolina.

Easy to recognize, roseroot becomes unmistakable when you scrape or bruise the large thick roots, as these then give off the agreeable aroma of expensive rose perfume.

The numerous stems of roseroot grow from 4 to 6 inches to about a foot high. They are thick with fleshy leaves, ranging in color from pale green to pinkish, that are either oblong or oval, smooth-edged or toothed. Dense tufts of reddish purple to yellow blossoms crowd the tops of the stems. Up to about 2 inches broad, these are composed of dozens of little flowers, each of which has four petals. These blossoms produce red and purple seed-filled capsules that have four or five prongs.

Good from summer to fall, the perennial roseroot and some of its close cousins are relished both in North America and in Europe as a boiled vegetable and as a salad plant. The succulent young leaves and stems, which are at their most tender before the plants flower, become pretty tough by the time the seed vessels appear.

But then, where the plants are abundant, you can boil up a feed of the big rough roots, season them with butter and pepper and a little salt, and enjoy them with your meat or fish. When they are young, the juicy stems with the leaves attached lend pleasant overtones to other wild greens, both raw and cooked.

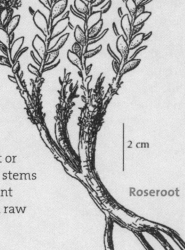

2 cm

Roseroot

SALSIFY *(Tragopogon* species)

The three species of salsify that thrive from coast to coast in this country and in southern Canada are also known as goatsbeard and as oyster plant. The latter name takes note of salsify's similarity in taste, to some palates, to that of the shellfish. To others, however, the roots have more the pleasant flavor of parsnips. The only secret is to get those roots while they are tender. The tops are used, too, both for salads and for cooked greens.

In many localities salsify is common along roadsides and in fields. Often growing 2 and 3 feet high, salsify is a tall perennial with a primary root that extends vertically downward. This becomes too pithy for use once the tall, leafy flowering stem develops the second year, producing either yellow or purple blooms not unlike large dandelion blossoms.

Also like dandelions, the leaves exude a milky juice when scraped or broken. They resemble wide blades of grass. Salsify is so good that the roots are grown commercially both on this continent and in Europe, the only difference between these and the wild variety being that the latter are usually smaller.

Salsify

Salsify roots can be a treat. Scrub them. Then scrape them. If you are preparing them beforehand, keep them in cold water along with a tablespoon of vinegar to prevent their discoloring. When ready to use, cut into ½-inch slices. Bring to a simmer in lightly salted water, in a covered saucepan, and cook until a table fork will easily penetrate the center of a test slab. Drain, salt and pepper to taste, and serve with melting butter or margarine.

SASSAFRAS *(Sassafras albidum)*

There is just one species of the familiarly fragrant sassafras that is native to North America. Ours is a small or medium-size tree, growing from New England to Ontario, Iowa, and Kansas, south to the Gulf of Mexico.

This member of the laurel family, which also includes several trees whose bark is powdered to provide cinnamon, is found along fences and roads, in abandoned fields, in dry woods, and in other open and semi-open places. Thickets often spring up from the roots. Famous for its supposed medicinal qualities soon after Columbus voyaged here, sassafras is now employed commercially mainly as a flavor. Privately, though, it is still widely used for everything from jelly to gumbo.

Sassafras
LEFT: **flowers.**
RIGHT: **twig with leaves and fruit.**

The very limber twigs and young shoots of the easily recognized sassafras are bright green and mucilaginous. The leaves, aromatic when crushed, grow in three shapes as shown in the drawing, all varieties sometimes stemming from the same twig. Also mucilaginous, they oxidize in the autumn to beautiful reds and oranges. Greenish-gold flowers, which have a spicy odor, appear with the leaves in the spring, the sexes on separate trees. Birds flock to the dark bluish fruits, nearly half an inch long, when they ripen on their thick red stems in the fall.

Sassafras tea, famous for centuries on this continent, where many people still drink it as a spring tonic, can be made by putting a palmful of preferably young roots into a pot with cold water and boiling them until the rich red color that you've learned by experience you like best is reached. Second and third extractions can be made from the same roots.

To dry and store sassafras root for later use in tea, choose just the bark of the young roots. Older roots can be employed, too, but it is best to scrape off the usual hard, rough covering first.

SHEPHERD'S PURSE (*Capsella* species)

Shepherd's purse is valuable to wild food seekers in that it is one of the more common of the wayside weeds, being found throughout most of the year in gardens, lawns, vacant lots, cultivated fields, and paths throughout most of the world where civilization has moved. It is quickly recognizable, and the tender young leaves, which, like others of the mustard family, are pleasingly peppery, may be enjoyed either raw or cooked. Indians even made a nutritious meal from the roasted seeds.

This wild green is familiar because of its flat triangular or heart-shaped seed pods, which, their broad bases uppermost, ascend the top parts of the stalks on short stems. A favorite food of blue grouse, these diminutive pouches develop from long clusters of tiny white flowers, each with twin pairs of opposite petals. Long green leaves, both smooth-edged and roughly toothed, grow in a rosette near the ground.

Growing so near to the earth and in such accessible places, these leaves are apt to pick up a lot of dust and grit, so it is best to gather them young and wash them well, afterward drying them in a towel. Otherwise, the dressing will slip off and form a pool in the bottom of the salad bowl. Tear, don't cut, these greens into bite-size pieces and toss them lightly with enough oil and vinegar, mixed 4 parts to 1, to coat them thoroughly. Arrange contrasting red tomato slices for trim; tomatoes tend to become too watery if tossed with the greens. Serve without delay.

These young greens, which vary considerably in size and succulence according to the richness of the soil

Shepherd's purse
TOP: **stalk with leaves and flowers.** BOTTOM: **rosette.**

where they grow, can also be carefully gathered, washed, and placed in a frying pan where a little bacon has been finely diced and partly fried. Cook just enough to wilt the leaves, then stir in some sour cream. Spoon out hot and divide the sauce over the servings.

Although the concentration of vitamins is greater in the green leaves, some people prefer the delicately cabbage-like flavor shepherd's purse takes on when blanched. Where, as so often happens, these edibles grow profusely near your home, you can experiment with blanching by anchoring paper bags over small groups of the young plants to exclude the sunlight.

The leaves, so bursting with vitamins but so low in calories, toughen as shepherd's purse matures. They can then be relegated to a small amount of boiling salted water, cooked until just tender, and dished out with the usual butter, margarine, vinegar, oil, hard-boiled egg, or other supplements.

Shepherd's purse, sometimes known as shepherd's heart or pick-pocket, is also used as a tea, a teaspoon to a cup of boiling water, 2 cups of which daily are said to stimulate sluggish kidneys. Pioneers sometimes soaked a handful of the leaves in water and used the latter to wash painful bruises.

SILVERWEED
(*Argentina anserina*)

The bright golden blossoms of silverweed are common in damp places, haunting seacoast and stream banks, tarrying about stagnant ponds, and even shoving up amid salt meadow grasses. The white undersides of the leaves are responsible for one of the common names of this edible. The roots, tasting like particularly good parsnips with overtones of sweet potato, have sometimes nourished people for months when other provisions were lacking.

Called *argentine* in French-speaking Canada, this food, which grows in Europe and Asia as well as on this continent, is also known as wild sweet potato, good tansy, wild tansy, cramp weed, and moor grass. It is luxuriant on the beaches and adjacent meadows of Alaska—where the natives and old-timers collect the fleshy roots in early spring as well as late fall—and extends over the roof of North America to Newfoundland. From there its range extends across the northern states and south along the Rocky Mountains to California and New Mexico.

Silverweed's relationship to the rose family is evinced by its lone, long-stemmed, five-petaled, inch-wide, bright yellow blossoms, which have the appearance of solitary roses. These eventually produce fruit that make one think of dry strawberries. The leaves, all produced from the roots, are long and featherlike, being composed of many stemless, toothed oblong leaflets that are shining green above and silvery below.

Silverweed

The roots, which on this continent were Indian favorites, are the parts used, although ruffed grouse, woodcock, rabbit, and mountain sheep feast on the foliage. Good both raw and cooked, these roots are thick and fleshy.

The easiest way to prepare them is by roasting or boiling.

It is reasonable that so popular an edible as silverweed should have assumed a certain position in the medicine chest. The pioneers found silverweed tea efficacious in allaying diarrhea. This beverage was made by steeping a teaspoon of leaves in a cup of boiling water. It was drunk cold, one or two cupfuls a day, a few sips at a time.

SLIPPERY ELM (Ulmus rubra)

Pour a cup of boiling water over a teaspoon of the shredded inner bark of the slippery elm. Cover and allow to steep until cool. Then add lemon juice and sugar to taste, and you'll have some of the famous slippery elm tea of pioneer days, still highly regarded as a spring tonic and as a plain pleasant drink in some parts of the country.

The slippery elm—also known as the red, gray, moose, and rock elm—abounds on bottomlands and on rich, rocky inclines in company with other hardwoods. A medium-size tree, generally some 40 to 70 feet tall with a trunk diameter from about 1 to 3 feet, it grows from Maine and southern Quebec to North Dakota, south to eastern Texas and northern Florida. Spreading branches provide broad, open, flattish crowns.

Slippery elm

The sharply toothed leaves, scratchy above and downy beneath, grow on short, hairy, stout stems. Growing from woolly, egg-shaped, blunt buds about ¼-inch long, the leaves become unsymmetrical, 4 to 8 inches long, and from 2 to 3 inches across the middle, where they are usually broadest. Dark green and dull, lighter on their under portions, they turn to beautiful masses of golden yellow in autumn. The bark is either grayish or dark reddish brown, becoming divided by shallow fissures and mottled by large, loose scales. The hairy twigs, incidentally, turn out to be mucilaginous when chewed.

The inner bark of branches, trunk, and root is extremely mucilaginous. Thick and fragrant, it is still widely gathered in the spring when, because of the rising sap, trees peel more readily. This whitish inner bark is then dried, as in a garret or a warm, half-open oven, and powdered as in a kitchen blender. It has demulcent and emollient as well as nutritive properties. Medically, it is still sometimes used for dysentery, diseases of the urinary passages, and bronchitis. For external application, the finely ground or powdered bark is mixed with enough hot water to make a pasty mass and used as a poultice for inflammations, boils, etc., and also in the form of both rectal and vaginal suppositories. More simply, the tea described in the first paragraph is sometimes used for coughs due to colds, one or two cupfuls a day, several cold sips at a time.

Many boys chew this intriguing bark. The Indians used it for food, some of them boiling it with the tallow they rendered from buffalo fat. In an emergency, it will provide life-saving nourishment today, and not at all unpleasantly, either raw or boiled.

SUMAC (*Rhus* species)

Sumac "lemonade" is just the thing to take the edge off a hard afternoon. Pick over a generous handful of the red berries, drop them into a pan, and mash them slightly. Cover with boiling water, and allow to steep away from any heat until the water is well colored. Then strain through two thicknesses of cloth to remove the fine hairs. Sweeten to taste, and serve either hot or cold.

Some Indian tribes liked this acidic drink so much that they dried the small one-seeded berries and stored them for winter use. Many settlers followed suit.

The rapidly growing staghorn sumac, also called the lemonade tree and the vinegar tree, is one of the largest species of the cashew family, commonly reaching 10 to 20 feet in height. It is easily recognized at any season because of the close resemblance of its stout and velvety twigs to deer antlers while these are still in velvet. It ranges from the Maritime Provinces to Ontario, south to Georgia and Missouri.

The bark of these shrubs or small trees, which often form thickets, is smooth. The satiny and often streaked wood, sometimes used commercially for such small objects as napkin rings, is green to orange in color. The fernlike leaves, about 14 to 24 inches long, are composed of eleven to thirty-one pointed leaflets from 2 to 5 inches in length. Dark green and smooth above, pale and sometimes softly hairy beneath, these flame into brilliant red in the fall.

The tiny, tawny green flowers grow in loosely stemmed clusters, one sex to a shrub or tree. The male clusters are occasionally 10 to 12 inches long. The female blossoms are smaller and extremely dense, producing compact bunches of berries. These are erect and so startlingly red that sometimes I've

Staghorn sumac
LEFT: **winter twig.**
RIGHT: **branch with leaves and fruit cluster.**

come upon a lone cluster suddenly in the woods and thought it was a scarlet tanager perched on a branch.

The hard red fruits are thickly covered with bright red hairs. These hairs are tart with malic acid, the same flavorsome ingredient found in grapes. Since this is readily soluble in water, the berries should be gathered for beverage purposes before any heavy storms, if possible.

Incidentally, the berries of the poisonous sumacs are white. However, there are other sumacs in the United States and Canada with similar red berries that provide a refreshing substitute for pink lemonade. All these red-fruited species are harmless.

One of them is the smooth or scarlet sumac, *Rhus glabra*, which grows from the Maritimes to Minnesota, south to Florida and Louisiana. This closely resembles the staghorn sumac, except that it is entirely smooth, with a pale bluish or whitish bloom coating the plump twigs.

Another is the dwarf, shining, or mountain sumac, *Rhus copallina*, which grows from New England and Ontario to Florida and Texas. Although similar to the aforementioned species, it can be distinguished from all other sumacs because of peculiar wing-like projections along the leaf stems between the leaflets.

Indians made a poultice of the bruised leaves and fruit of the red-berried sumacs and applied it to irritated skin. An astringent gargle, made by boiling the crushed berries in a small amount of water, is still used for sore throats.

SUNFLOWER
(*Helianthus* species)

Almost two-thirds of the sunflowers that brighten the world, some sixty species, thrive in this country. Although they grow in every state, sunflowers spring up in greater abundance in the West, especially on the prairies. Indians used them everywhere, but it was here they were most useful to the tribes, often taking the place of maize.

However, sunflowers had, and have, many more uses. The Indians found they could boil the crushed seeds, then skim an extremely nutritious oil from the surface. This was used at mealtimes and in cooking. It was also one of this continent's earliest hair oils.

In medicine, the seeds were regarded as diuretic and the entire plant as antimalarial. The roots were boiled and the warm liquid used as a liniment. They were also supposed to be efficacious in snakebite remedies. A strong extract from wild sunflower roots was one of the original baths used to allay the severe inflammations that plague most who come in contact with poison oak and poison ivy.

Indians obtained black and purple dyes from the seeds and a brilliant yellow dye from the plants, with which to beautify clothes, baskets, and ornaments. As if that weren't enough, the stalks can be utilized in an emergency like those of the tall, widely cultivated hemp to give delicate, silky threads.

Sunflower

The American wilderness is well stocked with teas, but wild coffees are scarcer. Sunflowers give one of the latter. The Seneca were among the Indians roasting sunflower seeds hulls after the kernels had been extracted, and pouring hot water over them to produce a coffeelike beverage.

The stately forms of wild sunflowers, reaching up to some 6 feet tall but seldom rivaling the size of domesticated species, are common sights in open fields and meadows and along roads. A few tolerate woodland shade. One sunflower, *Helianthus annuus*, is the state flower of Kansas, growing as far west as California and western Mexico.

Sunflowers, which are annuals, are all relatively tall. Their stems, for the most part, are rough and stout. Their stemmed alternate leaves, shaggy on both sides, are coarse and toothed. The blossoms are made up of many ray and disk flowers; their total diameters in the wild plants range from about 3 to 6 inches, with disks from 1 to 2 inches broad. The disk flowers vary in color from brown and purple to yellow. The showy rays, often brilliantly turning fields into almost solid expanses of gold, usually number from about ten to twenty-five. Although the season of blooming is supposed to be later, they are sometimes seen blossoming gaily in early spring.

The agreeably oily seeds of the wild sunflowers are important to such game birds as snipe, quail, grouse, partridge, dove, and pheasant. Antelope, deer, and moose dine on the plants.

Sunflower seeds are nutritious and, particularly when roasted in an oven or beside a campfire, delicious. Because the tedious job of shelling does not fit in with the high-speed tempo of American living, we enjoy them far less in the United States than, for example, do millions in eastern Europe. However, there continues to be a steady demand for the little bags of toasted, salted nuts at candy counters across the nation.

The fact remains that in an emergency the wild seeds could make all the difference. This would be true whether or not you just ate them raw or, as Lewis and Clark found the Indians doing along the Missouri River, pounded the kernels to a fine meal to drink with water, to make into bread, to stir into soups as thickening, or to mix with marrow.

To shell sunflower seeds in quantity, first break them up, as with a rolling pin, hammer, or food chopper. Then scatter the results in a large container filled with water. Stir vigorously so as to bring all the kernels in contact with the fluid and to break the surface tension. The kernels will sink to the bottom. The shells will remain floating, for use as a wild coffee if you want. The nuts can then be briefly dried and roasted, as in an open oven pan, and used in any recipe calling for nuts. Or the entire mass of dried kernels can be ground or pounded into a fine meal.

SWEET FERN

(*Comptonia peregrina*)

The fragrant leaves of the sweet fern were used as a tea as far back as the American Revolution. This plant is actually a shrub, partial to open fields and upland slopes where trees are sparse or absent, often forming solid stands in such habitats. It is also found to a lesser degree in open woods. Deer browse on it, and game birds and rabbits sometimes seek it out for food. It grows from the Maritimes to Saskatchewan and Minnesota, south to North Carolina, Georgia, Tennessee, and Indiana.

Sweet fern LEFT: **branch with leaves.** RIGHT: **burr.**

This sweet-scented shrub, growing from 1 to 3 feet tall, has fernlike leaves that give it its name. These are deeply divided into many roundish sections, the edges of which are usually sparingly toothed. The male flowers, about an inch in length, grow in clusters at the ends of the slim branches in catkins approximately an inch long. The female flowers grow in egg-shaped catkins. The resulting bristly round burrs envelop hard, glossy, brown little nuts. If you don't mind getting your thumbnail yellow, these are easily exposed and enjoyed, especially during June and early July while they are still tender.

The dried aromatic leaves of the sweet fern, a teaspoon to each cup of boiling water, make a very pleasant tea. When you use them fresh, just double the amount.

I've also brewed this in the sun by filling a quart bottle with cold water, adding 8 teaspoons of the fresh leaves, covering the glass with aluminum foil, and setting in the sun. The length of time required depends, of course, on how hot the sunlight is. The several times I tried this in New Hampshire, about 3 midday hours were needed before the brew became sufficiently dark. Made this way, wild teas have no bitterness of acrid oils extracted by other methods. You can then strain it, dilute it to individual taste, and serve it with ice.

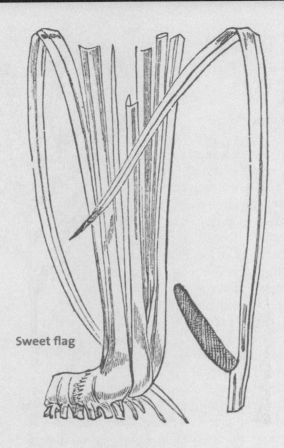

Sweet flag

SWEET FLAG
(Acorus calamus)

C andied sweet flag has somewhat the same aromatic
pungency as the now difficult-to-obtain candied ginger.
To make your own, cut the tender bases of the stalks into
very thin slices. Parboil in several changes of water to
moderate the strong taste.

Then simmer, stirring frequently, barely covered with a syrup
composed proportionately of 2 cups sugar to every cup of water,
until most of the sugar has been absorbed. Drain, dry apart from
one another on waxed paper or foil for several days, roll in
granulated sugar, and pack what you don't devour on the spot
in tightly closing jars.

The fleshy rootstalks were often used for this purpose in the days of wood fires, but they usually need to be kept on the back of a warm stove for several days to become sufficiently tender.

Sweet flag, a cousin of our friend the jack-in-the-pulpit, which also belongs to the arum family, grows in a wide band throughout southern Canada and the contiguous United States, as well as in Europe and Asia. You see broad stands of it in marshes, swamps, damp grasslands, and along stagnant waters, where it is also known as calamus, myrtle flag, sweet rush, and sweet grass. The latter two names were inspired not only by the flavor of the stalk's interior but by the pleasantly aromatic fragrance of the bruised foliage. This was a major reason why our pioneer ancestors often chose these leaves to spread cleanly on the floors of their cabins.

This aroma is one characteristic that distinguishes the edible from the blue flag, the state flower of Tennessee. Also, the sweet flag has glossy, yellowish green leaves, whereas those of the blue flag are both dull and bluish green. There is also the spicy pungency of the sweet flag's rootstock, a little of which is sometimes eaten raw as a remedy for indigestion.

Or you can make a tea from the roots, which can be dried and grated for the purpose. Stored in a tightly closed jar, these roots will keep for months. The recommended dosage is a teaspoonful to a cup of boiling water, drunk cold one or two cupfuls a day, several sips at a time. You may prefer this sweetened. In pioneer days it was held to be a remedy for sour or upset stomach, as well as a general stimulant to digestion.

The sharp, thin, swordlike leaves of the sweet flag grow up to about 4 feet tall. They sheathe one another tightly at the base, often beneath the surface of the ground or mud. Stout horizontal roots, with their unmistakable gingery taste, spread from the base in closely intertwined mats.

The flower stalk grows almost as tall as the leaves. About halfway up it, the spikelike spadix, several inches long and reminiscent of the "jack" of the jack-in-the-pulpit, grows off on an angle. This becomes closely covered with tiny yellowish-green flowers.

Raw sweet flag offers prime emergency food in the spring, when the partially grown flower stalks are edible and the interiors of the young plant stalks, crammed with half-formed leaves, are sweet and tasty enough to be taken home for salads.

WILD GINGER
(*Asarum* species)

Some of the Indian tribes regularly used wild ginger roots for flavoring. This plant, one of the better-known wildflowers, grows in fertile woods from the Maritime Provinces to Manitoba, south to North Carolina and Kansas. A related species follows the coast ranges from British Columbia down into California.

Wild ginger

Although the leaves are aromatic, emitting a pleasant fragrance when bruised or crushed, the roots are the part used and are milder than the unrelated ginger from the Orient. The plant is also known as Indian ginger, Canada snakeroot, and Vermont snakeroot—the latter two names resulting from the proclivity of the branching, easily gathered rootstalks to creep along the surface of the ground.

The beautiful long-stalked leaves of the wild ginger rise upon the rims of many a shaded stream, almost as if they enjoyed the gossiping of the brook as it gurgles past. These leaves, often heart-shaped and about 3 to 7 inches broad, have sharp points and broad bases. Deep green above, lighter below, the leaves are generally velvety with short hairs.

In the early spring a warm hue appears among the still undeveloped leaves. Presently a strange, dull bud—one to every pair of leaves—protrudes its long tip from their midst. The flowers eventually bloom in May, often on short stems so close to the ground that the purplish-red blossoms with their three long prongs are sometimes nearly invisible on the forest floor. These eventually develop seeds, nurturing them until they ripen.

There are two ways to use the roots of wild ginger, often gathered in early spring, after they have been well scrubbed. The first of these, common among the pioneers, is merely to dry them, grind them into a powder, and use them like the commercial spice they then resemble. Once regarded as efficacious in treating whooping cough, this is still commonly used in parts of eastern Canada as a remedy for flatulence. If you'd like to try it, just add ½ teaspoonful of the powdered or granulated root to a cup of boiling water. Drink this 2 tablespoons at a time, as often as necessary.

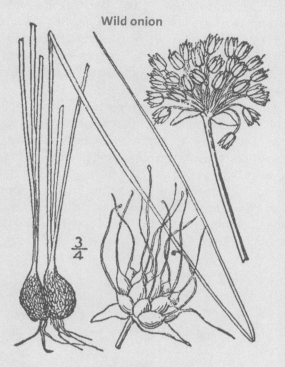

Wild onion

3/4

WILD ONION (*Allium* species)

Wild onions, including the leeks, the chives, and the garlics, grow wild all over North America except in the far northern regions. Indians used them extensively, not only for the provocative taste they impart to blander foods, but also as a main part of the meal. Settlers and frontiersmen soon followed suit.

When Père Marquette and his band journeyed from Green Bay, Wisconsin, in 1674 to near our present Chicago—whose name is taken from the Indian word "shikato," meaning place where wild onions are strong-smelling—their main food was wild leeks, probably *Allium tricoccum*, whose flat leaves, 1 to 3 inches broad, nod in the breezes from the Maritime Provinces to Iowa and Minnesota, south to the Carolinas.

For the most part, though, the wild onions have slender, quill-like leaves, similar to those of domestic varieties. They grow from bulbs. Flowers appear on otherwise naked shafts, arising like the ribs of an umbrella. The one characteristic on which to depend is the characteristic odor.

Although you probably won't like all the breed—especially not the strong-tasting field garlic, *Allium vineale*, which is an immigrant from Europe and which is beloved by cows in the East to the detriment of milk, cream, and butter—wild onions are all good to eat. The best way to find out your likes and dislikes is by trying them. Often you can use the entire plant.

However, have nothing whatsoever to do with any plants, wild or otherwise, that resemble the onion but do not have its familiar odor! Some bulbs whose appearance is superficially like that of onions are among the most concentrated of poisons. Your nose will be your own best protection.

Wild onions simmered until tender in a small amount of lightly salted water, then drained and topped with butter or margarine, or, for a change, mayonnaise, are fine fare. Save the liquid for soup or for other cooking.

Part II

ANIMALS

Chapter 1

Searching for Prey

MAMMALS Mammals are excellent protein sources and, for Americans, the most tasty food source. There are some drawbacks to obtaining mammals. In a hostile environment, the enemy may detect any traps or snares placed on land. The amount of injury an animal can inflict is in direct proportion to its size. All mammals have teeth, and nearly all will bite in self-defense. Even a squirrel can inflict a serious wound, and any bite presents a serious risk of infection. Also, a mother can be extremely aggressive in defense of her young. Any animal with no route of escape will fight when cornered.

Mammals provide a great source of meat and should not be overlooked as a viable food source. Signs that indicate the presence of mammals are well-traveled trails (usually leading to feeding, watering, and bedding areas), fresh tracks and droppings, and fresh bedding sign (nests, burrows, trampled-down field grass). Mammals can be eaten in any fashion desired. To eat most game, you'll first need to skin, gut, and butcher it.

LETTING PREDATORS HUNT FOR US If you are ever stranded and hungry, it may not be amiss to watch for owls, for spying one roosting in a quiet shadowy spot is not unusual, and it may be possible to steal close enough knock it down. Although not as large and plump as would seem from outward appearances, an owl nevertheless is excellent eating.

What is more likely, however, is that you may scare an owl from a kill and thus secure yourself a fresh supper. You may have equally good fortune, perhaps earlier in the day, with other predatory birds such as hawks and eagles. It is not uncommon to come upon one of these after it has just captured a partridge, hare, or other prey that is too heavy to lift from the ground. By running to drive the hunter away, you may thus secure a fresh meal.

Wolves, coyotes, and foxes may also be surprised at fresh kills that are still fit for human consumption. Such carnivores will seek new hunting grounds at the sight or scent of an approaching human being.

It is prudent to be aware of an owl's presence. With careful footsteps, you may get close enough to secure the bird as a source of food for yourself. More easily executed, though, is the heist of the owl's food. With good timing, you can easily scare an owl from prey that cannot readily be carried off by the startled bird.

HOW ABOUT BEARS?

Coming up to a bear's kill may be something else again. A wild bear probably won't dispute your presence. Then again it may, and although the chances are very much against this latter possibility, that is all the more reason not to take disproportionate risks.

If you are unarmed and really need the bear's meal, you will want to plan and execute your campaign with all reasonable caution. This will probably mean, first of all, spotting with the minutest detail preferably at least two paths of escape in case a fast exit should become advisable. This should not be too difficult where there are small trees to climb.

You'll then watch for your opportunity and if, for instance, the kill is a still-warm moose calf, build a large fire beside it, discreetly gathering enough fuel to last for several hours—until morning, if night be close at hand. You will take care in any event to be constantly alert, as bears, especially when they have gorged themselves, have a habit of resting near their food.

If you have a gun, you will be able to judge for yourself if the best procedure may not be to bag the bear itself. Fat is the single most important item in survival diets, and the bear is particularly well fortified with this throughout most of the year. Except usually for a short period in the spring, bear flesh is therefore particularly nourishing.

Many, most of whom have never tasted bear meat nor smelled it cooking, are prejudiced against the carnivore as a table delicacy for one reason or another. One excuse often heard concerns the animal's eating habits. Yet the most ravenous bear is a finicky diner when compared to such game as lobster and chicken.

It is only natural that preferences should vary, and if only for this reason it may be interesting to note that (a) many of our close acquaintances who live on wild meat much of the time relish plump bear more than any other North American game meat, with the single exception of sheep; and (b) furthermore, these individuals include a sizable number who, after long professing an inability to stomach bear meat in any form, found themselves coming back for thirds and even fourths of bear roast or bear stew under the impression that anything so savory must be, at the very least, choice beef.

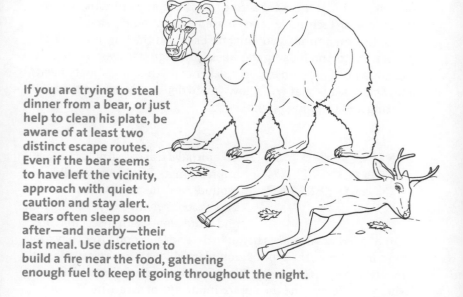

If you are trying to steal dinner from a bear, or just help to clean his plate, be aware of at least two distinct escape routes. Even if the bear seems to have left the vicinity, approach with quiet caution and stay alert. Bears often sleep soon after—and nearby—their last meal. Use discretion to build a fire near the food, gathering enough fuel to keep it going throughout the night.

HUNTING SMALL VS. LARGE ANIMALS

Unless you have the chance to take large game, concentrate your efforts on the smaller animals, due to their abundance. The smaller animal species are also easier to prepare. You must not know all the animal species that are suitable as food. Relatively few are poisonous, and they make a smaller list to remember. What is important is to learn the habits and behavioral patterns of classes of animals. For example, animals that are excellent choices for trapping, those that inhabit a particular range and occupy a den or nest, those that have somewhat fixed feeding areas, and those that have trails leading from one area to another. Larger herding animals, such as elk or caribou, roam vast areas and are somewhat more difficult to trap. Also, you must understand the food choices of a particular species.

TRACKING AN ANIMAL

Snares are excellent tools, since they work for you while you attend to other things. At times, however, it may be necessary for you to actually hunt down your game. If this should be the case, take the time to prepare before going out. Wear dark clothes, camouflage your skin with dirt or charcoal, cover your scent with smoke or pungent plants from the local area, and try to stay downwind from the animal. In addition, try to hunt at dawn or dusk, as this is the most active time for many animals. Any of the following techniques can be used to hunt wild game.

To stalk an animal, you must first see it. If there is none in sight, you'll need to find it using the tracks and sign it leaves behind. You don't need to be an expert tracker to do this. You simply need a few basic skills that will allow you to determine where the best hunting and trapping might be.

ANIMAL TRACKS AND PATTERN OF MOVEMENT

An animal's track is simply the impression its foot leaves on the ground. As time passes, this impression is changed by the sun, rain, and wind along with insect and other animal overlay. All tracks begin to deteriorate soon after they are made. In addition, the type of ground in which the track is made will directly impact its longevity. As a general guideline, use the following to help you determine the approximate age of an animal's track.

Crispness. Once an impression is made the effects of the sun and wind will begin to deteriorate its borders. The crisper its defined borders are, the fresher it is.

OVER TIME, THE WIND AND SUN WILL DESTROY
A TRACK'S CRISP BORDER.

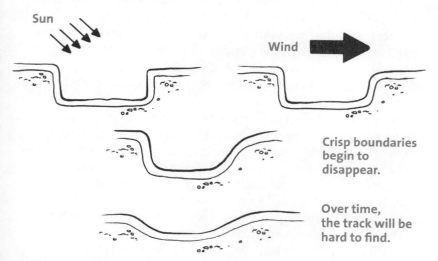

Sun

Wind

Crisp boundaries
begin to
disappear.

Over time,
the track will be
hard to find.

Weather. If there has been a recent rain or snowfall, you can determine if the track occurred before or after it happened. The same can be said for dew and frost. If there is crisp dew on the ground but the track is absent of it, this is a good indication that the track is fresh.

Evaporation. If you are in an area where the ground is dry but an imprint creates moisture, you can estimate how old the impression is based on the amount of moisture it still contains.

Vegetation. If a track has new undisturbed growth within it, then it is old. If an animal's track contains compressed and broken young vegetation, it is usually a good indication of recent passage.

Dislodged materials. Snow, dirt, sand, water, and so on will normally be sprayed forward in the direction of travel. As time passes, the displaced material will dry and harden and bond with its underlying surface, or it will evaporate.

For the purpose of this book, I am going to focus on three types of animal's tracks. These include rodents, rabbit and hares, and hoofed mammals. All three can provide an abundance of food for someone who is living in the wild.

Rodent Tracks

The white-footed mouse, gray squirrel, and woodchuck are all part of the rodent family. They all have a front foot with four toes with nails, three palm pads, two heel pads, and a vestigial thumb near the inner heel pad. Although these rodents have bigger hind feet, with five toes and nails, there are a few small differences between them. The white-footed mouse usually has three palm pads with two heel pads; the gray squirrel normally supports four palm pads with two heel pads; and the woodchuck is known to have three palm pads and two heel pads (one of which is hard to notice). Note: The heel pads on the hind feet of these rodents are rarely seen in their tracks.

Most rodents have a similar galloping pattern of movement. The woodchuck, however, tends to alternate between a galloping and a walking pattern. In the galloping pattern, the animal's front feet will hit the ground first and—as it continues its forward momentum—its hind legs will land in front of this position, allowing it to push off and continue its movement. Thus, when looking at these tracks, the imprints will normally show the hind feet ahead of the tracks created by the two front feet. In addition, the front feet tracks are usually side by side and closer together than the imprints made by the back feet. As mentioned, woodchucks are also known to use a walking pattern of movement. In this instance, limbs from opposite sides and ends of the body will move at the same time (for example, its front left and back right leg will move together), and as the animal moves, its hind track will usually land close to or partially on top of the front track.

TRACKS OF VARIOUS RODENTS

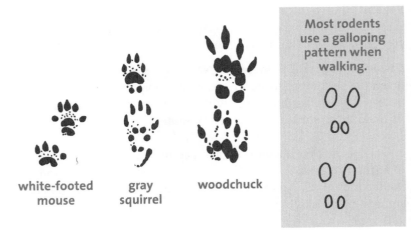

white-footed mouse

gray squirrel

woodchuck

Most rodents use a galloping pattern when walking.

Rabbit and Hare Tracks

The cottontail rabbit, snowshoe hare, and white-tailed jackrabbit are all part of the rabbit and hare family. They all have heavily furred feet with five toes and nails on the front feet and four toes with nails on the larger rear feet. The white-tailed jackrabbit is bigger than the cottontail and hare, and therefore its tracks tend to be bigger and more deeply imprinted. (This doesn't account for the size variance seen with young or female jackrabbits.) However, the snowshoe hare can spread its toes out as much as 4 inches when traveling on snow. Thus, its tracks can be quite impressive in size but not necessarily in depth. Note: The dense hair on a rabbit's or hare's foot makes it hard to see the animal's toe and toe pad marks (the toe pad marks are fairly small to begin with) when its tracks are made in snow.

> Rabbits and hares use a triangular galloping pattern of movement.

Like rodents, rabbits use a galloping pattern of movement (covered under rodents). Unlike the rodent, however, its front feet will land with one in front of the other. When looking at these tracks, the imprints will normally show a triangular pattern created when the hind feet land ahead of the two front feet, which are one in front of the other.

Hoofed Mammal Tracks

The white-tailed deer, elk, and moose are all hoofed mammals. They all have feet that consist of two crescent-shaped halves and two dewclaws (located behind and just up from the hoof). They all leave heart-shaped prints with the sharp end pointing in the direction of the animal's travel. Adult male tracks made by moose, elk, and deer decrease in size, in that order respectively. Elk tracks have a less drastic heart-shaped appearance, looking larger and wider then a deer's and smaller and rounder than a moose's.

> Hoofed mammals use a walking pattern of movement.

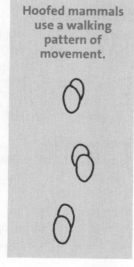

Hoofed mammals use a walking pattern of movement similar to that described for a woodchuck (see preceding).

With this type of movement, the animal's hind track will usually land close to or partially on top of the front track.

TRACKS OF VARIOUS HOOFED MAMMALS

white-tailed deer   elk   moose

UNDERSTANDING AND IDENTIFYING AN ANIMAL'S SIGN

The term "sign" simply refers to any vegetation or landscape changes that indicate the animal has been there. This can include scat, food remains, bedding areas, trail corridors through the woods, stunted vegetation, and damage to trees and shrubs. When tracking an animal, learning to identify its sign is probably more important than finding a track. The sun, rain, and wind along with insect and other animal overlay will all affect the crispness of a track. The animal's sign, however, has a greater impact on the landscape and deteriorates at a far slower rate, and thus may be the only indicator that an animal has been in the area. Here are a few basic ideas that may help.

Scat (droppings)
Every animal has droppings that are unique to it. Not only is scat useful in identifying that an animal is in the area, it can also help us determine how long ago it was there and what it has been eating. By taking the time to check the droppings for moisture, warmth, and content, you can provide yourself with a multitude of useful information.

Food remains
Squirrels will often leave mounds of pinecone scales on stumps or fallen logs. The abundance and freshness of these mounds will help you determine if squirrels are active in the area. Hoofed mammals and rabbits browse on saplings and leaves. A deer will often leave a frayed top, whereas rabbits leave it looking like it was cut at a 45-degree angle with a knife. A good indicator of recent

deer or rabbit activity would be a branch that has a fresh and white inner surface versus one that is brown and weathered.

Bedding areas

Rodents tend to live in underground dens or tree nests. If a nest is seen, watch for activity and look for other sign in the area. If an opening to an underground den is spotted, look for other sign in the area. Don't forget to evaluate the opening for spider webs or dead pine needles covering the entrance, as this usually indicates a lack of activity. Hoofed animals tend to disturb an area when they bed down. Bent-over grass, scraped dirt, and scraped snow are good indicators of a bedding area. If grassy, then look at how far the grass is displaced toward the ground. If it is not well worn, it may have been just a napping spot. If the snow has been scraped, does it look fresh or has there been a frost or new snowfall since the bed was created?

TRAIL SIGNS

Often an animal's trail can be easily identified, especially when looking for rabbits or hoofed animals. Animals, like humans, tend to take the path of least resistance whenever they can. After time, trails that lead from a bedding area to a water source can become very pronounced. A less traveled trail should be evaluated for recent activity by looking for vegetation displacement (vegetation that is bent, broken, flopped over, or pressed in), trees with displaced bark, pine needle movement, and recently broken twigs on the ground. Note: Broken twigs will usually lie in a V position with the point indicating the direction of the animal's travel, and any other displaced vegetation will usually do the same.

READING TRACKS AND FORESEEING ANIMAL MOVES

After someone has taken a fair share of squirrels and rabbits and has scored on a few deer as a lone stillhunter, he begins to develop something akin to the skill of an Indian hunter or frontiersman. He starts doing the right thing at the right time without thinking about it much. That type of skill can't be learned from any book, but there are some useful things that a book can point out.

Tracks in books appear on the page as they would in soft snow, damp sand, or mud, though clear prints are rare on the leaf-strewn forest floor or on hard, dry ground. The experienced tracker going into a new region seeks out likely areas where he can find clear prints in order to take his own census of the animals in the area. Good trappers are expert at it, and Indian hunters were good too. The trapper doesn't think in terms of exact numbers, but somehow the tracks that he finds tell him whether or not there are enough pelts in the area to make running a trapline there worthwhile.

TIPS ON HARD-TO-FOLLOW TRACKS

Tracks are often distorted, and you may see only disturbed leaves, clots of thrown-up earth, bent grass, broken twigs, and other clues running in a line. You often can't tell what animal made them unless you follow them for a while. The animal will probably cross a soft spot, and then you may find just one clear print of one foot.

THE PROBLEM OF DEAD-END TRACKS

After identifying the tracks and deciding to follow them, don't step right on the tracks. Sometimes a fox or coyote will suddenly reverse himself and step in his own tracks to get back to a piece of cover where he can jump aside. That leaves a baffling dead end for the tracker, especially if he has obliterated the animal's tracks by walking on them so that he can't backtrack and find the jumping-off place. Sometimes the track cannot be followed to the animal, but backtracking may lead to the animal's den or lie-up and a shot. If the hunter suddenly comes to a dead end in the tracks, the animal has backtracked in its own prints (or close to them) or has jumped to a leaning tree, log, stone wall, or other object well off the ground. Coons and foxes are experts at this. Do as the Indian hunters did. Look around at the dead end for such a means of escape, and if you don't find one, try backtracking. Sometimes you'll see one or two prints that you missed seeing on the original trail, and they may point in the opposite direction.

Some animals are very clever about entering water to throw a tracker off. If the tracks you're following enter a stream and do not come out again on the opposite side, the animal has probably walked along in the water for a while to throw the pursuer off. Many animals are quick to sense when a predator or a hunter is on their trail. Foxes, bears, and some other animals often circle back to identify their pursuer or get the scent.

CHANGING THE ANGLE OF VISION

The light is very important because of the shadows it throws. From one angle, the tracks may be almost invisible unless you look closely. From another angle with favorable light, the line of slight depressions or disturbed earth or leaves is clear because of the shadows that they cast. If tracks fade or disappear, try the Indian trick of moving from side to side to get the light right.

INTERPRETING AN ANIMAL'S LINE OF ADVANCE

In order to keep your eyes off the ground so that you can spot the animal ahead, it helps if you can deduce the line of advance and move from point to point. Deer, for instance, especially those with large antlers, will almost always take the easiest way unless pushed hard and trying to conceal themselves. They find it difficult to force their racks through thick cover. An otter on dry land will almost always be moving toward the nearest water. Foxes usually move from thick cover to thick cover, but sometimes pause on high ground to sun themselves and look around. During late fall, most bears are making beelines to nut groves, bee trees, berry patches, and other sources of food in their haste to fatten up before hibernation.

Move fairly fast from point to point, checking now and then to make sure that the line of prints is still there. Some Indian trackers were so good at this that they seldom looked at the tracks. They almost read the animal's mind, knowing what it was looking for or traveling toward, and they could follow the route more by knowing what the animal wanted than by doggedly following the prints that it had made.

If you lose the tracks, circling ahead will often cut through them again. Go back to the last prints, pause a while, and try to figure out the route. See if you can locate any terrain feature that would have caused a sudden change of direction. If so, it may be profitable to make a circle in that direction. Remember, though, that it is difficult to pick up a line of faint tracks or sign when you cut through it from the side. The tracks are under your eyes only for a few seconds as you move along, and you may have to make several circles.

STALKING AN ANIMAL

Once you have located your food source, if you intend to hunt it, you will need to use good stalking techniques. Staying downwind, move when the animal's head is down. I once heard that an animal (deer) will keep its head down for approximately 20 seconds while feeding and then lift it up to look around for movement. As a general rule, move for 10 seconds and then stop, staying perfectly still. Wait for the animal to pick up its head, look around, and start grazing again, before moving for another 10 seconds. If the animal looks up while you are moving, freeze. As long as you don't move, it will think you are a tree stump and will not comprehend that you're getting closer. If the creature is close to a creek, you may be able to move more quickly without it hearing you. In addition, realize that noise is bound to happen. The key is to freeze if you make noise, until you are sure the animal is comfortable. Getting close enough to use your weapon will take practice and skill.

DRIVING

Often done with a team of hunters, driving is a process of moving an animal into a waiting ambush. Several members of the hunting party actually make themselves known to the animal and walk toward it, constantly adjusting to ensure that the animal follows a certain path. This method works best when the creature can be funneled into a valley or similarly constricted location.

STAND (AMBUSH) HUNTING

Observe an animal's behavior, look for its sign, and select an ambush location that is downwind from the animal's approach.

WHEN TO FREEZE

A good trail-watcher stays as quiet as possible while waiting for game, but sooner or later you have to move your weapon to take a shot. Stillhunters and trackers must move along even if they do so slowly. At the first sight of the game, is it best to make an instant shot, or freeze in your tracks and raise your weapon in a deliberate manner? There is no exact answer in each situation, but there are a few things to bear in mind.

Moose, bear, mule deer, and most forest game have rather poor eyesight. Mountain and plains game—goats, sheep, and antelope—have excellent eyesight at all ranges. But all game is very sensitive to movement. If you remain still, the animal will probably not bolt if it doesn't get your scent. So you freeze in order to keep the animal where it is or in the hope that it will come closer. But now you must move your weapon to take the shot.

Surprising as it may seem, you can often move so that the animal seems unaware of the motion. It is nerve-racking to bring rifle into position in slow motion while a game animal is staring right at you, but it can be done. One old-timer tells how: "If the buck or moose is looking right at me, I wait a while, hoping he'll put his head down to feed or that he'll turn his head away. If he doesn't, and it looks like he'll stay put, I bring my rifle up so slowly that I can't see my arms moving." Practice that sometime for an exercise in control.

This slow movement is especially important to archers. A rifleman or a shotgunner can hope to get off a going-away shot even if the animal does come unstuck. The archer finds it very difficult to shoot accurately that fast. Deer are so very fast, for instance, that they often "jump the string." That is, they get out of the way in the slight time interval from the twang of the bowstring to the instant when the arrow arrives where the buck was; so many archers use string silencers—rubber buttons slipped on the bowstring that deaden the twang of the string. Many Indians used tufts of feathers for the same purpose.

CALLING Understanding that animals communicate with each other is the first step in learning how to call them in. I have often kissed the back of my hand (making a short smacking sound) or scraped two mussel shells together to attract a curious squirrel. Changing how I kiss my hand by making a long-drawn-out squalling sound can draw predators who think I am a hurt rabbit. This sound has also been known to catch the attention of a moose if it is done just right. Banging antlers together often attracts deer during their rutting season. Some hunters have perfected the art of attracting elk or duck by blowing on a blade of grass. Take the time to listen to the creatures in your area and practice different techniques of imitating their sounds. If perfected, you can draw the animal to your location—making the hunt a lot easier.

THE SECRETS OF SUCCESSFUL CALLING Hunters must spend a lot of time listening carefully to the sounds of game if they want to be successful callers, as one experienced guide on the shore of Chesapeake Bay well knew. One day the guide and a partner were sitting in a duck blind. It was a calm, quiet day, and ducks were going over at an elevation appropriate to transatlantic jets. The hunters had a good decoy rig out, but it seemed hopeless to expect a shot. Finally, one pair of black ducks came down out of the north. They were low enough, but they seemed to be about a mile away. The guide's partner whipped his wooden duck call out of his pocket and sucked in air in preparation for a mighty series of quacks.

The old-timer grabbed his companion's arm before the latter could blow and shook his head. Then he made a most astonishing noise with his mouth—heek-heek, heek-heek, he called, high-pitched and slightly plaintive like a split clarinet reed. The pair of blacks wavered and swung around into the hunters' rig. Two shotgun shells later, the two sportsmen had the makings of a fine meal.

"Fred," said the guide's partner, "that didn't sound any more like a black duck than a fog horn. What were you trying to imitate?"

The old-timer only glanced at his fellow-hunter oddly for an instant while the Labrador retrieved the birds. Then he revealed the secret of his success. "Son," he said, "I was imitating a drake black duck—which you likely never listened to before. The hen blacks sound off and quack, quack just like most ducks on a farm pond, but the drake, he makes the sound I made. I saw you puffing up to blow those loud highball quacks, and I don't think the ducks would have come to that. The season's been open for a while now, and everybody's been quacking at those blacks from here to Hudson Bay. Most people think the black goes quack because that's all they ever really hear. Now you really listen to a flock some time when you get the chance, and then you'll hear the drakes going heek-heek, just like me. The birds don't hear hunters calling like that so often; so they'll come to it."

This wily guide could recognize ducks at a great distance from the blind and then make the appropriate calls in time to bring them in. His big spread of mixed geese and duck decoys helped too, of course.

Good Indian callers had similar skills, and many northern Indians still show astonishing ability to get birds when less-experienced white guides fail. The northern Cree of Canada take a big toll of Canada geese by calling them to crude brush blinds built on shore. These hunters are so expert that they call high-flying flocks of wily Canada geese to their shotguns by barking out "ee-ronk, ee-ronk, ee-ronk" with mouth and throat. When you hear Canadas "barking," you'll wonder how a human throat and mouth can produce the same noise.

Calling waterfowl was an art among the Indians long before the white man arrived in North America. Until about thirty years ago, few white men tried to call birds or animals, except, of course, those moose callers who learned from the Indians to use the birchbark horn and those few hunters who lived in areas where the turkey was still abundant. Nowadays, calling has become very popular, and a wide variety of manufactured calls is available.

LEARNING ANIMAL COMMUNICATION SYSTEMS To call well, you must have some idea of the means of communication used by birds and animals. From the chickadee to the moose, birds and animals communicate with each other in one way or another. As hunters who have listened to them carefully know, some wild creatures carry on conversations, accented for emotion as well as meaning.

Squirrels that chatter and chase up and down tree trunks and scamper madly over the rustling leaves, pausing from time to time with menace or "follow me" on their expressive faces, are not just romping. They are communicating. Male squirrels confront each other for a moment and communicate by definite signs. One animal retreats. The pursuer is then recognized as the master of the other and has first choice of available food and females.

Foxes, wolves, and some other animals mark their regular runways by urinating on stones, trees, and boulders to attract or warn off others of their kind by means of scent. The beaver perfumes clay and mud patties with his glandular castor scent to attract females. Mink use their musk glands to communicate, and male cottontail rabbits leave signs of their presence by rubbing their chins on a stump or tree. Few woodsmen can ignore the devastating scent left by a wolverine that forces its way into a cabin. Even snakes leave scent trails and follow others that interest them.

Sometimes a hunter calls perfectly, knowing that the quarry is nearby, but gets no response. It is often his scent that disturbs the animal, or it may be an alarming scent from another animal. Indians have long known that the sounds made by animals and birds are only one part of the entire communication pattern, and that a hunter's call must fit in with it. Indians would never attempt, for instance, to call in a wild turkey if a red-tailed hawk or other large predatory bird were circling overhead.

Hoofed animals paw the ground, stamp their feet, and snort to signal impatience or anger and to warn off an intruder. The bellow of a moose or the belling of an elk conveys two meanings— the search for a mate and a challenge to fight other males. These animals also communicate with each other by rattling their antlers against trees, branches, or bushes. Whitetail deer and antelope communicate with their flashing flags and rumps. When a deer's flag goes up or a pronghorn's rump hairs stand erect and flash white, the animal is warning that danger is present. When you see those signals, it's almost always useless to try a stalk. Beaver and muskrats communicate by diving into the water with a warning splash. The beaver also slaps the water with his flat tail to signal danger.

CALLING BIRDS

Any novice hunter learning to communicate with crows soon discovers that the birds have several distinct calls with definite variations in rhythm and loudness. Each one has a definite meaning. This is evident when a novice crow caller sounds the alarm call instead of the rally call. Grackles communicate through their calls and chatter, but they also signal with eyes, beak, head, wings, and tail.

When calling most birds, one is always right to give the signature call of the species in order to arouse interest and inform the bird that others of its kind are within hearing. During the breeding season, male songbirds perch and sing. The male bird does not sing out of sheer joy. The songs are territorial signals, warning off other male birds of its own kind and notifying other intruders that the singer has established his boundaries. The calls also attract the female. If you imitate the territorial song or call of a songbird, the male bird often comes quickly to investigate or even to attack the intruder, and you may attract a female. That's the time when you may get an interesting photograph, and it's a good way to draw small birds out of thick cover where photography is difficult.

A low, unspecific warbling or whistling sometimes has a similar effect, and it may attract females as well as males during the breeding season and afterward. One mechanical call consists of two disks that rub against each other when they are rotated. The resulting squeaks and warbles sound like no particular bird, but they arouse curiosity. Many birds respond either by singing or coming to investigate. If you can recognize the various responses, you can locate the various species. Indians often whistled and warbled in this way to call in predatory birds and animals that hoped to prey on nestlings.

Many birds are known by names based on their calls; for instance, the killdeer, a big plover, calls kill-dee, kill-dee, usually when in flight, and the bobwhite's name is based on its signature call. Going through a standard bird guide and checking the names of the birds against the notations on the sounds they make will give you a large vocabulary of calls. You may already know the names and appearance of many birds. If you find that the name is based on the sound the bird makes, you are adding greatly to your knowledge.

TYPES OF CALLING

There are three general types of calling. In one of them, the caller imitates the sounds made by the bird or animal that he wishes to attract. In calling predators, the caller most often imitates the calls of the prey. For instance, the most popular call for foxes, coyotes, and birds of prey is the sound of a dying rabbit. A third type of calling depends on making noises that simply arouse curiosity. The Indians depended on these curiosity calls, and by experience, learned that low tapping, scratching, quiet and indistinct whistling, or blowing on a wide blade of grass or a leaf held between the base and tip of the thumbs, as shown in the drawing, often works. This type of quiet calling is often effective when the caller really does not know what kind of bird or animal to expect. The sounds are not human, but they represent no specific animal or bird.

The sounds made by the predators themselves can sometimes be used to advantage. The Indians often imitated the call of a hunting hawk to freeze quail, squirrels, rabbits, and other small game so that they would stay still long enough for an easy shot with a bow.

Holding leaf in position for calling

Aboriginal callers were often more successful than white men because the natives had an astonishing range of vocal sounds in their languages that the white caller found it very difficult to imitate. These sounds were often used to decoy animals and birds.

The Salish hunters of the Northwest Coast could place a stiff leaf between the teeth and blow on it to imitate the bleat of a fawn—a sure call for wolves, wildcats, and other predators as well as does and even bucks. The Salish hunters also made effective calling devices for moose and elk from the hollow stalks of sunflowers and from hollow bones.

Good Indian callers could keep up a regular conversation with the quarry. They often called from blinds or thick cover, but if the game would not come to the blind, the hunter would leave it and stalk the animal, meanwhile keeping up the animal's interest with intermittent calling. Of course, the volume of the call had to be reduced as the hunter and the game came closer and closer together.

MANUFACTURED CALLS

Modern manufactured calls are available for almost every purpose, and their complexity and prices vary greatly too. For a beginner, a hard-rubber, mouth-operated call is satisfactory since he doesn't have the necessary skills to use the finely made hardwood calls. With mouth-operated calling devices, the instrument should incorporate some means of varying the pitch. If the call is capable of only one pitch, there's no possibility of adjusting it higher or lower if you find that the single pitch is off.

When mouth-operated calls are used in cold weather, saliva often enters them and freezes, silencing the call or altering the pitch. Moisture from the breath may also accumulate and freeze. Most good calling devices can be taken apart and wiped free of moisture. Calling devices that operate with vibrating reeds should be easy to take apart so that the reed can be cleaned and dried or replaced. If the call is a one-piece device, blow into it backward from time to time to clear out moisture. It's best to carry two calls on a hunting trip so that if one freezes or clogs, the other is ready.

Some calling devices depend on friction to make the sounds. Typical of this type are the cedar-box calls used for turkeys. These devices require the use of two hands, and make it difficult to hold a camera or a gun. Some calling devices are operated by squeezing a rubber bulb to force air through a reed. A few hunters do not squeeze these calls with their fingers. Instead, they place them under a foot or a knee and gently squeeze the bulb that way, leaving both hands free.

Mouth-operated calls should be light enough so that they can be held in the mouth without the use of the hands. A lanyard loop around the neck helps when you drop the call out of your mouth to use binoculars, camera, or weapon. Some calling devices can be inserted entirely inside the mouth. One turkey call consists of a vibrating diaphragm that is pushed up against the roof of the mouth and blown. It's very popular with archers, who usually like to have both hands free to keep an arrow on the string.

HOW TO ELIMINATE HUMAN ODORS

Many Indian tribesmen took ritual baths in order to cleanse themselves before hunting. Some of them even spent long periods in steam baths made by plunging red-hot stones into water in dugouts. The Indians believed that this cleansing of the flesh made them more acceptable to the gods and that hunting success would be granted. The elimination of the sour human odor that is easily detected by game was probably more important, however. Indian hunters did not smoke or eat while on stand or stillhunting because the odor of tobacco and food is alarming to most game animals, though they may not connect it with man.

Some modern hunters who must come close to the game imitate the Indians in this and will not bring their deer-hunting clothes into the house. They believe that the clothes would pick up the thick indoor odors inside. The Indian's rule still stands; it's not wise to smoke a cigar, pipe, or cigarette on deer stand, or to break out a salami sandwich if you're waiting for a fox or coyote.

SCENT CLUES THAT ANIMALS LEAVE BEHIND

The human nose is not a precise instrument, and few hunters claim that they use it to find game, but sometimes it does work. In heavy cover, you may catch a whiff of the very distinctive smell given off by elk. The odor of rotting meat after a bear, a mountain lion, or some other predator has made a kill sometimes leads a hunter to a productive area. The urine of most game animals has a very powerful, acrid smell, and Indians could sometimes locate a big moose by first catching the odor of its urine and then seeing the tracks.

Fresh-spilled blood has a distinct, sweetish, almost overwhelming smell. You may smell blood after a shot at a big-game animal before you actually see it. A fleeing wounded animal often lies down to try to regain its strength, and in its terror, it usually urinates freely. If you are tracking a wounded animal and catch the combined odor of fresh blood and acrid urine, you may be close to your quarry.

Men who live a great deal of their lives outdoors are much more adept at using the sense of smell to hunt than the average city dweller. In the city, the smells of gasoline, motor exhaust, millions of people, cooking, and all sorts of manufacturing processes blunt a human being's sense of smell. In clean air, it is possible to smell many animal odors, and some big-game kills have been made because the hunter smelled the animal even before he saw it or its tracks.

SCENT LURES FOR GAME

Indian hunters sometimes used female deer scent made from the glands to attract buck deer, and concentrated deer scent is available in bottled form today. Trappers also use artificial and natural concentrates to attract animals to their sets. For instance, professional predator trappers working for the government often keep coyotes captive to collect urine for use on their traps.

How game scents attract animals is something of a mystery. Sometimes they work, and sometimes they don't. Female deer scent of the animal in heat sometimes attracts buck deer during the rut. If the buck is not breeding any longer, he may lose his caution when he smells the scent on the hunter's clothes because he believes that he is dealing only with a harmless doe. And that may be the secret of animal scents. When the hunter sprinkles his clothes, particularly his boots, with them, it masks the human smell and the smell of cooked foods and tobacco. One western hunter used to douse himself with buck lure before going after Columbia blacktail deer. He once was sitting in a clump of brush when he was amazed to see a coyote coming in from downwind. Normally, a coyote would never approach a man from that direction, but this one did, and the hunter shot him. Presumably, the coyote was investigating the enticing scent of doe deer in hopes of picking up an injured animal and never caught the masked human scent. Varmint hunters may be missing a good bet by not masking their own odors when calling. However, only a few have tried it, and their results were not conclusive.

THE ART OF BECOMING INVISIBLE

An elaborate blind isn't always needed. Instead, the hunter may take advantage of natural cover such as reeds or brush. "Hides"—a term used in England—are used by many hunters who must move around because they cannot expect the game they await to show up near a permanent structure. Outdoorsmen who live where game is so abundant that an elaborate blind is not needed use similar temporary, often portable, hides. In Alaska and the Canadian North, few indigenous peoples build complicated permanent blinds. These hunters more often pile up a rough semicircle of ice and snow or force evergreen boughs into the ground when hunting waterfowl. Elaborate waterfowl blinds are used farther south where the migrating birds follow specific flyways and are more wary after encountering many hunters on the flight south.

THE IMPORTANCE OF HIDING HANDS AND FACE Indian hunters relied more on hides and clever concealment than they did on any form of blind or camouflage. You often see a white man afield at a distance as three white dots when he is wearing dull clothing. Face and hands stand out vividly. A good outdoorsman knows that his chief problem in a blind or when using camouflage is to conceal his human form. The white of hands and face and, at close range, the contrast between the white of the eye and the dark pupil are the chief giveaways. Waterfowl hunters almost always keep their faces hidden until the last moment before shooting, and turkey hunters favor face nets of dark makeup.

BREAKING UP THE HUMAN OUTLINE Indians often decorated their bows with colorful designs and often painted their faces and bodies with decorative patterns. At close range these patterns showed up clearly, especially when very bright paint was used, but at longer range these bright patterns were difficult to pick out. Bright colors break up the human outline, and since the Indian did not show white hands and face, he was well concealed in his paint.

There is a lesson here for the modern hunter. Unless you are hunting color-sensitive game such as wild turkeys and waterfowl, your outline is more important than the colors you use. Bulky, loose clothing is better than well-fitting, tighter clothing.

HOW MOVEMENT ALARMS GAME

To most game animals and birds, movement is much more noticeable than color. A careless gesture or a nervous shifting of the leg on a deer stand will often spook an oncoming buck. Indians seldom used branches or leaves tied to the headdress or body, since leafy branches sway and accentuate movement. A nod of the head that would go unnoticed by the game is exaggerated when the branches move. The branches or twigs also increase the height of the hunter. It's difficult to keep low with several inches of foliage sticking up over your head and shoulders. Good hunters know that they should look around a boulder, a hummock, or a log—not over them—and that is harder to do with leafy camouflage on head and shoulders.

Camouflage is of little concern to those who hunt big game with firearms. In most states and provinces, the law requires the firearms hunter to wear bright clothing during the big-game season. The water-fowler, varmint hunter, bowhunter, and photographer, on the other hand, use camouflage a great deal.

Chapter 2
Outwitting Small Game

RABBITS, HARES, AND SQUIRRELS PROVIDE GOOD hunting throughout the United States. Probably more hunters learn their craft by going after these animals than any other, and this was true of the young Indian, who learned a great deal about deer and elk hunting by using his first bow on the elusive squirrel and the erratic rabbit and hare.

RABBITS In the spring particularly, those years when rabbit cycles are near their zeniths, the young lie so fearlessly that a dog will step over one without scenting it, and all an individual has to do, if he wants, is to reach down and pick the youngster up.

Adult rabbits themselves depend so much on camouflage that at any time if you pretend not to see one and continue strolling as if going past, it is frequently possible to come close enough to do some immediately accurate throwing with a ready stone.

Tularemia, or rabbit fever, is occasionally a threat in some localities and in one respect the disease is a little harder to avoid when not hunting with a firearm, for one precaution can be to shoot only rabbits that appear to be lively and in good health. The germs of rabbit fever are destroyed by heat, however, and another safeguard is to handle the animal with covered hands until the meat is thoroughly cooked.

Rabbits are unusually easy to clean. One method is to begin by pinching up enough of the loose back skin to slit it by shoving a knife through. Insert your fingers and tear the fragile skin apart completely around the rabbit. Now peel back the lower half like a glove, disjointing the tail when you come to it and finally cutting off each hind foot. Do the same thing with the top section of skin, loosening it finally by severing the head and two forefeet. You can then, as you've already possibly found, pull the animal open just below the ribs and flip out the entrails, retrieving heart and liver. You may also want to cut out the small waxy gland between each front leg and the body.

Hunting Cottontails

The cottontail rabbit is small, 14 to 16 inches long, and weighs no more than two or three pounds. The white puffy tail, distinguishing the cottontail from the larger hares, is clearly visible even at a distance when the animal is going away fast. Local variations of the cottontail include the New England variety, the desert cottontail, the swamp rabbit, and the marsh rabbit. The ranges of these animals often overlap. For the hunter, the animals are much the same and inhabit similar territories, except for the swamp rabbit and the marsh rabbit, both of which favor freshwater swales in the South.

In Europe, rabbits live by the thousands in large warrens and dig their own burrows. They dig so many holes in a confined area that they often undermine roads, railroad right-of-ways, and even airfields. In the United States, rabbits and hares do not live crowded together, and they rarely dig their own burrows. Instead, they establish forms—nests in depressions in the ground often lined with soft grasses and the fur of the doe. Sometimes, however, cottontails take refuge in burrows dug by other animals, the woodchuck in particular. If this happens when you are hunting, it's almost useless to try to dig the rabbit out since it will use the escape hole made by the chuck. Digging out rabbits or almost any form of game is illegal in most states.

In the United States and Canada, the term "hare" includes the arctic hare, the snowshoe hare (sometimes called the snowshoe rabbit), and the various jackrabbits of the West. Among the latter are the black-tailed jack, the white-sided jack, and the white-tailed jack. All species of hare are larger and heavier than the various forms of cottontail. The white-tailed jack may be as long as 28 inches, and weigh as much as 10 pounds. The meat of the jacks is stringy, tough, and almost without flavor. The Indians and most white men prefer the flesh of the cottontail. Arctic hares and the snowshoe rabbit (varying hare) are good eating.

In upper New York State and the area around the Great Lakes in the United States and Canada, the hunter may be confused when he brings down a big hare resembling the black-tailed jackrabbit but with no black on its rump. This is the European hare, long escaped from the hutches of early settlers and gone wild. Eastern Indians soon discovered that this hare is flavorful and big enough to be meaty.

Walking Them Up

Walking them up, or flushing rabbits by walking in their territory, assures a well-filled bag if the hunter knows the terrain and where rabbits are likely to be found. After a slight

Cottontail rabbit

snow, look for tracks to locate concentrations of them. Even when there is no snow, you can often locate the well-worn runways that the cottontail establishes in thick cover such as briar patches, thick clumps of berry bushes, and other dense vegetation. Overgrown pastures and fields near woods and other fringe areas are always a good bet.

Cottontails prefer thorny bushes or vines for cover because they can run below the thorns, though dogs, foxes, coyotes, and larger birds of prey find it difficult to negotiate that kind of cover. Some Woodland Indians wore full-length rawhide leggings that resembled the chaps worn by cowmen for this kind of hunting. Nowadays, cottontail hunters often wear heavy leather-faced trousers.

The cottontail has only two defenses against predators and hunters—concealment and a fast escape. The well-camouflaged cottontail can hide in a clump of dry grass or leaves which seems too small to conceal even a mouse. If you look for the large, dark eye, you may spot the rabbit.

Bolting the Cottontail

To bolt the cottontail from its hide, try the Indian trick of taking a few steps and then standing stock still for a minute or two. The rabbit may panic and break cover. If two or three hunters work together, walking a stretch of cover abreast, it's best for all of them to pause and wait at frequent intervals. Good hunters, who know how to walk and stop, can often get their limits out of a single

Cottontail rabbit tracks

abandoned pasture, while the man who insists on walking miles may pass through the same territory without getting a single shot..

Locating the Runways

In heavy cover, it may be possible to trail-watch for cottontails. Go through the cover slowly some time when you are not hunting or when the season is closed and look for the runways. The best place to stand is where two or more runways cross, and when you go out with your gun or bow, try to stay downwind. You'll often find tufts of rabbit hair caught on thorns and branches if the runway is used often. Sitting on a good runway early in the morning or late in the afternoon when cottontails are on the move will often put a few of them in the bag.

SQUIRRELS There are five kinds of tree squirrels in the United States, and the range of some of them extends into Canada.

The most common is the familiar gray squirrel of the East, which becomes almost tame where hunting is not permitted. It can be a nuisance as well. In the wild, the gray squirrel is a clever, wary game animal. These animals weigh about one pound.

Many squirrel hunters have never seen a fox squirrel because they have grown scarce in some areas, although the overall range of the fox squirrel is about the same as that of the gray. These animals have much more red in their fur and are sometimes called big red squirrels or red-tailed squirrels. They weigh from about 2¼ to 2¾ pounds. The fox squirrel is so large that he looks as big as a marten to the man who is used to hunting grays. The fox squirrel is much clumsier in trees than the gray or any other tree squirrel, and that may be the reason why this animal is almost extinct in some parts of his range. A hunter usually has little difficulty in hitting a fox squirrel, and predators find it an easy prey.

The tiny red squirrel is edible too, but is so small that few men hunt him. It is only about 10 inches long and the tail makes up 4 to 6 inches of this length. The average weight is less than half a pound.

The reddish-pelted animal, often called chickaree, is a woods sentinel. The red squirrel seems unafraid of hunters, perhaps because he is seldom hunted, and scolds intruders noisily. Often a deer stalk is spoiled by a nervous chickaree scolding the silent stillhunter, who should try to get away from red as quickly as possible. Even then, red may follow, scolding the hunter and

Gray
squirrel

Gray
squirrel
tracks

alerting every deer for hundreds of yards. Indian hunters often
avoided his scolding by moving silently and staying away from
nut trees and den trees where he was likely to be found or by
screaming like a hunting hawk. This scares a chickaree and makes
him freeze until the hunter passes by. The hawk scream must be a
perfect imitation in order to avoid frightening off the deer or other
game you are hunting.

The red squirrel is regarded as vermin in many states and no
limit or closed season is imposed, though a few states do classify
him as a game animal. He is destructive and eats nestlings and
eggs. Reds also seem to be able to kill off the larger gray squirrel in
certain areas and take over that more valuable animal's range.
They do this by raiding the nests of gray squirrels and killing the
kits to eat, but sometimes a tiny red squirrel pursues the larger
gray adult and bites at his rear. Sometimes the red manages to do
an effective castration job.

Hunting the red squirrel is good conservation. Where there is
no limit, a dozen or more in the stew pot make an excellent meal.
Woodland Indians often used them for food when other game
was scarce.

There is a California gray squirrel, and there are two forms of
tassel-eared squirrels that inhabit the area along the Colorado
River, but few westerners hunt squirrels for food. The few who do
are almost always from back East. Western hunters are missing a
good bet when they disdain tree squirrels as game.

Most tree squirrels are subject to melanism, and albinos are to
be found. In some areas, you may run across glossy-black gray
squirrels. These are melanistic, though some southern hunters
insist that they are a separate species.

Squirrels' Favorite Foods

All tree squirrels eat nuts, fruits, berries, seeds, some soft twigs and bark, a few kinds of fungus, and some farm crops, especially corn. The primary food of the fox squirrel and the gray is nuts, and you'll almost always find these animals among oaks, beech trees, hickories, and other nut trees. Since the Indians gathered many different kinds of nuts for their own food, an Indian squirrel hunter had an advantage over most modern urban hunters. While gathering nuts, he kept an eye open for a flaunting tail. If you want to hunt squirrels successfully, one good way to prepare yourself is to study trees so that you can recognize nut-bearers at a distance. When you can pick out a black walnut among the other trees in a grove, you'll probably find squirrels in it if it is nut-bearing at the time.

Squirrels can bite deeply enough to make a nasty wound. If you stun or wound a squirrel, don't pick it up too soon. The Indians often finished off squirrels by pressing a foot firmly on the animal's shoulders below the neck so that the squirrel could not bite the moccasined foot. The pressure stopped the heart and lungs. This method works well with other small game.

Stillhunting for Squirrels

Stillhunting for squirrels is primarily a matter of recognizing good country in which to hunt them and stalking in silence. Some stillhunters use squirrel calls to imitate the contented sounds that the animals make when they have found abundant food. Indian hunters often tapped and rubbed two round, smooth pebbles together to imitate a squirrel chewing on a nut shell to get at the meat inside. Most of the time, those two sounds will bring squirrels to the feast through the treetops. Since the squirrels usually travel fairly high in the treetops, the hunter seldom has to worry about his scent reaching the animals. A good stillhunter moves silently through the woods, but should pause often to conceal himself and call. Sometimes the squirrels will not come but they will answer, and then the hunter stalks them.

Hunting Squirrels in Pairs

The gray squirrel is an expert at keeping a tree trunk between himself and the hunter. If you're on one side of the tree, the squirrel almost always seems to be on the opposite side. He often climbs the tree on that side until he reaches the crown and then jumps to another tree without being seen. Indians often hunted squirrels in pairs, and modern hunters often do the same. When two hunters approach a nut tree and a squirrel whisks around to the other side, one man remains where he is, weapon ready, and the other quickly moves around the tree. One or the other will usually get a shot. If there is a third man in the party, he backs off a few yards so that he can see the topmost branches. Often he is able to pick off the squirrel if it is out of sight of the two other men.

Indian Ruses for Fooling Squirrels

If you're hunting alone, it sometimes helps to prop up your coat and perhaps your hat on a bush near the tree. When you go around the trunk, the squirrel will usually circle around too. When he sees your coat and hat, he may become alarmed and freeze for an instant, so that you may get a shot.

Some Indian hunters carried a long fiber cord or thong. When the squirrel dodged around the trunk, the Indian hitched the line to a sapling or bush before he went around the trunk. When the squirrel came around to his original position, the Indian pulled on the line to shake the bush or sapling violently. This often held the squirrel's attention so that the hunter could fire. Modern squirrel hunters who use this trick often tie a short stick to the end of the line. It's quicker to hitch the stick behind a low fork in a bush than it is to tie the line.

Sitting for Squirrels

Some hunters find it pays off to sit for squirrels. Take up a favorable position near or in a grove of hardwoods and remain quiet. If you can conceal yourself, so much the better. Some Indians lie prone on the ground on their backs and shoot from that position, and many shotgunners and riflemen do the same. Putting leaves over yourself to break up your outline helps, and some men carry a camouflage ground cloth that they throw over themselves, but that's dangerous in heavily hunted squirrel groves.

If you know of a den tree, try sitting for squirrels there. As a rule, a den tree has large hollows where branches have broken off and the stub has rotted out, or the trunk may be hollow. Some hunters sit near a den tree and then use their calls to make the alarmed sounds that squirrels make when they spot a predator or a hunter. That often brings the squirrels running to the shelter of the den tree, and the hunter may be able to take as many as three or four of them as they come.

Squirrels sometimes ignore the discharge of a rifle or a shotgun. After a shot, remain still, and the animals will begin to move again in fifteen minutes or so. If you are sitting for squirrels, it's wise to let cleanly killed animals lie until you are finished hunting in that area. Mark where they fall by noting bushes, branches, or stones near the animal and wait until you are finished before picking up the kill. The less you move, the better.

Squirrel hunters sometimes concentrate so much on watching tree trunks and high branches that they miss squirrels on the ground. If berries and fruits are available on low bushes or have fallen to the ground, or if the nuts are falling, you may find squirrels almost underfoot if you walk quietly enough.

Some squirrel hunters have the unsportsmanlike habit of firing a charge of shot into every squirrel nest they see in hopes of knocking a squirrel out of them. These leafy breeding nests are almost always empty by the time the hunting season starts.

Best Squirrel Hunting Weather

On windy, cold days or when rain or snow is falling, squirrels remain at home and wait the weather out; so it's wiser to hunt on calm, rather warm days, and the best time is early in the morning or late in the afternoon. Squirrel hunting, as the Indians knew, is usually good just after a cold snap or a storm has ended because the denned-up animals come out to make up for lost time in their feeding.

If you hunt during bad weather, the middle of the day is sometimes productive. The squirrel stays at home until hunger drives him to feed, and that's usually later in the day than usual. If the weather is bad during the forenoon but improves later in the day, that's the time to be out with gun or bow.

PORCUPINES

Porcupines, like thistles and nettles, are better eating than it might seem reasonable to expect. The slow moving, dull-witted rodent is in human estimation often a nuisance, being so ravenous for salt that practically anything touched by human hands will whenever possible be investigated by sharp inquisitive teeth.

The sluggish porcupine is the one animal that even the greenest tenderfoots, even weak with hunger, can kill with a weapon no more formidable than a stick. All one usually has to do to collect a meal is reach over the animal, which generally presents the raised quills of back and tail, and strike it on the head. Being so low in intelligence, the hedgehog requires a lot more killing than might be expected.

These big, blundering rodents with their many quills grow to nearly a yard in length and may weigh over forty pounds. The barbed quills—about 32,000 of them—give an adult porcupine the

Porcupine

look of a black, elongated pincushion with white streaks. Porcupines like to sit in the high branches of a tree and sway back and forth in the wind. They are so large that it's quite possible to mistake one high in a tree for a bear cub.

To defend himself, porky pokes his unarmed face into shelter such as the space under a log or between ground and a boulder and lashes out with his quill-armed tail. If he's unusually aggressive, he'll "charge" suddenly backward toward the enemy, but will likely lumber back to his improvised shelter.

The fisher (pekan), a big tree-climbing weasel, is about the only woods animal that manages to dine regularly on porcupines. The lightning-fast fisher turns the porcupine over onto his back and bites at the unprotected underside. Coyotes can do it too. One coyote engages porky's attention, and the other rushes in from the side and flips him over; then one or both may get in a killing bite.

The quills are hollow and enable the porcupine to float with ease, but he spends most of his time aloft eating tree bark and tender twigs, which makes him hated by tree farmers and timber companies. The porcupine will often work his way right around a trunk, eating bark as he goes. That girdles the tree and kills it. He also likes to eat canoe paddles, axes, and tool handles for the salty sweat on them.

The laws in some places prohibit the killing of porcupines except by a man who is lost in the woods and starving. The porcupine is so slow that a man can easily kill one with a club. If the bark and twig supply holds up, a porcupine will stay in a small clump of trees for an entire year, and he may stay in one small area for his entire life. If Indians saw a porcupine and had no immediate need for meat, they would note its location. When other game grew scarce, they often had several porcupines pinpointed and could kill them as needed. Since the porcupine does not hibernate, he is accessible all year round.

Porky lives in a stub hole in a tree, a cleft in the rocks, a cave, a hollow under tree roots or boulders—any shelter that doesn't require too much work to make it comfortable. Indian women often dug or rooted him out for the sake of his quills. The quills were used in the handsome decorative work on the buckskin garments of Woodland and other Indians. The quills take dye readily, and the women dyed them in many colors. Then they were cut into varied lengths and sewn onto garments in decorative patterns.

Porcupine tracks

How Indians Pulled Porcupines from their Dens

At times, Indians dug porky out, but usually it was enough to pull him out of his den with a stick. The hunter took a supple length of sapling about an inch thick and split one end of it to form four or more long, flexible "fingers." The porcupine stick was shoved into the den until contact was made, and then the stick was pushed and twisted until the ends caught in the animal's quills. The porcupine was then dragged out of the hole and killed with a club. If you try the same procedure, be sure about the identity of the animal in the hole. It may be a skunk. Tracks and sign near the den will usually identify the animal inside.

Dealing with Quills

Porcupines cannot, of course, shoot their quills, but any that are stuck in the flesh by contact should be pulled out immediately, for their barbed tips cause them to be gradually worked in and out of sight. Dogs are common victims. I had a big Irish Wolfhound who became so infuriated at the genus that, with no regard for himself until later, he killed every porcupine he could find.

If you're alone in the bush with a dog in such a disagreeable predicament, you'll probably have to do as I did; lash the pet as motionless as possible against a tree, and use your weight for any necessary additional leverage. Pincers can be improvised by splitting a short branch. At any rate, each of the perhaps hundreds of quills has to come out, or death may be the least painful result.

This danger from quills is one reason why it is a poor practice to cook a porcupine by tossing it into a small fire. Very often all the quills do not burn off. The best procedure is to skin out the porcupines by first turning it over so as to make the initial incision along the smooth underneath portion. Many who've dined on this meat consider the surprisingly large liver uncommonly toothsome.

WOODCHUCKS

The common chuck that burrows under boulders and stumps in almost every pasture in the eastern states and southern Canada is a surprisingly big and bold animal. A large adult weighs ten pounds or a little more, and he is well armed with strong rodent teeth and earthmoving claws.

The woodchuck feeds early and late on tender green vegetation including timothy, hay, alfalfa, and garden crops. His burrows are a constant hazard to horses and cattle.

Where Chucks Dig Their Burrows

The woodchuck's burrow is usually dug on rather high, dry ground, and it must be close to green ground vegetation, for the chuck does not climb trees and does not range far from home to feed.

Indian youngsters used to stalk woodchucks to demonstrate their stalking skill and courage. While the chuck was feeding outside his burrow, the would-be brave tried to place himself between the chuck and the entrance to the hole and then kill him with club or bow. The chuck is a brave animal, and the Indian youngster often found it difficult to stand up to the animal's angry growls and menacing jaws and meet its headlong charge.

Bowhunters often try this trick today, and find that the chuck hasn't changed. He is still one of the few animals in North America that will charge boy, man, or dog and bite when he attacks.

The Cree, Ojibway, and Algonquin all hunted the chuck for practice in stalking

Woodchuck

Woodchuck tracks

and shooting and for food when other game was scarce. A young chuck, carefully cleaned and cooked, is a tasty dish, and some modern hunters eat them. Today, the chuck is a valued animal in many areas because he provides a living target for long-range riflemen who go after him with the latest in flat-shooting firearms equipped with rifle scopes. Almost everywhere, farmers welcome the chuck hunter because he thins out these crop-eating rodents and helps to cut down on the number of dangerous chuck holes in the pastures.

BEAVER Beaver was something I had very much wanted to eat ever since I was a boy and had read Horace Kephart's regretful observation: "This tidbit of old-time trappers will be tasted by few of our generation, more's the pity." It was a lean black-haired trapper, Dan Macdonald, who gave me the opportunity some years later, and as beaver are one of the principal fur animals along the upper Peace River I've been fortunate enough to be able to enjoy *amisk* many times since.

The meat is so sustaining that anyone lost and hungry is markedly fortunate to secure it. Beaver cuttings on trees, which indicate the presence of the amphibian, are easily recognized by

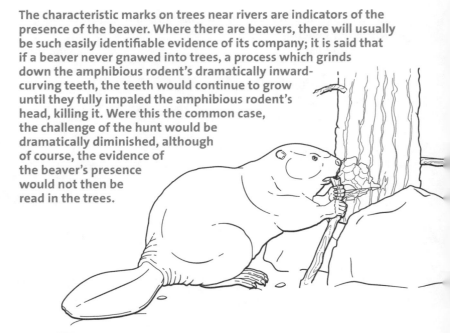

The characteristic marks on trees near rivers are indicators of the presence of the beaver. Where there are beavers, there will usually be such easily identifiable evidence of its company; it is said that if a beaver never gnawed into trees, a process which grinds down the amphibious rodent's dramatically inward-curving teeth, the teeth would continue to grow until they fully impaled the amphibious rodent's head, killing it. Were this the common case, the challenge of the hunt would be dramatically diminished, although of course, the evidence of the beaver's presence would not then be read in the trees.

the marks left by the large sharp teeth that have kept gnawing around and around, biting continually deeper until the wood is severed. Because beaver don't know how trees will fall, the animal is occasionally found trapped beneath trunk and branches.

If you have a gun and enough time at your disposal to wait for a sure shot, an often productive campaign is to steal to a concealed vantage on the downwind side of a beaver pond. The furry animal may then be seen swimming and shot in the head. If you have a choice and not much ammunition, wait to bag the biggest one you can. Beaver, the largest rodents on this continent, weigh up to fifty pounds or more.

Beaver quarters seem almost incommensurably delicious when you're hungry from outdoor exertion, although with the larger adults the meat does, even though you may be reluctant to heed it, have a tendency to become somewhat fibrous and stringy when cooked. The meat has a distinctive taste and odor somewhat resembling that of plump turkey. A sound idea in an emergency is to supplement it with lean flesh such as rabbit, so as to take the fullest possible advantage of the fat.

A beaver tail looks surprisingly like a scaly black fish whose head has been removed. Tails may be propped up or hung near a cooking fire whose heat will cause the rough black hide to puff and to separate from the flesh, whereupon it can be peeled off in large flakes.

The beaver tail is so full of nourishing oil, incidentally, that if set too close to a blaze it will burn like a torch. The meat is white and gelatinous, and rich enough that one finds himself not wanting too much of it at a time.

OTHER SMALL GAME

On occasion, the Indians hunted several other small animals with bow and arrow or firearms. Muskrats and beaver were sometimes hunted, and the Indian trapper would do almost anything to rid himself of a raiding wolverine. Most often, though, the beaver, muskrat, wolverine, lynx, mink, marten, sable, river otter, the various weasels, and other small fur-bearers were and still are taken with traps and snares rather than firearms. The Aleuts of Alaska did hunt the sea otter from kayaks with harpoons, and after the Russian fur traders arrived, they sometimes used firearms too. The sea-otter trade led to the exploration of Alaska and Russian colonization there. It is interesting to know that the pursuit of this valuable fur-bearer by Indian hunters working for the Russians led to the early exploration of the western coast just as the lust for beaver pelts led to the exploration of much of the American and Canadian West.

LEMMINGS FOR EMERGENCY DIETS

Lemmings have been found valuable as an emergency food by members of the Royal Canadian Mounted Police on extended patrols. Lemmings are the little stub-tailed mice that when reaching the ocean on their migrations, occasionally start swimming in the possible belief that it is just another pond or lake.

"In winter they nest on or near the ground, deep in snowdrifts," say Mounted Police sources, "and you will have to dig for them. In summer, you can find them by overturning flat rocks. You can get them by setting snares of very fine wire along the runways. Lemmings are constantly preyed upon by shrews, weasels, foxes, and owls." These animals are edible, too.

Chapter 3

Trapping and Snaring Animals for Food

FOR AN UNARMED SURVIVOR OR EVADER, OR WHEN the sound of a rifle shot could be a problem, trapping or snaring wild game is a good alternative. Several well-placed traps have the potential to catch much more game than a man with a rifle is likely to shoot.

To be effective with any type of trap or snare, you must
- Be familiar with the species of animal you intend to catch.
- Be capable of constructing a proper trap.
- Not alarm the prey by leaving signs of your presence.

There are no catchall traps you can set for all animals. You must determine what species are in a given area and set your traps specifically with those animals in mind.

Look for the following:
- Runs and trails.
- Tracks.
- Droppings.
- Chewed or rubbed vegetation.
- Nesting or roosting sites.
- Feeding and watering areas.

SNARES ARE SIMPLE AND EFFECTIVE Even if you do have a firearm, you may want to set a few snares, the principles of which are as simple as they are primitive. With a strong enough thong or rope, you can snare deer and larger animals. With nothing huskier than horsehair or light fishing line, squirrels and rabbits can be caught. A snare is, in effect, a slip noose placed with the object of tightening about and holding a quarry if the latter inadvertently moves into it.

"The size of the snare depends on the size of the animal you are trapping," as the Hudson's Bay Company notes in the instructions it encloses in its own emergency kit. "For example, on a rabbit trail the loop should be about 4 inches in diameter and hang from 1½ inches to 3 inches above the ground."

Let us assume, for the sake of illustration, that you want to snare a rabbit for the pot. You can see that they, like other animals, follow regular paths. You will endeavor, therefore, to hang the slip noose so that the rabbit will run headfirst into it and quickly choke himself.

You may want to go one step further and narrow the trail at that particular spot. This you can accomplish in one of several ways. You can drop a branch or small tree as naturally as possible across the track, making a narrow slit in it in which to suspend the noose. You can shove a few sticks into the ground to serve as a funnel. You can block the bottom, top, and sides of the runway with brush except for a small opening where the loop awaits.

All possible guile will be employed to make everything seem as congruous as possible, an achievement whose necessity increases in direct proportion with the intelligence of the prey sought. Trappers customarily prepare snares months ahead and leave them with the nooses harmlessly closed until fur season, to blend with the surroundings. Small pot animals, however, can usually be snared by beginners with a minimum of artifice.

A quick way to collect squirrels, for instance, is to lean a pole against a conifer under which there is considerable squirrel sign and at six or so points on the pole attach small nooses. A squirrel scampering up the incline runs his head into the waiting loop and falls free. Its dangling there does not seriously deter other squirrels from using the same route and being so caught themselves.

You can tie one end of the snare to a stationary object such as a pole or tree. You can tie it, particularly if snow makes tracking easy, to a drag or a weight such as a chunk of deadwood. Preferably, as shown in the accompanying illustrations of snares that have proved particularly effectual, you can bend a sapling and arrange a trigger so that the animal will be lifted off its feet and, if not choked as humanely as is possible under the conditions, at least rendered helpless enough for us to catch.

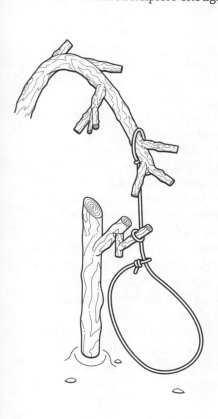
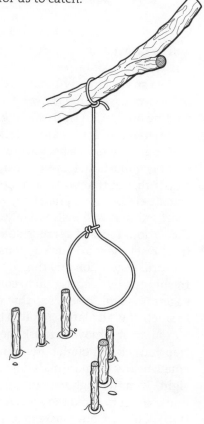

Fasten a noose from a sturdy yet flexible tree limb. Bow the branch down while, at the noose end, looping the rope around another limb nearer the ground. The loop should be tight enough that it sustains the bent branch tautly in place, but loose enough to easily unravel. In an animal's struggle to free itself from the snare, the loop will likely come undone, triggering the high branch to shoot upward as the noose's grip tightens around the hostage's neck.

A keen eye will discern the tracks or paths of forest-dwelling animals. Many follow regular paths. To further influence the route of your quarry so that its path leads to your dinner plate, you can use readily available materials, such as sticks, to create a gauntlet that funnels into a well-set snare.

POSITIONING TRAPS AND SNARES

Position your traps and snares where there is proof that animals pass through. You must determine if it is a "run" or a "trail." A trail will show signs of use by several species and will be rather distinct. A run is usually smaller and less distinct and will only contain signs of one species. You may construct a perfect snare, but it will not catch anything if haphazardly placed in the woods. Animals have bedding areas, watering holes, and feeding areas with trails leading from one to another. You must place snares and traps around these areas to be effective.

For an evader in a hostile environment, trap and snare concealment is important. It is equally important, however, not to create a disturbance that will alarm the animal and cause it to avoid the trap. Therefore, if you must dig, remove all fresh dirt from the area. Most animals will instinctively avoid a pitfall-type trap. Prepare the various parts of a trap or snare away from the site, carry them in, and set them up. Such actions make it easier to avoid disturbing the local vegetation and thereby alerting the prey. Do not use freshly cut, live vegetation to construct a trap or snare. Freshly cut vegetation will "bleed" sap that has an odor the prey will be able to smell. It is an alarm signal to the animal.

You must remove or mask the human scent on and around the trap you set. Although birds do not have a developed sense of smell, nearly all mammals depend on smell even more than on sight. Even the slightest human scent on a trap will alarm the prey and cause it to avoid the area. Actually removing the scent from a trap is difficult, but masking it is relatively easy. Use the fluid from the gall and urine bladders of previous kills. Do not use human urine. Mud, particularly from an area with plenty of rotting vegetation, is also good. Use it to coat your hands when handling the trap and to coat the trap when setting it. In nearly all parts of the world, animals know the smell of burned vegetation and smoke. It is only when a fire is actually burning that they become alarmed. Therefore, smoking the trap parts is an effective means to mask your scent. If one of the above techniques is not practical, and if time permits, allow a trap to weather for a few days and then set it. Do not handle a trap while it is weathering. When you position the trap, camouflage it as naturally as possible to prevent detection by the enemy and to avoid alarming the prey.

Traps or snares placed on a trail or run should use channelization. To build a channel, construct a funnel-shaped barrier extending from the sides of the trail toward the trap, with the narrowest part nearest the trap. Channelization should be inconspicuous to avoid alerting the prey. As the animal gets to the trap, it cannot turn left or right and continues into the trap. Few wild animals will back up, preferring to face the direction of travel. Channelization does not have to be an impassable barrier. You only have to make it inconvenient for the animal to go over or through the barrier. For best effect, the channelization should reduce the trail's width to just slightly wider than the targeted animal's body. Maintain this constriction at least as far back from the trap as the animal's body length, then begin the widening toward the mouth of the funnel.

USE OF BAIT

Baiting a trap or snare increases your chances of catching an animal. When catching fish, you must bait nearly all the devices. Success with an unbaited trap depends on its placement in a good location. A baited trap can actually draw animals to it. The bait should be something the animal knows. This bait, however, should not be so readily available in the immediate area that the animal can get it close by. For example, baiting a trap with corn in the middle of a corn field would not be likely to work. Likewise, if corn is not grown in the region, a corn-baited trap may arouse an animal's curiosity and keep it alerted while it ponders the strange food. Under such circumstances it may not go for the bait. One bait that works well on small mammals is the peanut butter from an MRE (meal ready to eat) ration. Salt is also a good bait. When using such baits, scatter bits of it around the trap to give the prey a chance to sample it and develop a craving for it. The animal will then overcome some of its caution before it gets to the trap.

If you set and bait a trap for one species but another species takes the bait without being caught, try to determine what the animal was. Then set a proper trap for that animal, using the same bait.

Note: Once you have successfully trapped an animal, you will not only gain confidence in your ability, you also will have resupplied yourself with bait for several more traps.

BASIC SNARES AND TRAPS

Once placed, snares and traps continue to work while you can tend to other needs. It shouldn't take much to find the indigenous animals' superhighways. These trails are located in heavy cover or undergrowth, or parallel to roads and open areas, and most animals routinely use the same pathways. Although several snares are covered in this section, for squirrel and rabbit-size game a simple loop snare is the best method of procurement in all climates.

SIMPLE LOOP SNARE

An animal caught in a simple loop snare will either strangle itself or be held secure until your arrival. To construct this type of snare, use either snare wire or improvised line that's strong enough to hold the mammal you intend to catch. If using snare wire, start by making a fixed loop at one end. To do this, bend the wire 2 inches from the end, fold it back on itself, and twist or wrap the end of the wire and its body together, leaving a small loop. Twist the fixed loop at its midpoint until it forms a figure eight. Fold the top half of the figure eight down onto the lower half. Run the free end of the wire through the fixed loop. The size of the snare will determine the resultant circle's diameter. It should be slightly larger than the head size of the animal you intend to catch.

Four steps for constructing a simple loop snare.

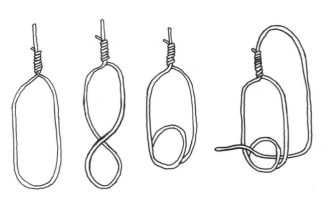

If using improvised line, make a slipknot that tightens down when the animal puts its head through it and lunges forward.

Avoid removing the bark from any natural material used in the snare's construction. If the bark is removed, camouflage the exposed

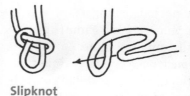

Slipknot

wood by rubbing dirt on it. Since animals avoid humans, it's important to remove your scent from the snare. One method of hiding your scent is to hold the snaring material over smoke or underwater for several minutes prior to its final placement. Place multiple simple loop snares, at least fifteen for every animal you want to catch, at den openings or well-traveled trails so that the loop is at the same height as the animal's head. When placing a snare, avoid disturbing the area insofar as possible. If establishing a snare on a well-traveled trail, try to use the natural funneling of any surrounding vegetation. If natural funneling isn't available, create your own with strategically placed sticks (again, hide your scent). Attach the free end of the snare to a branch, rock, or drag stick—a big stick that either is too heavy for the animal to drag or will get stuck in the surrounding debris when the animal tries to move.

Check your snares at dawn and dusk. Always make sure any caught game is dead before getting too close.

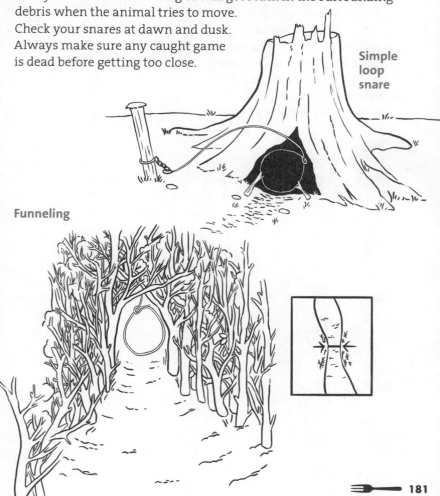

Simple loop snare

Funneling

ONE-PIN TOGGLE TRIGGER

The one-pin toggle trigger is primarily used to procure small game in a deadfall-mangling snare.

To construct a one-pin toggle, find one straight 8- to 12-inch-long branch that can be easily cut in two. Cut across its diameter, creating two pieces that respectively measure one-third and two-thirds of its length. Create a small notch across the center of the cut end of each branch so that a small twig can sit between the pieces when they are placed back together. This twig will provide the trigger to the one-pin toggle.

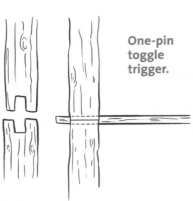

One-pin toggle trigger.

To use the one-pin toggle, place the twig between the two pieces and place it perpendicular to the ground with the longer piece up. Laying a large rock against the upper end of the toggle provides enough weight to arm the trigger and hold it all together. The device is tripped when the twig is moved. This can be facilitated by having it placed in the direct travel pattern of an animal or by putting food on the twig.

TWO-PIN TOGGLE TRIGGER

The two-pin toggle trigger is primarily used to procure small game in a strangling snare.

To construct a two-pin toggle, procure two small forked or hooked branches that ideally fit together when the hooks are placed in opposing positions. If unable to find two small forked or hooked branches, construct them by carving notches into two small pieces of wood until they fit together.

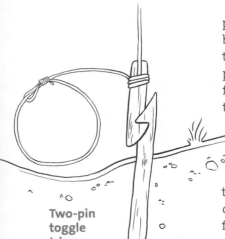

Two-pin toggle trigger

To use a two-pin toggle, firmly secure one branch in the ground so that the fork is pointing down. Attach the snare to the second forked branch, which is also tied to a sapling or other device so that when the trigger is tripped, the animal is captured or strangled. To arm the snare, simply bend the sapling and bring the two-pin toggle together. The resultant tension will hold it in place.

TWITCH-UP STRANGLE SNARE

An animal caught in a twitch-up strangle snare will either strangle itself or be held securely until your arrival. The advantage of the twitch-up snare over the simple loop snare is that it will hold your catch beyond the reach of other predatory animals that might wander by. To construct this type of snare, begin by making a simple loop snare out of either snare wire or strong improvised line. Find a sapling that, when bent to 90 degrees, is directly over the snare site you have selected.

You'll need to construct a two-pin toggle trigger to attach the sapling to the snare while holding its tension. Procure two small forked or hooked branches that ideally fit together when the hooks are placed in opposing positions. If unable to find such branches, construct them by carving notches into two small pieces of wood until they fit together.

To assemble the twitch-up snare, firmly secure one branch of the trigger in the ground so that the fork is pointing down. Attach the snare to the second forked branch, which is also tied to the sapling at the location that places it directly over the snare when bent 90 degrees. To arm the snare, bend the twig and attach the two-pin toggle together. The resultant tension will hold it in place. Adjust the snare height to the approximate position of the animal's head.

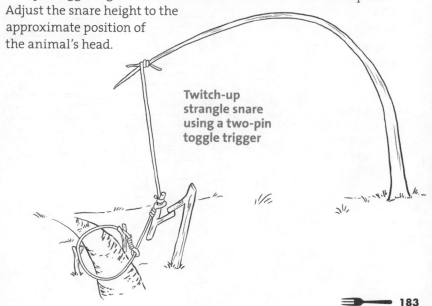

Twitch-up
strangle snare
using a two-pin
toggle trigger

When an animal places its head through the snare and trips the trigger, it will be snapped upward and strangled by the snare. If you're using improvised snare line, it may be necessary to place two small sticks into the ground to hold the snare open and in a proper place on the trail.

BOX TRAP

A box trap is ideal for small game and birds. It keeps the animal alive, thus avoiding the problem of having the meat spoil before it's needed for consumption. To construct a box trap, assemble a box from wood and lines, using whatever means are available. Be sure it's big enough to hold the game you intend to catch. Create a two-pin toggle trigger as described earlier for the twitch-up strangle snare, by carving L-shaped notches in the center of each stick. For the two-pin toggle to work with this trap, it's necessary to whittle both ends until they're flat. Be sure the sticks you use are long enough to create the height necessary for the animal or bird to get into the box. Take time to make a trigger that fits well.

Set the box at the intended snare site. Secure two sticks at opposite ends on the outside of one of the box's sides. Tie a line to each stick, bring the lines under the box, and secure them to the middle of the lower section of your two-pin toggle. Connect the two-pin toggle together, and use it to raise the side of the box that's opposite the two stakes. Adjust the lines until they're tight and about 1 inch above the ground. Bait the trap. When an animal or bird trips the line, it'll be trapped in the snare.

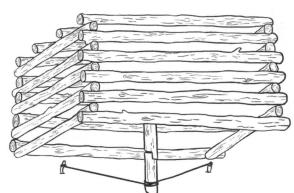

A box trap created using an L-shaped two-pin toggle trigger

APACHE FOOT SNARE

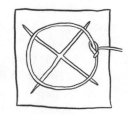

The Apache foot snare is a trap that combines an improvised device that can't easily be removed when penetrated with a simple loop snare made from very strong line. This snare is most often used for deer or similar animals and is placed on one side of an animal trail obstacle, such as a log. The ideal placement is directly over the depression formed from the animal's front feet as it jumps over the obstacle.

To improvise the device that the animal's foot goes through, gather two saplings, one 20 inches and the other 14 inches long, and eight sturdy branches that are ½ inch in diameter and 10 inches long. Lash each sapling together to form two separate circles, and sharpen one end of each of the eight branches to a blunt point. Place the smaller circle inside the larger, and evenly space the branches over both so that the points approach the center of the inner circle. Lash the sharpened sticks to both of the saplings.

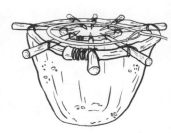

To place the snare, dig a small hole at the depression site, lay the circular device over it, and place the snare line over it. When an animal's foot goes through the device, it will be unable to get it free. As it continues forward, the strong, simple loop snare will tighten down on its foot. When constructing a snare like this, I often use a three-strand braid made from parachute cord, but any strong braid will work. The free end of the snare line should be secured to a large tree or other stable structure.

Apache foot snare

Camouflage the snare with leaves or similar material. Any large animal caught in this snare should be approached with caution.

TREADLE SPRING SNARE

Use a treadle snare against small game on a trail. Dig a shallow hole in the trail. Then drive a forked stick (fork down) into the ground on each side of the hole on the same side of trail. Select two fairly straight sticks that span the two forks. Position these two sticks so that their ends engage the forks. Place several sticks over the hole in the trail by positioning one end over the lower horizontal stick and the other on the ground on the other side of the hole. Cover the hole with enough sticks so that the prey must step on at least one of them to set off the snare. Tie one end of a piece of cordage to a twitch-up or to a weight suspended over a tree limb. Bend the twitch-up or raise the suspended weight to determine where you will tie a trigger about 2 inches long. Form a noose with the other end of the cordage. Route and spread the noose over the top of the sticks over the hole. Place the trigger stick against the horizontal sticks and route the cordage behind the sticks so that the tension of the power source will hold it in place. Adjust the bottom horizontal stick so that it will barely hold against the trigger. As the animal places its foot on a stick across the hole, the bottom horizontal stick moves down, releasing the trigger and allowing the noose to catch the animal by the foot. Because of the disturbance on the trail, an animal will be wary. You must therefore use channelization.

TREADLE SPRING SNARE

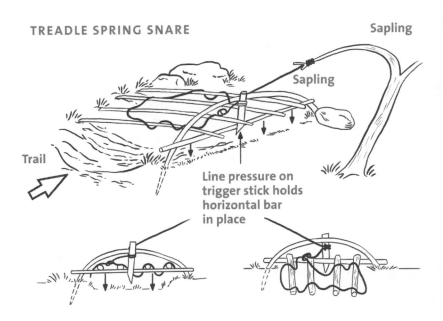

Sapling

Sapling

Trail

Line pressure on trigger stick holds horizontal bar in place

DRAG NOOSE

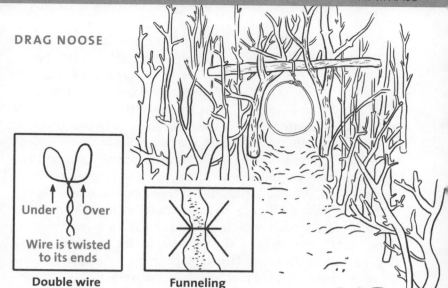

Under | Over

Wire is twisted to its ends

Double wire locking loop

Funneling

DRAG NOOSE Use a drag noose on an animal run. Place forked sticks on either side of the run and lay a sturdy crossmember across them. Tie the noose to the crossmember and hang it at a height above the animal's head. (Nooses designed to catch by the head should never be low enough for the prey to step into with a foot.) As the noose tightens around the animal's neck, the animal pulls the crossmember from the forked sticks and drags it along. The surrounding vegetation quickly catches the crossmember and the animal becomes entangled.

Noosing wand

NOOSING WAND A noose stick or noosing wand is useful for capturing roosting birds or small mammals. It requires a patient operator. This wand is more a weapon than a trap. It consists of a pole as long as you can effectively handle, with a slip noose of wire or stiff cordage tied at the small end. To catch an animal, you slip the noose over the neck of a roosting bird and pull it tight. You can also place it over a den hole and hide in a nearby blind. When the animal emerges from the den, you jerk the pole to tighten the noose and thus capture the animal. Carry a stout club to kill the prey.

OJIBWA BIRD POLE

An Ojibwa bird pole is a snare used by native Americans for centuries. To make it effective, place it in a relatively open area away from tall trees. For best results, pick a spot near feeding areas, dusting areas, or watering holes. Cut a pole about 6 feet long and trim away all limbs and foliage. Do not use resinous wood such as pine. Sharpen the upper end to a point, then drill a small-diameter hole into the side of the pole 2 to 3 inches down from the top. Cut a small stick 4 to 6 inches long and shape one end so that it will almost fit into the hole. This is the perch. Plant the long pole in the ground with the pointed end up. Tie a small weight, about equal to the weight of the targeted species, to a length of cordage. Pass the free end of the cordage through the hole, and tie a slip noose that covers the perch. Tie a single overhand knot in the cordage and place the perch against the hole. Allow the cordage to slip through the hole until the overhand knot rests against the pole and the top of the perch. The tension of the overhand knot against the pole and perch will hold the perch in position. Spread the noose over the perch, ensuring that it covers the perch and drapes over on both sides. Most birds prefer to rest on something above ground and will land on the perch. As soon as the bird lands, the perch will fall, releasing the overhand knot and allowing the weight to drop. The noose will tighten around the bird's feet, capturing it. If the weight is too heavy, it will cut the bird's feet off, allowing it to escape.

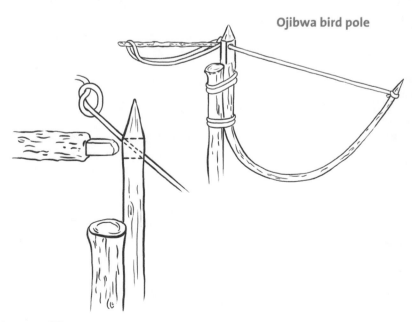

Ojibwa bird pole

Squirrel
pole

SQUIRREL POLE

A squirrel pole is an efficient means by which to catch multiple squirrels with minimal time, effort, and materials. Attach several simple loop snares to a 6-foot-long pole, then lean the pole onto an area with multiple squirrel feeding signs; look for mounds of pinecone scales, usually on a stump or a fallen tree. The squirrel will inevitably use the pole to try to get to his favorite feeding site.

BOW TRAP

A bow trap is one of the deadliest traps. It is dangerous to man as well as animals. To construct this trap, build a bow and anchor it to the ground with pegs. Adjust the aiming point as you anchor the bow. Lash a toggle stick to the trigger stick. Two upright sticks driven into the ground hold the trigger stick in place at a point where the toggle stick will engage the pulled bow string. Place a catch stick between the toggle stick and a stake driven into the ground. Tie a trip wire or cordage to the catch stick and route it around stakes and across the game trail where you tie it off. When the prey trips the trip wire, the bow looses an arrow into it. A notch in the bow serves to help aim the arrow.

Warning: This is a lethal trap. Approach it with caution and from the rear only!

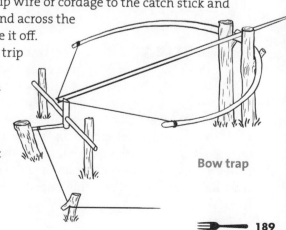

Bow trap

PIG SPEAR SHAFT

To construct the pig spear shaft, select a stout pole about 8 feet long. At the smaller end, firmly lash several small stakes. Lash the large end tightly to a tree along the game trail. Tie a length of cordage to another tree across the trail. Tie a sturdy, smooth stick to the other end of the cord. From the first tree, tie a trip wire or cord low to the ground, stretch it across the trail, and tie it to a catch stick. Make a slip ring from suitable material. Encircle the trip wire and the smooth stick with the slip ring. Emplace one end of another smooth stick within the slip ring and its other end against the second tree. Pull the smaller end of the spear shaft across the trail and position it between the short cord and the smooth stick. When tripped, the catch stick pulls the slip ring off the smooth sticks, releasing the spear shaft across the trail and impales the prey against the tree.

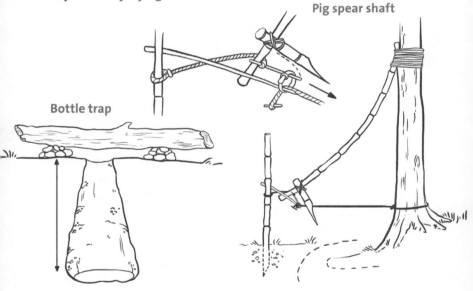

Pig spear shaft

Bottle trap

BOTTLE TRAP

A bottle trap is a simple trap for mice and voles. Dig a hole 12 to 18 inches deep that is wider at the bottom than at the top. Make the top of the hole as small as possible. Place bark or wood over the hole with small stones under it to hold it up 1 to 2 inches off the ground. Mice or voles will hide under the cover and fall into the hole. They cannot climb out because of the wall's backward slope. Use caution when checking this trap; it is an excellent hiding place for snakes.

Chapter 4
Weapons

HANDHELD WEAPONS Handheld weapons include rocks, throwing sticks, spears, bolas, weighted clubs, slingshots, and rodent skewers. Skill and precise aim are the keys to success when using these devices, and acquiring them requires practice.

Rocks

Hand-size stones can be used to stun an animal long enough for you to approach and kill it. Aiming toward the animal's head and shoulders, throw the rock as you would a baseball.

Throwing Stick

The ideal throwing stick is 2 to 3 feet long and thicker or weighted on one end. Holding the thin or lighter end of the stick, throw it in either an overhand or sidearm fashion. For best results, aim for the animal's head and shoulder.

Spear

To make a straight spear, procure a long, straight sapling and sharpen one end to a barbed point. If practical, fire harden the tip to make it more durable by holding it a few inches above a hot bed of coals until it's brown.

To make a forked spear, procure a long, straight sapling and fire harden the tip. Snugly lash a line around the stick 6 to 8 inches down from one end. Using a knife, split the wood down the center to the lash. To keep the two halves apart, lash a small wedge between them. (For best results, secure the wedge as far down the shaft as possible.) Sharpen the two prongs into inward-pointing barbs.

Flint-knapped tips can also be used to create a spear. To make one, attach a bone or rock tip to the front of your spear.

A throwing spear should be between 5 and 6 feet long. To throw a spear, hold it in your right hand and raise it above your shoulder so that the spear is parallel to the ground. Be sure to position your hand at the spear's center point of balance. (If left-handed, reverse these instructions.) Place your body so that your left foot is forward and your trunk is perpendicular to the target. In addition, point your left arm and hand toward the animal to help guide you when throwing the spear. Once positioned, thrust your right arm forward, releasing the spear at the moment that will best enable you to strike the animal in the chest or heart.

Using a spear to procure fish is a time-consuming challenge but under the right circumstances can yield a tasty supper. When using a spear you'll need to compensate for difference in light refraction above and below the water's surface. In order to obtain proper alignment, you'll need to place the spear tip into the water before aiming. Moving the spear tip slowly will allow the fish to get accustomed to it until you are ready. Once the fish has been speared, hold it down against the bottom of the stream until you can get your hand between it and the tip of the spear.

A forked spear made from a long sapling can also be used as a rodent skewer. To use it, thrust the pointed end into an animal hole until you feel the animal. Twist the stick so that it gets tightly snagged in the animal's fur. At this point, pull the animal out of the hole. Realize the rodent will try to bite and scratch you, so keep it at a distance. Use a club or rock to kill it.

Wooden forked spear

Bola

A bola is a throwing device that immobilizes small game long enough for you to approach and kill it. To construct a bola, use an overhand knot to tie three 2-foot-long lines together about 3 to 6 inches from one end. Securely attach a ½-pound rock to the other end of each of the three lines. To use the bola, hold the knot in your hand, and twirl the lines and rocks above your head or out to your side until you have attained adequate control and speed. Once this is accomplished, release your grip when the bola is directed toward the intended target.

Weighted Club

A weighted club can not only be used to kill an animal at close range but is also a valuable tool for meeting other survival needs. To construct one, find a rock that is 6 to 8 inches long, 3 to 4 inches wide, and about 1 inch thick. Cut a 2- to 3-foot branch of straight-grained wood that is 1 to 2 inches in diameter. Hardwood is best, but softwood also works. Snugly lash a line around the stick 6 to 8 inches down from one end. Split the wood down the center and to the lash with a knife. Insert the stone between the wood and as close to the lashing as possible, and secure the rock to the stick with a tight lashing above, below, and across the rock. You can also use a strong forked branch and secure the rock between the two forked branches. Use the weighted club in the same fashion as a throwing stick.

Bola

Slingshot

A slingshot is a fairly effective tool for killing small animals. To construct one, you'll need elastic cord, bungee cord, or surgical tubing, as well as webbing or leather to make a pouch. Cut a strong forked branch with a base 6 to 8 inches long and forked ends 3 to 5 inches long. Carve a notch around the top of each forked end, ½ inch down from the top. Cut two 10- to 12-inch pieces of elastic cord or line and secure them to the forked ends by wrapping one end of each cord around the carved notches, then tightly lashing them in place. Cut a piece of webbing or leather 3 inches long and 1 to 2 inches wide. Make a small centered hole ½ inch in from each end. Using the free end of the two elastic cords, run ½ inch through the hole in the webbing or leather. Secure each cord to the webbing

Weighted club

or leather by lashing it in place or tying a knot in the cord. To use the slingshot, hold a marble-size rock in the slingshot's pouch between the thumb and pointer finger of your right hand. Place your body so that your left foot is forward and your trunk is perpendicular to the target. Holding the slingshot with

Improvised sling-shots are effective weapons for procuring small game.

193

a straightened left arm, draw the pouch back toward your right eye. Position the animal between the forked branches, and aim for the head and shoulder region. Release the rock.

Rodent Skewer

A forked spear made from a long sapling can be used as a rodent skewer. To use it, thrust the pointed end into an animal hole until you feel the animal. Twist the stick so that it gets tightly snagged in the animal's fur, then pull the animal out of the hole. The rodent will try to bite and scratch you if it can, so keep it at a distance. Use a club or rock to kill it.

Rodent skewer

Rabbit Stick

One of the simplest and most effective killing devices is a stout stick as long as your arm, from fingertip to shoulder, called a "rabbit stick." You can throw it either overhand or sidearm and with considerable force. It is very effective against small game that stops and freezes as a defense.

FIREARMS

Few who go into the matter will dispute that the ideal diet for the average individual stranded in the North American wilderness with inadequate food supplies is meat. Fat, rare meat will keep the human body supplied with all the vitamins, minerals, and other food substances necessary for the fullest enjoyment of peak health. Other wild foods will also accomplish this, but none in most instances as easily or as satisfactorily. The challenge of survival will therefore in all likelihood be easier to meet if you have a firearm and ammunition. Suppose you have some choice in those two matters? Should you take a revolver, automatic pistol, shotgun, or rifle? What caliber? What type of ammunition?

You're considering the extreme problem of securing enough food to maintain strength indefinitely under primitive conditions, let us remember, perhaps for weeks and possibly for months without any outside help. The question viewed in that light becomes largely a matter of mathematics. What weight ammunition used with how heavy a firearm can reasonably be depended upon, pound for pound, to give you the most food?

Handguns, you will probably agree after following such reasoning a little farther, are not worth their weight and bulk as survival weapons if you have any choice in the matter. You can kill with them, certainly. The point is, because of inadequacies in such firearms themselves, no matter how expert you may be you cannot be sure of killing with them. You can hunt a month, even in ordinarily good country, and see only one moose. Your life can depend on your securing that one moose.

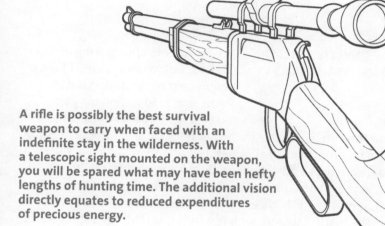

A rifle is possibly the best survival weapon to carry when faced with an indefinite stay in the wilderness. With a telescopic sight mounted on the weapon, you will be spared what may have been hefty lengths of hunting time. The additional vision directly equates to reduced expenditures of precious energy.

The best survival weapon, it follows, is a flat and hard shooting rifle. There is no need to say that it should be rugged, accurate, and durable. Neither is it necessary to add that a shotgun is no fit substitute, for although having about the same displacement and heft as a rule, it shoots bulkier ammunition at much smaller prey.

It would be hard to begrudge the additional few ounces of a good telescopic sight, if only because of the often vital minutes one adds to each day of the most productive hunting periods. You will probably also want to include a light sling, such as a Whelen, if only for purposes of carrying.

As for ammunition, for several evident reasons, you'll want one shot to do the job whenever possible. You are therefore apt to prefer the explosive effect of a high-velocity, hollow point cartridge.

SURVIVAL WEAPONS FOR A GROUP

Suppose two or three of you each has a choice of survival weapons. Should one select a revolver, another a scatter gun, and the third the flat-shooting and hard-hitting rifle? Some such diversification, at first thought, would not seem unreasonable. However, the same objections to handguns and shotguns would still prevail. You can see, upon consideration, that the probability of success would be greater if all had a rifle apiece, enabling you to spread out and hunt separately.

These rifles should all be identical, so that the parts of one or even two could be used to repair the third.

WHAT AND WHERE TO SHOOT

The first axiom of surviving by hunting, following the weight for weight formula to its inevitable conclusion, is to rely on big game. You will want to aim from the steadiest position possible for the vital region that affords the most margin for error, usually the chest.

Some member of the deer family is what anyone really bogged down in the North American wilderness is most apt to turn to for sustenance. The adult male, as any sportsman knows, is fattest just before the mating season, which, varying according to species and climate, commences roughly in early autumn. The male then becomes progressively poorer. At the end of the rut, the prime male is practically without fat even in the normally rich marrows.

The mature female is the choice of the meat hunter once the rutting season is well under way. She remains preferable until approximately early spring. Then the male once again becomes more desirable. Generally speaking, older animals have more body fat than younger ones.

DIFFERENT PROBLEMS AND DIFFERENT PLACES

The fact that a variety of different types of firearms are included in the survival kits issued in quantity by various groups does not conflict with the preceding statements. Particularly as such outfits are made up en masse with the knowledge that only a very minor percentage of them will ever need to be used, qualifications such as expense and weight are far more important considerations than they would be otherwise.

The basic problem is different, however, in country such as the interior of Panama, where there is abundant small game but few or no big game animals. In such a region, a functional weapon for living off the country is a rifle such as the .22 Hornet. If you wanted to diversify your ammunition so as to be in a position to destroy a minimum of meat, you could also carry a supply of reduced-recoil reload ammo having ballistics similar to those of the .22 long rifle cartridge.

AIMING FOR THE VITAL AREAS OF GAME

Most novice hunters have very little idea of the anatomy of animals and therefore they do not place their shots properly. The best possible training, of course, is to skin and cut up game animals or help someone do it, as Indian youngsters did.

The placement of the heart and lungs of four-footed animals is quite low in the chest. Not knowing this, many hunters place their shots too high. From the side, the total lung-heart area of a deer is only about 10 inches high and about 14 inches long—a small target at 200 or more yards, and a very small target for the archer at almost any range.

VITAL AREA OF THE WHITE-TAIL DEER

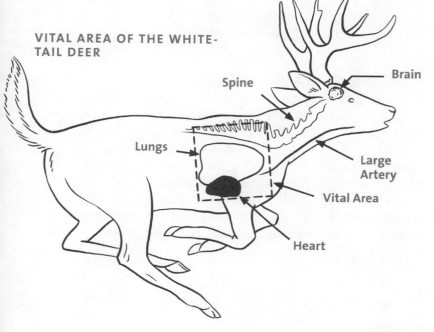

Spine

Brain

Lungs

Large Artery

Vital Area

Heart

As shown in the drawing, the line formed by the rear of the upper leg cuts the heart-lung area in half when viewed from the side. Placing a bullet or an arrow on that line at just the right height may pierce the lung on the near side, the upper part of the heart, and the lung on the other side. Most hunters describe this shot as hitting "just behind the shoulder." The use of the word "shoulder" is deceptive. It gives the impression that the vital area is high in the chest because most people think in terms of human anatomy. Almost all four-footed animals have the vital organs in the lower two-thirds of the body. If you are a little high with a rifle, you may smash the spine above the lungs, but that's hard to hit and it's easy to shoot high over the animal's back.

GOING-AWAY SHOTS It is rare to find a wary game animal standing still broadside to the hunter. Most often, game animals are going away from the hunter, and that fact poses something of a problem, particularly for archers. If a deer, elk, antelope, or other nondangerous game runs straight away from the hunter, there are only two possible targets. You can aim at the neck (including the back of the head), intending to kill by cutting or smashing the spinal column or the brain, or you can aim directly between the hams, fairly high, to drive the bullet right through the intestinal tract and into the heart-lung area. Both are difficult shots even for a skilled hunter firing an accurate, high-powered rifle.

SHOOTING FROM ELEVATED STANDS When shooting with firearms from an elevated stand in a tree or on a steep hillside, the best target is usually the middle of the back. Try to angle your shot downward toward the heart-lung area. If you are slightly forward of the animal, aim right at the top of the shoulders. From the side, angle in just to the near side of the spine. All these shots make a humane kill if you are using an adequate rifle, and if the shot can be centered, you may smash the backbone before the bullet even reaches heart or lung.

AVOIDING INJURY FROM WOUNDED ANIMALS

Approach all "dead" game with caution. The stories of careless deer hunters mutilated on the antlers of seemingly dead deer are legion, and many other animals are dangerous when wounded. Even the inoffensive pronghorn antelope can injure a man severely with his sharp hoofs if he kicks convulsively just as the hunter bends over the motionless animal or kneels down beside it. The safest approach is from the animal's back as it lies on the ground. In some cases, the nature of the wound is quite conclusive. A solid hit in a vital area or a dislocated or shattered spine is usually apparent to the eye, but take no chances. Gently touch the animal's eye with the muzzle of your gun or the tip of an arrow. Even an unconscious animal will blink if it is still alive. If the animal does blink, put another bullet into it or use another arrow.

If you are anxious to save meat, the neck just below the skull is a good place for a finishing shot with firearm or bow, but that mars the animal's cape for purposes of taxidermy. Some hunters cut the throat of every big game animal that they put down in order to make sure that it is dead and bleed it, but that mars the cape too. If you want a head-and-neck mount, it's probably best to put another bullet or arrow into the heart-lung area.

Following up a wounded game animal is a difficult and sometimes dangerous task, especially if you have shot the animal in rough country just before sunset. Good sportsmanship demands a quick, merciful kill. In addition, you'll avoid a lot of troublesome tracking if you shoot well enough to anchor the animal.

Every time a humane hunter fires a shot, he investigates the results even if he believes that he has missed. Game is too scarce today to be wasted, and even in frontier times wild meat and hides were too valuable for a hunter to waste an animal.

Before making any move to follow a wounded animal, take a few minutes to look at the lay of the land and think about the nature of the hit. You may save yourself hours of difficult, perhaps dangerous tracking by figuring out where the animal is likely to go.

Look for blood on the ground, grass, or leaves, and don't give up until you have followed the animal's tracks or general line of flight for a considerable distance. If the animal has gotten into thick cover, and you can't see a clear blood trail or tracks, it often pays to zigzag back and forth as you follow its general direction.

Chapter 5
Other Hunting Methods

BINOCULARS Just the other afternoon I sat on a bluff, sunlight glinting into my eyes from the meandering Peace River, and surveyed an open hillside a little more than a mile away. It seemed untenanted, and yet when I directed my binoculars on it I could see a medium-size cinnamon bear gorging himself on saskatoons.

If I had needed meat, which I didn't, or wanted the glossy fur, which as a matter of fact I preferred to see on the bear, it would not in all likelihood have been too difficult to circle to within easy shooting distance. Yet although visibility was as good as could be expected where mountains rise in high wilderness as untouched as themselves, the berry bushes so camouflaged the bear that even knowing where he was I still couldn't make him out without the telescope.

The point is that when binoculars and other such glasses as are fully capitalized upon, they are surpassed only by the firearm itself in importance in the matter of securing game for survival. If bringing down an animal can mean the difference between life and death, and particularly if your own life is not the only one so dependent, you're not going to attempt a needlessly dramatic offhand shot. The same principle holds true in glassing the country for game. You'll find yourself holding the glasses as steadily as possible, utilizing any available support, sitting if you can, and even sprawling prone with the lenses resting on a log if afforded that opportunity.

An area, as one soon appreciates, is best scrutinized section by overlapped section. Any object that may conceivably be some part of an animal is patiently watched for minutes for any sign of movement. Even if none is distinguished, before shifting the field of vision you'll probably fix that particular spot in mind so as to study it later to see if any detail has changed.

You'll get the habit, likely as not, of carefully scanning game trails for as far as you can see. You'll give particular notice to the types of cover where you know an animal may be lying and to the particular vegetation on which you are aware one may be feeding. Shores, as everyone knows, are especially well traveled, and you have perhaps more than once spotted moose dipping ungainly heads to drink, or have spied bears and maybe even mountain goats swimming.

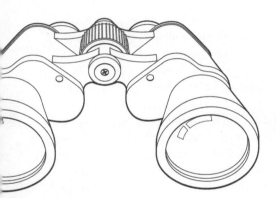

Game animals are often naturally well camouflaged to blend with their habitat. When scanning the country-side, a pair of trusty binoculars will help discern that slight movement in the brush, a possible indication of game that may represent the meal of meat that sustains your survival.

THE LAW OF SURVIVAL

Few will disagree that practices ordinarily contrary to both game regulations and good sportsmanship are justified in extreme emergencies by the more ancient law of survival. Under ordinary circumstances many of the methods of securing food herein described are illegal practically everywhere, and reasonably so, for a certain repugnance accompanies even the contemplation of some, while at best their successful commission in moments of stress will not be joined by any satisfaction except that resulting from the thus fulfilled instinct to stay alive.

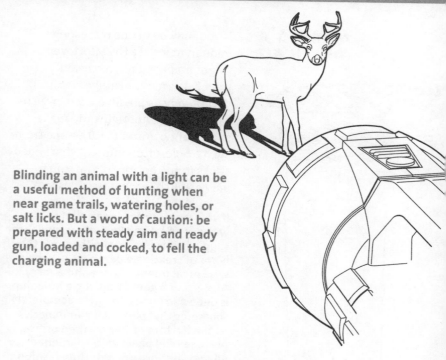

Blinding an animal with a light can be a useful method of hunting when near game trails, watering holes, or salt licks. But a word of caution: be prepared with steady aim and ready gun, loaded and cocked, to fell the charging animal.

JACKING One of these generally forbidden practices is jacking, in part the act of attracting and holding an animal's eyes at night by the beam of a light. Deer are among the big game creatures that can be readily spotted and held in this fashion long enough to be shot. Bears, on the other hand, will sometimes fall backward in their haste to scramble out of the way.

Likely places for jacking are on the downwind sides of well-used game trails and watering holes. Licks are occasionally found where the ground is so tremulous that you may sleep in brush or tall grass until awakened by the quivering caused by the animal's weight. Strategically located trees are particularly favored locations, both because of the deceptive way one's scent is dissipated and because of the often increased visibility afforded by a seat high amid branches.

Procedure for any reasonable contingency should be well thought out ahead of time, for it will be necessary to move and hold the light so as to see both animal and sights. The darker the night is, as a matter of fact, the better in many respects it will be for jacking. During nights when the northern lights are bright or when the moon is large, on the other hand, you may be able to distinguish and shoot a game animal without additional illumination, particularly if you have a good light-gathering telescopic sight.

MAKING A DEATH PIT

If you may be in one place long enough to justify the effort, you might prepare a pit in a heavily traveled game trail and cover it as deceptively as possible with branches and leaves. Aborigines, to make sure that no animal will escape from such a hole, often implant sharpened sticks in the bottom of the trap to pierce anything that tumbles in.

If you are stranded indefinitely, without rifle, in a place where evidence suggests it is bustling with game, the labor of creating a death pit may be a wise investment of time and energy. At signs of a game trail, dig a hole that is deep and wide enough to completely submerge that particular game species. At the bottom of this earthen orifice, place several posts with sharpened edges pointing upward. Then fashion a grillwork of sticks that will hold, at ground level, a scattering of leaves and grass or any available natural camouflage, thus disguising the hole with an appearance of solid ground.

BESIEGING A BURROW

Distasteful as it may be to him, a starving man is occasionally forced to smoke small animals from places of concealment. Sometimes an animal can also be driven to within reach of a club by quantities of water being poured into a burrow.

The opening may be such that it will be possible to impale the creature on a barbed pole or to secure it by twisting a forked stick into its hair and skin. Frequently, you may be able to dig with some success. You may also have some luck by spreading a noose in front of the hole, hiding a short distance away, and jerking the loop tight when the quarry ventures out.

Chapter 6
Methods for Preparing Game

N ORDER TO EAT YOUR CATCH, YOU'LL FIRST NEED to skin, gut, and butcher most game. Always do this well away from your camp and your food cache. Before skinning an animal, be sure it is dead. Once you're sure, cut the animal's throat and collect the blood in a container for later use in a stew. If time is not an issue, wait thirty minutes before starting to skin. This allows the body to cool, which makes it easier to skin and also provides enough time for most parasites to leave the animal's hide.

COLD-WEATHER SKINNING In cold weather, when temperatures drop to freezing or lower at night, skinning isn't really necessary. Besides, leaving the hide on prevents drying and helps keep the meat clean, which can be especially helpful in horse-packing and other backcountry situations where you can't handle the meat as carefully as you'd like. Leave the hide on until you take the animal to cold storage or to camp. There you can skin and bag it under clean conditions.

WARM-WEATHER SKINNING

In hot weather—say with daytime temperatures higher than sixty degrees and nighttime temperatures no lower than forty—skinning promotes the needed cooling and could save the meat. During hot late-summer bow seasons, I suggest skinning an animal immediately in the field. While doing that, you need to bag the meat to keep it clean and to keep flies off. I recommend that you always carry lightweight cheesecloth game bags for that purpose when early-season hunting.

COOLING THE CARCASS

To promote cooling, hang the carcass in the shade or drape it over a log so air can circulate on all sides. Medium-size animals such as deer and antelope will cool well this way, although it's a good idea to open up the hip and shoulder joints for quicker cooling. Big animals such as elk should be quartered; they cool very slowly otherwise. Bone sour, the result of slow cooling, is particularly common in the hip joints and shoulders. To prevent that, slice down the insides of the back legs to open up the hip joints and cut under the front legs to open up a space between the legs and the chest.

GLOVE SKINNING

Glove skinning is the method most often used for skinning small game. Hang the animal from its hind legs, and make a circular cut just above the ankle joints. Don't cut through the tendon. To avoid dulling your knife by cutting from the fur side, slide a finger between the hide and muscle, and place your knife next to the muscle so that you cut the hide from the inside. Cut down the inside of each leg, ending close to the genital area, and peel the skin off the legs until you reach the animal's tail. Firmly slide a finger under the hide between the tail and spine until you have a space that allows you to cut the tail free. Follow the same procedure on the front side. At this point, the hide can be pulled down and free from the animal's membrane with little effort. Avoid squeezing the belly, as this may cause urine to spill onto the meat. Pull the front feet through the hide (inside out) by sliding a finger between the elbow and the membrane and pulling the leg up and free from the rest of the hide. Cut off the feet. The head can either be severed or skinned, depending on your talents.

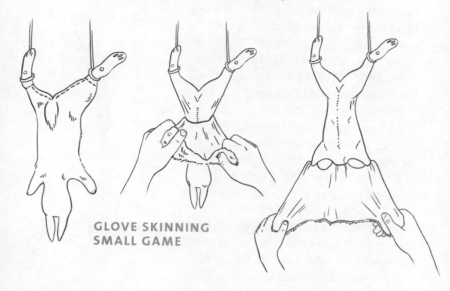

GLOVE SKINNING SMALL GAME

SKINNING SMALL GAME

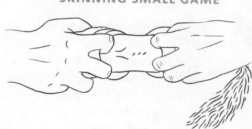

1. Cut the hide around the body.

2. Insert two fingers under the hide on both sides of the cut and pull both pieces off.

3. Separate the ribs from the backbone. There is less work and less wear on your knife if you break the ribs first, then cut through the breaks.

SKINNING LARGER GAME

A larger animal can be hung from a tree by its hind legs or skinned while lying on the ground. To hang it by its hind legs, find the tendon that connects the upper and lower leg, and poke a hole between it and the bone. If musk glands are present, remove them. These are usually found at the bend between the upper and lower parts of the hind legs. Free the hide from the animal's genitals by cutting a circular area around them, and then make an incision that runs just under the hide and all the way up to the neck. To avoid cutting the entrails, slide your index and middle fingers between the hide and the thin membrane enclosing the entrails. Use the V between the fingers to guide the cut and push the entrails down and away from the knife. The knife should be held with its backside next to the membrane and the sharp side facing out, so that when used, it cuts the hide from the non-hair side. Next, cut around the joint of each extremity. From there, extend the cut down the inside of each leg until it reaches the midline incision. You should attempt to pull off the hide using the same method as for small game. If you need to use your knife, cut

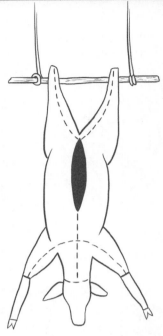

Skinning large game

toward the meat so as not to damage the hide. Avoid cutting through the entrails or hide. If skinning on the ground, use the hide to protect the meat, and don't remove it until after you gut and butcher the animal. Once the hide has been removed, it can be tanned and used for clothing, shelter cover, and containers.

GUTTING LARGER GAME

To gut an animal, place the carcass, belly up, on a slope with the head higher or hang it from a tree by its hind legs. Make a small incision just in front of the anus and insert your index and middle fingers into the cut, spreading them apart to from a V. Slide the knife into the incision between the V formed by your two fingers. Use your fingers to push the internal organs down, away from the knife, and as a guide for the knife as you cut up the abdominal cavity to the breastbone. Avoid cutting the bladder or other internal organs. If they are punctured, wash the meat as soon as possible. Cut around the anus and sex organs so that they will be easily removed with the entrails.

Remove the intact bladder by pinching it off close to the opening and cutting it free. Remove the entrails, pulling them down and away from the carcass. To do this, you will need to sever the intestines at the anus. Save the liver and kidneys for later consumption. **Caution: If the liver is spotted, a sign of disease, discard all internal organs and thoroughly cook the meat.** Cut through the diaphragm and reach inside the chest cavity until you can touch the windpipe. Cut or pull the

> **Note:**
>
> When cutting the hide, insert the knife blade under the skin and turn the blade up so that only the hide gets cut. This will also prevent cutting hair and getting it on the meat.

windpipe free and remove the chest cavity contents. Save the lungs and heart for later consumption. All internal organs can be cooked in any fashion but are best when used in a stew.

If you intend to eat the liver, you'll need to remove the small black sac, the gallbladder, as it's not edible. If it breaks, wash the liver immediately to avoid tainting the meat. Since fat spoils quickly, it should be cut away from the meat and promptly used. The fat is best in soups.

BUTCHERING GAME

To butcher an animal, cut the legs, back, and breast sections free of one another. When butchering large game, cut it into meal-size roasts and steaks that can be stored for later use. Cut the rest of the meat along the grain into long, thin strips about ⅛ inch thick, to be preserved by smoking or sun drying. Don't forget the head: the meat, tongue, eyes, and brain are all edible, as is the marrow inside bones. Keep the bones, brain, sinew, hoofs, and other parts. Each will serve many different survival needs.

LARGER GAME

Cut larger game into manageable pieces. First, slice the muscle tissue connecting the front legs to the body. There are no bones or joints connecting the front legs to the body on four-legged animals. Cut the hindquarters off where they join the body. You must cut around a large bone at the top of the leg and cut to the ball-and-socket hip joint. Cut the ligaments around the joint and bend it back to separate it. Remove the large muscles (the tenderloin) that lie on either side of the spine.

Cook large meat pieces over a spit or boil them. You can stew or boil smaller pieces, particularly those that remain attached to bone after the initial butchering, as soup or broth. You can cook body organs such as the heart, liver, pancreas, spleen, and kidneys using the same methods as for muscle meat. You can also cook and eat the brain. Cut the tongue out, skin it, boil it under tender, and eat it.

MEAT CARE

Allowing meat to spoil through neglect or ignorance is worse than losing a wounded animal. From mid-October on, meat care isn't a major problem in northern latitudes because fall weather will cool meat quickly. If you're hunting close to home, you can drag a deer out to your car and take it home for processing. But in the West, many bow seasons open in August, when the weather is too hot for quick meat cooling. Under these conditions you can find yourself in the backcountry, where you can't get meat to a cooler for several days. In those situations you must know how to handle an animal.

The key is to get body heat out of a carcass. It's not air temperature that spoils meat, but internal body heat. Hot weather keeps body heat from dissipating rapidly enough to prevent spoilage. Field-dressing (gutting) the animal is the first step.

FIELD-DRESSING DEER

To field-dress a deer, lay the animal on its back and slit the hide along the belly from chin to anus, being careful not to cut into the stomach or intestines. (If you plan to cape the deer for mounting, cut only from the brisket to the anus.) Cut the windpipe and esophagus at the chin and loosen them from the neck so they can be pulled into the body cavity. Next, cut around the anus to loosen it so the intestines can be pulled out through the body cavity. Reach into the body cavity and cut the diaphragm loose from the inside of the rib cage. Roll the deer onto its side and pull the viscera onto the ground. You may have to cut additional connective tissue loose inside to get everything out. Wipe the inside of the body cavity with a clean rag. If any internal organs have been punctured, contaminating the inside of the deer, wash the body cavity thoroughly with clean water and then wipe it dry.

BONING

If you have to pack animals a long way on your back, boning the meat (that is, removing all the bones) can reduce the weight you have to carry. Boning also enhances cooling. When boning an animal in the field, you must have game bags available to keep the meat clean.

Boning helps to reduce weight and speeds cooling. With the animal lying on its side, start by skinning the upper half of the animal from head to tail. Then cut off the front leg. (This is easy to do because it's held in place only by muscle.) Bag the leg to keep it clean.

Remove the back leg next. Start on the inside of the pelvis and work toward the back, slicing the meat cleanly from the pelvic bone. Soon you'll come to the hip joint. Push hard on the leg to break this joint open, and then continue to cut along the pelvis until the entire back leg comes loose. Bag the leg. To reduce weight further, you can later remove the bones from the front and back legs.

Finally, slice the meat off the ribs. Start at the brisket and work around the body to the backbone, much as you'd fillet a fish. Rib meat, flanks, backstrap, and neck come off in one big piece. You can cut this into two or three pieces to keep weight down.

When you've finished the top side, flip the carcass over and do the same on the other side. In hot weather, you must bag meat to keep off flies. Hang the meat in the shade, or if daytime temperatures are too hot, hang the meat at night and wrap it in sleeping bags during the day to keep it cool.

BONES MAY MEAN SALVATION A lot of us, given the time, capitalize on the food value inherent in bones in two ways: Small bones go into the pot to thicken stews and soups, and we may also like to chew on the softer of these, particularly if we are lounging around a campfire. Larger marrow bones are opened so that their soft vascular tissue can be extracted.

The mineral-rich marrow found in the bones of animals that were in good physical condition at demise is not surpassed by any other natural food in caloric strength. What is, at the same time, the most delectable of tidbits is wasted by the common outdoor practice of roasting such bones until they are on the point of crumbling. A more conservative procedure is to crack them at the onset, with two stones if nothing handier is available. The less the marrow is then cooked, the more nutritious it will remain.

All this is something to consider if any of us, when desperate for food, happens upon the skeleton of a large animal.

PRESERVING MEAT Meat processors say life begins at forty (forty degrees, that is), so if nighttime temperatures are dropping to forty degrees or lower, you can keep meat in the field for several days. The best way, especially if daytime temperatures are getting too warm, is to hang the meat at night without the game bags to cool it thoroughly. Then in the morning re-bag the meat, stack it on a clean tarp, and cover it with sleeping bags. With a good layer of bags, the meat temperature will rise no more than three to four degrees during the day. After sundown, hang it again for re-cooling. You can keep meat in the field for a week or more this way, even if daytime temperatures rise to sixty degrees or higher. This is also a good way to transport meat in your vehicle on a long drive home.

If you can't cool meat to forty degrees or lower at night, then you need to get it into cold storage within three days. If you're going into the backcountry, always line up packing services ahead of time, so you know you can get the meat out. If you follow these steps, you end up with great table fare, the sign of a successful hunter.

CAN LIVE MEAT SPOIL TOO QUICKLY TO BE CONSUMED?

One often hears it suggested that when any bird or animal has been unduly harassed before death, as may be considered to be the case if, for example, it has been run to ground by wolves, its meat is no longer fit to eat. Such conclusions are false, however, and are more attributed to fancy than fact. Although it is true that the amounts of lactic acid in the muscle tissues of such animals is higher than those not chased by their predators and that the rate of spoilage is faster, this meat is still quite safe to eat if cooked well and immediately.

WHICH PARTS OF MEAT TO EAT

You will probably want to eat most of any animals you can secure if short of food. Some parts that are high in vitamin A, such as the liver, have been recognized as a specific cure for night blindness. But any section of plump fresh meat is a complete diet in itself, affording all the necessary food ingredients even if you dine on nothing but fat rare steaks for week after month after year.

BLOOD

Animals should not be bled any more than can be helped if food is scarce. Whether they should be so handled at other times is a matter largely of circumstances and of personal personal opinion. Blood, which is not far removed from milk, is unusually rich in easily absorbed minerals and vitamins. Our bodies need iron. It would require the assimilation of ten ordinary eggs, we are told, to supply one man's normal daily requirements. Four tablespoons of blood are capable of doing the same job.

Fresh blood can be secured and carried, in the absence of handier means, in a bag improvised from one or another part of the cleaned entrails. One way to use it is in broths and soups, perhaps enlivened by a wild vegetable or two.

LEATHER AND RAWHIDE

The skin of the animal is as nourishing as a similar quantity of lean meat. Baking a catch in its hide, although ordinarily both a handy and tasty method of occasionally preparing camp meat, is therefore a practice you should not indulge in when rations are scarce.

Rawhide is also high in protein. Boiled, it has even less flavor than roasted antlers, and the not overly appealing and yet scarcely unpleasant look and feel of the boiled skin of a large fish. When it is raw, a usual procedure naturally adopted in emergencies is to chew on a small bit until mastication becomes tiresome and then to swallow the slippery shred.

Explorers speak of variances of opinion among individual members of groups as to whether or not leather, generally footwear or other body covering, should be eaten. When you are so situated that to reach safety you will need to walk, retaining your foot protection should of course come first. If you are cold as well as hungry, you will stay warmer by wearing the rawhide than you would by sacrificing it to obtain a little additional heat via the digestive system. If the article in question is made of commercially tanned leather, the answer will be simpler indeed, for such leather generally has scant if any food value.

Chapter 7
What About Birds?

BIRDS FOR FOOD Almost all birds are edible. If nests are near, eggs may also be available for consumption. Birds are commonly found at the edge of the woods where clearings end and forests begin, on the banks of rivers and streams, and on lakeshores and seashores.

Birds can be snared, caught with a baited hook, or on occasion clubbed. The Indians often trapped and hunted birds such as eagles, turkeys, hawks, and the large woodpeckers to obtain feathers for decoration and for fletching arrows. The feathers of the turkey, turkey buzzard, and various geese were used a great deal for fletching.

Small birds were seldom taken with bow and arrow, though some young hunters took them with very light, pronged spears or with arrows with blunt points that killed or stunned by impact. Boys of the Plains tribes were taught to snare birds with nooses made of horsehair. The small nooses were tied about 6 inches apart on a stick that was placed on the ground. Seeds or grain were scattered as bait. Some birds nearly always got their legs entangled in these snares, and the watching boys ran from cover to kill them before they could escape. The stick to which the nooses were tied acted as a drag.

CAPTURING BIRDS All species of birds are edible, although the flavor will vary considerably. You may skin fish-eating birds to improve their taste. As with any wild animal, you must understand birds' common habits to have a realistic chance of capturing them. You can take pigeons, as well as some other species, from their roost at night by hand. During the nesting season, some species will not leave the nest even when approached. Knowing where and when the birds nest makes catching them easier. Birds tend to have regular flyways going from the roost to a feeding area, to water, and so forth. Careful observation should reveal where these flyways are and indicate good areas for catching birds in nets stretched across the flyways. Roosting sites and watering holes are some of the most promising areas for trapping or snaring.

Nesting birds present another food source—eggs. Remove all but two or three eggs from the clutch, marking the ones that you leave. The bird will continue to lay more eggs to fill the clutch. Continue removing the fresh eggs, leaving the ones you marked.

TYPES OF BIRDS	FREQUENT NESTING PLACES	NESTING PERIODS
Inland birds	Trees, woods, or fields	Spring and early summer in temperate and arctic regions; year round in the tropics
Cranes and herons	Mangrove swamps or high trees near water	Spring and early summer
Some species of owls	High trees	Late December through March
Ducks, geese, and swans	Tundra areas near ponds, rivers, or lakes	Spring and early summer in arctic regions
Some sea birds	Sandbars or low sand islands	Spring and early summer in temperate and arctic regions
Gulls, auks, murres, and cormorants	Steep rocky coasts	Spring and early summer in temperate and arctic regions

PREPARING BIRDS Pluck all birds unless they are scavengers or seabirds, which should be skinned. Leaving the skin on other kinds of birds will retain more of their nutrients when cooked.
Cut the neck off close to the body. Cut open the chest and abdominal cavity, and remove the insides. Save the neck, liver, heart, and gizzard, which are all edible. Before eating the gizzard, split it open and remove the stones and partially digested food. Cook in any desired fashion. Cook scavenger birds a minimum of twenty minutes to kill parasites.

QUAIL By studying the habits of quail, California Indians learned that the western forms of this game bird like to follow a low fence, natural hedge, or line of brush rather than fly over it. To trap the quail, they attached nooses made of fine thongs to bushes or branches at openings in the runways and also placed the nooses where the runways ended. Sometimes the Indians baited the ground near the nooses. Every few days, boys or women removed the birds caught in the snares, which were then reset.

TURKEYS An odd, simple trap was used to catch the wary wild turkey. Two poles were driven into the ground about 10 feet apart. A much lighter pole was tied between the two uprights about 14 inches above the ground. The trap was then baited with grains of maize. Knowing the habits of the birds, the Indians knew the direction of their approach and scattered corn under the length of the pole and 6 to 12 inches beyond it. A few women and boys then hid nearby and stayed quiet. When the turkeys reached the trap and began feeding on the grain, they soon had to stretch their necks beneath the crossbar to reach the grain. A wild turkey does not seem to be able to withdraw its head from under a low horizontal pole. The hidden trappers rushed from their blind and snatched the self-trapped birds.

GEESE Canada geese, snow geese, and blue geese were trapped in an equally simple way. A trench about 18 feet long, 18 inches deep, and 14 inches wide was dug in the ground. Kernels of maize were sparingly scattered along the length of the trench, and the trench trap was ready. The trappers took cover close to the trap. When the geese flew in, they began to eat the grain at the ends of the trench, then continued into the trench itself in search of more corn. When several geese were in the trench, the trappers rushed from cover and seized the birds. The geese could not fly away because they did not have enough room to spread their wings in the narrow trench.

GETTING BIRDS WITHOUT GUNS Game birds such as ptarmigan and grouse promise feasts for anybody lost in the wilderness, especially as a few stones or sticks are often the only weapons needed to catch one. If one misses the first time, such fowl usually will afford a second and even a third chance to be captured. When they do fly, they generally go only short distances and may be successfully followed, particularly if this is done casually and at such a tangent that it would seem as if one were strolling on past.

It goes without saying that no sportsman finds any amusement in indiscriminate killing; it follows with equal reason that when survival is at stake and when wild meat may mean life itself, otherwise distasteful means of securing meat may be justified, even though regrets for their necessity may remain.

Any bird, as a matter of fact, will furnish good eating in an emergency.

Because bevies of grouse tend to fly and flutter close to the ground for short distances only, a casual pursuit with a few good stones or sticks may lead to an important feast. The birds will usually allow the hunter a few opportunities to get reasonably close enough to them so that his chances of success are quite high.

The only difference is that some are more tender and plump, and to different palates better-tasting than others. Colonies afford particular opportunities. Even ripe eggs should not be overlooked when one needs food.

SUCCESSFUL BIRD TRAPS

Traps also work well with birds. A stick fence put up in a narrowing spiral and baited will sometimes catch, in its center, fowl such as quail.

Bird Tunnel Trap

Dig a funnel-shaped tunnel that narrows at its end. Using bait such as bird seed or berries, create a trail that leads to the back of the tunnel. The bird will enter the tunnel while eating the seed and, once done, will be unable to back out since its feathers will become wedged in the tunnel's walls. This trap is most effective for birds that have guard feathers on their heads; a quail is a good example.

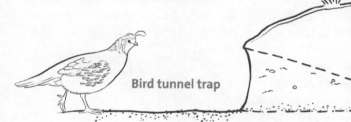

Bird tunnel trap

Bird Hole Trap

In a piece of wood, cut a small circle that is barely big enough for a bird's head to get through. Like the tunnel trap, this design works best on birds with guard feathers. Securely place the wood over a small hole and use seed, fruit, or other bird bait to lead the fowl toward the trap. Be sure to place some on the board and at the bottom of the hole. When the bird puts its head through the wood, its feathers will become wedged when it tries to withdraw it head. Note: This can be used with a jar, but its slick sides make it less effective.

Bird hole trap

SCAVENGERS EASILY CAUGHT

Gulls and other scavenger birds can be easily although unpleasantly caught by a man who is desperate enough for food. A short stick or bone sharpened at both ends is secured in the middle by a line, preferably tied to something limber such as a sapling, and is then concealed in some bait such as a decomposed fish. When a bird swallows the bait, jerk the line to position the stick sideways in the bird's gullet and pull it toward you.

MAKING AND USING A BOLA

One can improvise a bola, a missile weapon consisting primitively of stones attached to the ends of thongs. Although the Spanish are generally most often thought of in connection with the bola, the Inuit also use a device of this type, consisting of several cords about a yard long with a small weight at the extremity of each.

The bola is grasped at the center from which all cords radiate, and the weights are twirled above the head. Twirled and released at flying birds, the spinning strings often twist around one or more and bring them to the ground.

Bolas are typically made by tying one end of a string or rope to the middle of a slightly longer string or rope, approximately a yard long. Lash a stone that fits comfortably in the palm of your

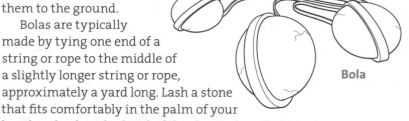

Bola

hand to the detached end of the shorter length; likewise, secure slightly larger weights to the ends of the longer length. When ready for action, grasp the middle stone in a firm grip, swing the two larger ones into a rapid-moving circular motion, aim the rock in hand at the target, and fire away. Another technique is to grasp the contraption at the center from which multiple lengths radiate, twirling several weights attached to the ends of each length above your head. Also, variations of this weapon can be made from a stick in place of the short rope length; this is firmly held as the stones spin above it like the rotors of a helicopter.

Chapter 8

Insects as a Food Source

"I T IS NEXT TO IMPOSSIBLE TO STARVE IN A wilderness," says George Leopard Herter, of Herter's, Inc., sporting goods manufacturer, importer, and exporter:

If no game, fish, mollusk, etc. are present, you are still in no danger.

Insects are wonderful food, being mostly fat, and are far more fortifying than either fish or meat. It does not take many insects to keep you fit. Do not be squeamish about eating insects, as it is entirely uncalled for. In parts of Mexico, the most nutritious flour is made from the eggs of small insects found in the marshes. In Japan, darning needles or dragon flies are a delicacy. They have a delicious delicate taste, so be sure to try them.

Moths, mayflies, in fact about all the insects found in the wools, are very palatable. The only ones I ever found that I did not care for were ants. They contain formic acid and have a bitter taste. Some aborigines have capitalized on the ants' acidity by mashing them in water sweetened with berries or sap to make a sort of lemonade. The eggs and the young of the ant are also eaten.

A small light at night will get you all the insects you need to keep you in good condition. If the weather is too cold for flying insects, kick open some rotten logs or look under stones and get some grubs. They keep bears fat and healthy and will do the same for you.

A BUG DIET Many cultures around the world eat bugs as part of their routine diet. Pan-fried locusts are considered a delicacy in Algeria and several Mexican states. In Malaysia, bee larvae are considered a special treat. Our phobia about eating bugs is unfortunate, as they provide ample amounts of protein, fats, carbohydrates, calcium, and iron. Compared with cattle, sheep, pigs, and chickens, bugs are far more cost effective to raise and have far fewer harmful effects related to their rearing.

Although bugs are not harvested for food in the United States, those of us who purchase our foods at the store are eating them every day. The FDA allows certain levels of bugs to be present in various foods. The accepted standards allow up to 60 aphids in 3½ ounces of broccoli, 2 to 3 fruit fly maggots in 200 grams of tomato juice, 100 insect fragments in 25 grams of curry powder, 74 mites in 100 grams of canned mushrooms, 13 insect heads in 100 grams of fig paste, and 34 fruit fly eggs in every cup of raisins.

A study done by Jared Ostrem and John VanDyk for the entomology department of Iowa State University comparing the nutritional value of various bugs to that of lean ground beef and fish showed the following results per 100 grams:

BUGS ARE A GREAT SOURCE OF FOOD

	PROTEIN (g)	FATS (g)	CARBOHYDRATES (g)	CALCIUM (mg)	IRON (mg)
Crickets	12.9	5.5	5.1	75.8	9.5
Small grasshoppers	20.6	6.1	3.9	35.2	5.0
Giant water beetles	19.8	8.3	2.1	43.5	13.6
Red ants	13.9	3.5	2.9	47.8	5.7
Silkworm pupae	9.6	5.6	2.3	41.7	1.8
Termites	14.2	n/a	n/a	0.050	35.5
Weevils	6.7	n/a	n/a	0.186	13.1
Lean ground beef (baked)	24.0	18.3	0	9.0	2.09
Fish (broiled cod)	22.95	0.86	0	0.031	1.0

Bugs can be found throughout the world, and they are easy to procure. In addition, the larvae and grubs of many insects are edible and easily found in rotten logs, underground, or under the bark of dead trees. Although a fair number of bugs can be eaten raw, it is best to cook them in order to avoid ingesting unwanted parasites.

FINDING INSECTS The most abundant life-form on earth, insects are easily caught. Insects provide 65 to 80 percent protein, compared to 20 percent for beef. This fact makes insects an important, if not overly appetizing, food source. Insects to avoid include all adults that sting or bite, hairy or brightly colored insects, and caterpillars and insects that have a pungent odor. Also avoid spiders and common disease carriers such as ticks, flies, and mosquitoes.

Rotting logs lying on the ground are excellent places to look for a variety of insects, including ants, termites, beetles, and grubs, which are beetle larvae. Do not overlook insect nests on or in the ground. Grassy areas, such as fields, are good areas to search because the insects are easily seen. Stones, boards, or other materials lying on the ground provide the insects with good nesting sites. Check these sites. Insect larvae are also edible. Insects such as beetles and grasshoppers that have a hard outer shell will have parasites. Cook them before eating. Remove any wings and barbed legs also. You can eat most insects raw. The taste varies from one species to another. Wood grubs are bland, while some species of ants store honey in their bodies, giving them a sweet taste. You can grind a collection of insects into a paste. You can mix them with edible vegetation. You can cook them to improve their taste.

WORMS Worms (Annelida) are an excellent protein source. Dig for them in damp humus soil or watch for them on the ground after a rain. After capturing them, drop them into clean, potable water for a few minutes. The worms will naturally purge or wash themselves out, after which you can eat them raw.

TERMITES By tearing open a rotten log, you may uncover a calorie-laden feast scurrying for cover. Comprised of up to 38 percent protein, termites also are rich in iron, calcium, and essential essential fatty and amino acids. Resembling pale ants, they can be eaten raw or roasted in a dry pan, where they sometimes acquire a shrimp-like flavor.

CRICKETS If you avoid the brightly colored species, crickets and grasshoppers are generally safe to eat. Also, 100 grams of cricket contain two times the protein of the same amount of beef and 15 percent more iron than spinach. Remove the heads, legs, and wings and cook thoroughly to kill any parasites. They are easier to hunt early in the morning, when colder temperatures make them slower.

Part III
FISH

Chapter 1
The Importance of Fish

FRESHLY CAUGHT FISH PROVIDE A COMPLETELY
balanced diet when sufficiently fat and not overcooked.
The main difficulty with subsisting exclusively on fish
arises from the fact that in calories they are often far less
nourishing than one might expect.

There are no poisonous freshwater fish. However, the catfish
species has sharp needlelike protrusions on its dorsal fins and barbels.
These can inflict painful puncture wounds that quickly become
infected. And it is best to cook all freshwater fish to kill parasites.

Fish represent a good source of protein and fat. They offer some
distinct advantages to the survivor or evader. They are usually more
abundant than mammal wildlife, and the ways to get them are silent.

UNDERSTANDING FISH

To be successful at catching fish, you
must know their habits. For instance,
fish tend to feed heavily before a
storm. Fish are not likely to feed after
a storm when the water is muddy
and swollen. Light often attracts fish at night. When there is a
heavy current, fish will rest in places where there is an eddy, such
as near rocks. Fish will also gather where there are deep pools,
under overhanging brush, and in and around submerged foliage,
logs, or other objects that offer them shelter.

Fish are commonly found in almost all sources of water. The best times to fish are just before dawn or just after dusk, at night when the moon is full, and when bad weather is imminent. Fish tend to be close to banks and shallow water in the morning and evening hours. In addition, fish can be found in calm deep pools (especially where transitions from ripples to calm or calm to ripples occur); under outcroppings and overhanging undercuts, brush, or logs; in eddies below rocks or logs; and at the mouth of an intersection with another stream. Avoid fish that have slimy bodies, bad odor, suspicious color (gills should be pink and scales pronounced), and/or flesh that remains indented after being pressed.

CATCHING AND EATING FISH

Some methods of fish procurement include fishing tackle, gill nets, spears, poisons, and even your bare hands. To prevent spoilage, prepare the fish as soon as possible. Gut the fish by cutting upward on its abdomen and then removing the intestines and large blood vessels (kidneys) that lie next to the backbone. Remove the gills and, when applicable, scale and/or skin the fish. On bigger fish you may want to fillet the meat off the bone. To do this, cut behind the fish's gill plates on each side of its head and slide the knife under the meat next to the backbone. Keeping the knife firmly placed against the backbone, begin slicing toward the tail. Next, hold the tail's skin and slide the knife between the skin and meat, cutting forward using a slight sawing motion.

USING YOUR COMMON SENSE

By applying everyday common sense to your fishing, you should be able to catch fish or at least improve your chances of finding them. Like anything you do, you can do it well only if you spend some time evaluating the conditions or circumstances surrounding the situation and making sound judgments to accomplish the results you're after. To succeed, you must have the facts or knowledge necessary to make your decision.

To catch fish, you must apply the same kind of thinking. You first have to find them, and to find them you need to know something about them. You need to know what affects them and you must learn to recognize their habits. Once you learn a few of these facts, you can make some judgments necessary to find and catch them.

The following list gives a few important facts that you'll need when you're trying to locate fish, regardless of the type of waters you will be fishing.

- Ninety percent of all waters contain no fish.

- Fish are creatures of habit; once you learn their habits, you can find them.

- Fish require some form of cover (structure) in which to live.

- Fish require some form of cover (structure) in which to move about (migration routes) when they search for food.

- Fish concentrate in areas where cover (structure) is available.

- Most game fish are in deep water most of the time (greater than 8 or 10 feet deep).

EARLY SEASON FISHING

After the first warming trends of spring, just after ice-out (in March or April), try some of the following tips.

When to Fish

The time of day for early season fishing is critical for the best results. The following illustrations can be used as a general rule.

EARLY MORNING: 6:00 TO 9:00 AM

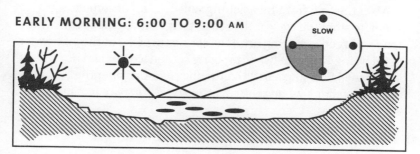

Cool water temperature and low angle of the sun's rays, which bounce off the water, provide little action.

LATE MORNING TO EARLY AFTERNOON: 9:00 AM TO 1:00 PM

Sun starts to penetrate water, surface starts to warm up.
Often produces, but could be irregular.

AFTERNOON TO EARLY DUSK: 1:00 TO 5:00 PM

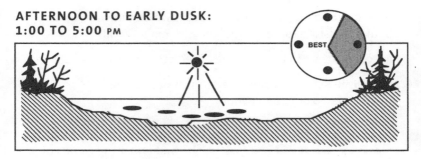

Sun's rays at maximum penetration. Best time to fish, when air and
water temperatures are warmest.

Cold Fronts

During the early season, cold fronts are one of the key factors that
will affect fishing.

After the cold front hits, fishing will drop off or come to a
complete stop. The cycle will repeat itself with the next warming
trend and keep repeating until the spring turnover of the lake water.

Knowing where to fish after early season ice-out can be
determined by using a little common sense. Consider the
following factors when selecting the water you plan to fish.

Best Places

- small lakes
- ponds
- quarries

Best Water

Remember, darker bottom areas such as mud flats and shallow, silt-covered areas absorb heat and warm up quicker than light-bottomed areas such as sand or gravel. Most early season fish will seek out the warmest water.

MIDSEASON FISHING

Here are just a few tips to try during the summer months (mid-June through mid-September) when the fishing slows down.

When to Fish

During the summer, as a general rule, early morning and late evening are the best times to fish.

EARLY MORNING: 4:30 TO 9:00 AM

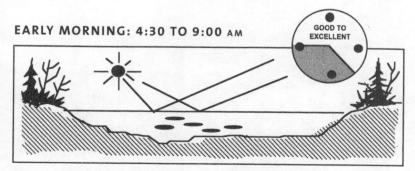

Fish are active just before daybreak (4:30 AM) until about 9:00 AM. Fishing will be excellent.

MID-MORNING TO LATE AFTERNOON:
9:00 AM TO 5:00 PM

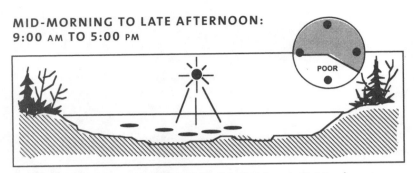

Fish are inactive during most of the day (9:00 AM to 5:00 PM). Most species will be in deep water.

SUNSET TO EARLY EVENING:
6:00 TO 9:00 PM

Fish are again active when the sun starts to set (6:00 to 9:00 PM). Excellent fishing.

During the summer months, fish are harder to catch for two main reasons.

1. The food chain is at its peak.

2. Fish are harder to find due to abundant cover.

Summer Stagnation

During midseason, most lakes go through what is called the summer stagnation cycle. The surface water warms to well over 39.2°F and floats on the heavier water below. Most lakes stratify into three layers, as

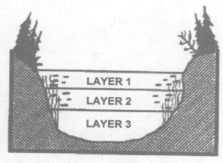

shown at right. The top layer is the warmest, the second is cooler, and the third is cold and low in oxygen. Most fish species prefer the middle layer, but they all venture into the upper layer during feeding sprees.

Wind Effect

Wind can matter during the hot days of midseason fishing. Strong winds can push cooler offshore water close in to shore, bringing in bait fish and predators to

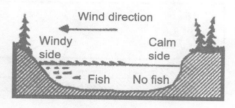

feed. The bait fish will be attracted to insects blown into the water by the wind, which in turn will attract the larger predators.

The next time you're tempted to fish the calm side of the lake where you may be more comfortable, remember that you may have better luck on the windy side.

LATE-SEASON FISHING

The following are just a few tips to try during the fall months (late September through ice-up), when the fall turnover is in process.

When to Fish

Water temperature is the most important factor to consider during this period. Daylight hours are shorter, limiting the warming effects of the sun. Conditions will be similar to early spring fishing. As a general rule, most fish will be scattered throughout the lake, feeding near the surface.

EARLY MORNING:
DAYBREAK TO 9:00 AM

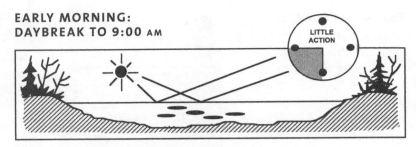

Cool water temperature and little sun penetration into water results in poor action.

LATE MORNING:
9:00 AM TO NOON

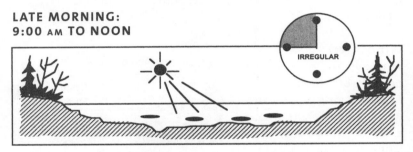

Fish are active in shallow warmer water. Often produces, but fishing is irregular.

AFTERNOON TO EVENING:
12:00 PM TO 6:00 PM

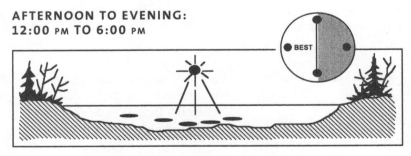

Surface waters are the warmest, and fish are active, including deep-water species. Best fishing.

During the fall season, fish become more active. They feed more often and migrate away from their summer haunts.

Concentrations of Bait Fish

Warmest Water

Heat from the sun will be the single most important factor that governs fish activity on most lakes in the fall. Fish will seek the warmer surface waters or the shallows.

To find active fish consistently in the fall, fish areas having concentrations of bait fish.

Fall Turnover

During the fall season, the surface water cools until it becomes heavier than the water beneath it. It sinks and mixes with the deeper water until all the water has the same temperature. This process will continue until ice-up and most fish will be scattered through-out the lake, feeding near the surface.

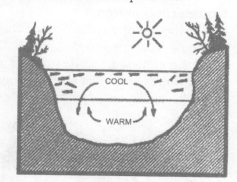

Best Waters

As is true in the spring, darker bottom areas such as mud flats or slit-covered areas will attract more fish because they absorb heat and warm the water around them.

During the late fall season, fish continue to feed much better in very clear water.

When fishing around the time of fall turnover, be willing to change lakes. Some lakes have longer turnover periods than others.

SEASONAL LAKE TURNOVERS

A body of water goes through an annual cycle of temperature changes paralleling the seasons. Knowing what the water conditions are and how they affect the fish during each season change can improve your chances of a better catch. The following illustrations depict each season change and the effects on the fish.

Spring Turnover

After ice-out, surface water warms from 32°F to its maximum density at 39°F. The heavier surface waters then sink and mix with the deeper, lighter waters. As the stagnant deep water reaches the surface, it is charged with oxygen by the spring winds and warmed by the sun, repeating the cycle until the water temperature is uniform throughout the lake.

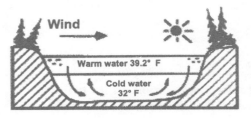

Most fish will be found in the shallower areas of the lake where the waters warm more quickly.

Summer Stagnation

During the summer, surface water warms and rapidly becomes less dense than the water below it. It floats on top of the colder water throughout the entire summer without mixing with the deeper waters. The upper layer of water will vary between 2 and 10 feet in depth, depending on the size of the lake.

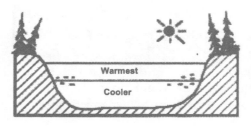

Most fish will be found just below the warm surface band of water.

Fall Turnover

In the fall season, the surface water cools until it approaches the temperature of the lower water beneath it. When it cools and becomes heavier, it sinks and mixes with the deeper waters until all the water has the same temperature. This process continues until the water reaches 32°F or freezes up.

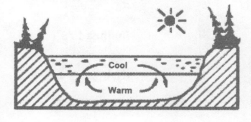

During this cooling period, most fish will be scattered throughout the lake.

WATER TEMPERATURE In most cases, fish activity is governed by water temperature. It affects their movements and spawning and is an important factor to consider during the various seasons. Most fish prefer a particular water temperature and seek out the depths that suit them best. Learn those depths and you'll catch more fish.

FISHING BY DEGREES The following chart shows the temperature that specific species of fish prefer. Although you may not find the exact water temperature, most fish will be found in the water closest to the temperature listed on the chart on the next page.

WATER TEMPERATURE
BY DEGREES

Carp 78°F

Catfish 76°F

Bullhead 78°F

White Bass 76°F

80°

75°

Bluegill 75°F

Largemouth Bass 73°F

70°

Crappie 71°F

Smallmouth Bass 70°F

65°

Walleye 69°F

Perch 68°F

Muskie 67°F

60°

Brown Trout 60°F

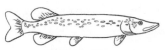

Northern Pike 55°F

55°

Rainbow Trout 55°F

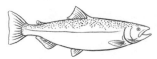

Chinook Salmon 55°F

50°

Coho Salmon 55°F

Lake Trout 50°F

Chapter 2
Where to Fish

READERS OF THIS BOOK ARE GENERALLY
seeking food in a survival situation. Thus fore-
knowledge of where fish may most easily be found
will be helpful.

**POND, LAKE,
AND RESERVOIR
FISHING**

Pond Fishing
Ponds are usually excellent fishing
waters. They have abundant growth,
which provides cover for bait fish
as well as a variety of game fish.
The game fish population in a pond can include bass, pike, pickerel,
perch, panfish, and, in some areas, members of the trout family.
Most ponds are either creek- or spring-fed, both of which provide
excellent water quality.

Lake Fishing
Lakes vary in size, shape, and depth. They provide the same sort of
food and cover for the fish population as do most ponds. They can
also be fished in the same areas as a pond, and can include bass,
pike, pickerel, perch, panfish, and, in some areas, trout as the
principal species. Most lakes are creek-, spring-, or river-fed.

Reservoir Fishing
Reservoirs or impoundments also vary in size, shape, and depth.
They provide the same sort of food and cover for the fish population

as most lakes and ponds. They can also be fished in the same areas as a pond or lake, and can include most game fish species, depending on their location in the various parts of the country. Most reservoirs or impoundments are creek-, stream-, or river-fed.

Most ponds, lakes, and reservoirs can be fished from shore or from a boat using a variety of equipment such as spinning gear, cane poles, bait-casting gear, or a fly-fishing outfit.

POND, LAKE, AND RESERVOIR LOCATIONS

Various areas to try in a typical pond, lake, or reservoir are described below and keyed to the illustrations on the following pages.

1. Stream or River Mouths

Excellent areas to try, as incoming water brings in a variety of food that attracts both bait fish and game fish.

2. Stream or River Channels

In most ponds, lakes, or reservoirs formed by the damming of a stream or river, the original streambed or riverbed will have the deepest water. The deep water will be home for most fish, which will use the channel as a migratory route to and from the shallows as they search for food. The edges of the channel's breaklines formed by the original stream or river are excellent areas to try.

3. Submerged Rock Piles

In shallow water they attract spawning fish. In deep water they provide cover and are excellent areas if there is access to deeper water.

4. Points

Look for the point that has easy access to deep water. Fish the tip as well as corners.

5. Humps or Ridges

The edge of a hump of ridge provides excellent breaklines to fish. Shallow humps attract spawning fish in the spring. Deep humps are most productive in the summer and fall.

6. Spillway or Dam

Both above and below the spillway or dam are excellent areas to try. Some of the largest fish in a lake, pond, or reservoir lurk around the spillway.

7. Deep Holes or Springs

Most any of the game fish may hold along the edges of the breakline, or some species may suspend at mid-depth over the hole.

8. Submerged Tree Stumps or Fallen Trees

These are excellent areas depending on the amount of shade provided and access to deeper water or a breakline.

9. Weed Beds or Lily Pads

These areas are also excellent, depending on access to deeper water. Inside edges (shallow) are most productive in the spring or fall. Outside edges are used as a breakline or migratory route.

10. Reeds

Reeds are excellent areas in early spring for bass or pike, particularly if they connect to marshy areas or they are located at the mouth of a feeder creek.

11. Old Road Beds

Old road beds are good areas to try that provide breaklines as migratory routes to and from shallow water when fish are in search of food.

POND FISHING LOCATIONS

LAKE FISHING LOCATIONS

1. **Stream or River Mouths**
2. **Stream or River Channels**
3. **Submerged Rock Piles**
4. **Points**
5. **Humps or Ridges**
6. **Spillway or Dam**
7. **Deep Holes or Springs**
8. **Submerged Tree Stumps or Fallen Trees**
9. **Weed Beds or Lily Pads**
10. **Reeds**

RESERVOIR OR IMPOUNDMENT FISHING LOCATIONS

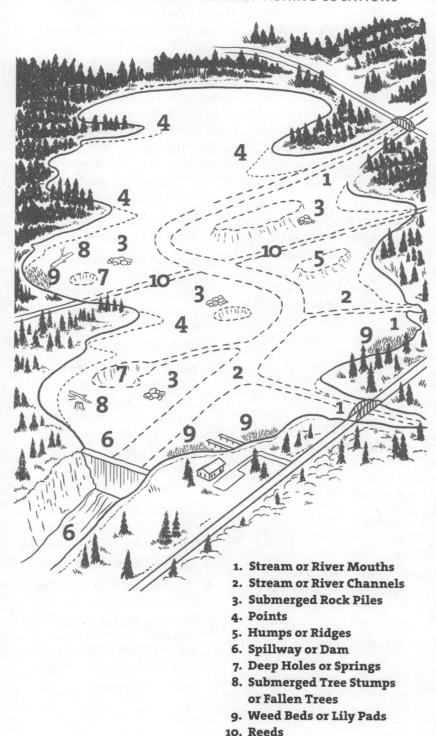

1. **Stream or River Mouths**
2. **Stream or River Channels**
3. **Submerged Rock Piles**
4. **Points**
5. **Humps or Ridges**
6. **Spillway or Dam**
7. **Deep Holes or Springs**
8. **Submerged Tree Stumps or Fallen Trees**
9. **Weed Beds or Lily Pads**
10. **Reeds**

STREAM AND RIVER FISHING

Streams and rivers can provide excellent fishing waters if fished properly. The game fish population in a river or stream can include most any species, depending on where it's located. The most important factors to consider when fishing a river or stream are the current and structure that affect it.

Most fish-holding locations will be areas where the fast-moving water passes some form of structure, which will slow the water down and also provide cover for the fish. A few places to try are described below and illustrated on the following page.

1. Dams or Spillways

Both above and below the dam or spillway are excellent areas to try. Fish the rip-rap areas above the dam or spillway along the shoreline, and the first bank eddies at the base or below the dam or spillway.

2. Humps

Humps provide excellent staging areas for spawning walleyes and saugers during early spring. They also provide holding areas for both catfish and walleyes. Upstream humps, closest to the dam or spillway, provide the best results.

3. Eddies

Eddies provide cover and the best potential to produce a mixed stringer of most species found in the river or stream. They can be fished from either the shore or from a boat.

4. Points or Bars

Points or bars along the shore-line can be holding areas for a variety of species. They cause the current to form eddies or holes on the downstream side, which are excellent areas to try.

5. Bays or Backwaters

These are excellent areas to try during early spring. Bays and backwaters provide spawning areas for walleye, bass, and northern pike.

6. Main Channel Edges

Main channel edges downstream for a mile below a dam or spillway are excellent areas to try. They will hold large catfish most any time and female walleyes prior to spring spawning.

7. Outside Bends

Outside bends along the shoreline are excellent holding areas for bass and crappies.

8. Stream or Creek Mouths

Stream or creek mouths are excellent areas to try during early spring for northern pike. They also will hold the same pike throughout the summer season.

9. Boulders or Rock Piles

Downstream sides will provide cover for a variety of species which will lie in ambush waiting for food to be washed down by the river or stream current. Fishing above the boulders or rocks and allowing the current to take your bait past the holding areas will provide the best results.

10. Islands

Islands are excellent areas to try along the sides away from the main channel. Favorite spawning areas for crappies during early spring. Also good for northern pike along the downstream points.

STREAM AND RIVER FISHING LOCATIONS

Chapter 3
Catching Fish

THE WORLD IS COVERED WITH WATER, AND FISH should not be overlooked as a food source. Various methods of procuring fish include using fishing tackle, bare hands, chop fishing, spearing, and using a net.

FISHING TACKLE   If you have fishing tackle, use it. If you don't, you'll need to improvise. Crude tackle isn't very useful for catching small fish like trout but has proven somewhat effective with larger fish like carp, catfish, and whitefish.

MAKESHIFT FISHING   Just because you don't happen to have a hook and line doesn't mean you can't catch fish. Unravel a bit of sweater, for instance. Tie on a small strip of bright cloth. The corner of a handkerchief will do—when the fish closes his mouth over the cloth, give the line a tug. There is a reasonable chance, especially where fishing is virgin, that you'll flip the quarry out on the bank. This doesn't always work, of course, but fish won't always take regular bait either.

HOOKS MADE ON THE SPOT You can devise almost any number of different types of hooks. A bent pin really works, as many a youngster has learned, the only trick being to maintain pressure so that the fish won't slip off. An open safety pin is a somewhat larger hook of the same variety. Bent nails have been used with considerable success.

The art of fishing did not commence with the patent of the first steel fishhook, and any number of fishing devices can be provided without a trip to the sporting goods store. A simple pocketknife, for example, can easily be converted into a sturdy fishhook by using a wooden wedge to maintain an angled blade, and then lashing the contraption together and covering it entirely with bait. Likewise, by whittling some of the plentiful material furnished by the woods themselves, a variety of fishing devices can be made. As has been proven by numerous indigenous societies that survived solely on fish diets, effective makeshift hooks, rods, reels, and lines can be fashioned entirely from provisions not made in the factory.

You can also cut hooks from wood, preferably wood that is hard and tough. Whittle out the shank first. Lash one or more sharp slivers so that they slant upward from the lower end. You can even add a barb by lashing another sliver even more acutely downward from the top. Thorns, if available, can also be utilized. Fish bones, too, will furnish both serviceable points and barbs. To make a wooden hook, cut a piece of hardwood about 1 inch long and about ¼ inch in diameter to form the shank. Cut a notch in one end in which to place the point. Place the point (piece of bone, wire, nail) in the notch. Hold the point in the notch and tie securely so that it does not move out of position. This is a fairly large hook. To make smaller hooks, use smaller material.

You can make field-expedient fishhooks from pins, needles, wire, small nails, or any piece of metal. You can also use wood, bone, coconut shell, thorns, flint, seashell, or tortoise shell. You can also make fishhooks from any combination of these items.

IMPROVISED FISH HOOKS

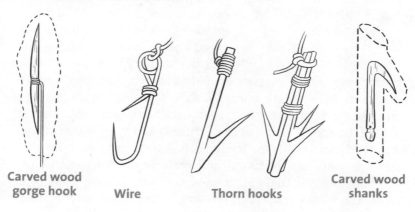

Carved wood gorge hook

Wire

Thorn hooks

Carved wood shanks

SKEWER, SHANK, AND SAFETY PIN HOOKS

Some commonly used hooks are skewer and shank hooks (made from bone, wood, or plastic) and safety pin hooks.

Skewer hook

A skewer hook is a sliver of wood, bone, or plastic that is notched and tied at the middle. When baited, this hook is turned parallel to the line, making it easier for the fish to swallow. Once the fish takes the bait, a simple tug on the line will turn the skewer sideways, lodging it in the fish's mouth.

Shank hook

A shank hook is made by carving a piece of wood or plastic until it takes on the shape of a hook that is notched and tied at the top. When the fish swallows the hook, a gentle tug on the line will set it by causing the hook end to lodge in the fish's throat.

Safety pin hook

A safety pin can be manipulated to create a hook. Depending on the size of the safety pin, this system can catch fish of various sizes and is a good option.

HOW TO MAKE A FISHING LINE

Fishing lines can be improvised in numerous ways. One method is to unravel a piece of fabric and to knot lengths of four or so threads together at frequent intervals. Another is to cut around and around a section of leather, forming a continuous lace.

Line can be more scientifically made, after cutting or raveling any fabric or fiber that may be available so as to procure a number of long strands. Take four of these threads and fasten them at one end. Hold two threads in each hand. Roll and twist each strand clockwise between the thumb and forefinger of each hand, while turning those held in the right hand counterclockwise around those secured in the left. This twisting and winding must be done tautly, so that the completed line will not unravel.

Depending on the lengths of thread, conclude each of the four strands about 2 inches apart so as to make the splicing on of fresh strands easier. About an inch before any thread stops, twist on a new strand to replace the one just ending.

Unravel strands of thread from a sweater or other garment, and twist two strands together into a strong, taut single length. Take another double stranded length and twist them together at intervals, continuing to splice in additional lengths near the ends of the last one. In this way, you can make a durable fishing line of substantial length.

This procedure can be continued, so long as materials hold out, to make a line of any length. The same operation that will provide a small cord for ordinary fishing can be employed with a dozen or more strands to manufacture a fishing line capable of landing a tuna or big lake trout.

IMPROVISED FISHING LINES

If you don't have fishing line, use a 10-foot section of improvised cordage. Although you could attach your line to a single pole, I'd advise setting out multiple lines tied to the end of one or several long, straight branches. Sticking these poles into the ground allows you to catch fish while attending to other chores. The goal is to return and find a fish attached to the end of your line.

To attach a standard hook, safety pin, or fixed loop to your line, use an improved clinch knot. All other improvised hooks can be attached to a line using any knot. Following are the steps to attach a hook with a clinch knot.

1. Run the free end of the line through the hook eye and fold it back onto itself.

2. Wrap the free end up and around the line six or seven times.

3. Run the line's free end down and through the newly formed loop just above the hook eye.

4. Finally, run the line through the loop formed between the two lines twisted together and the free end that just went through the loop next to the hook eye.

5. Moisten the knot, and pull it tight. Cut the excess line.

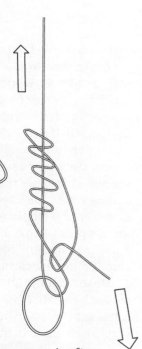

Improved clinch knot

BUTTONS AND SPOONS

A metal button or spoon is often successful as a lure. So is any small bright bit of metal. In its emergency kit the Hudson's Bay Company, with characteristically commendable frugality, includes a tablespoon with a hole drilled in its handle so that a hook can be wired in place for trolling or gigging.

A button securely fastened at the end of a makeshift line will catch and reflect light as it sways and shifts beneath the current of a stream, and possibly lure some of the more curious fish to its odd presence. A fish may even close its mouth over the bait, in which case a quick tug is required for the slim chance the jaw will remain clamped just long enough to steal it away from the water.

FINDING THE BEST BAIT Various insects, and even fuzzy seeds resembling these, will catch fish. Widely efficacious are grasshoppers, which when available can themselves be gathered with particular ease at night with the aid of a light.

"Experiment with bait," the Hudson's Bay Company advises any of its employees who may be in distress. "Look for bait in water, for this is the source of most fish food. Insects, fish, examine the stomach and intestines. See what it was feeding on and try to duplicate it. If it is crayfish (form of fresh water crab), turn over the rocks in the stream until you get one."

Incidentally, if you succeed in finding many crayfish, there's your meal, for once they are cooked by being dropped into boiling water, the lower portion is easily sucked free of the shell. One way to catch these is by driving a school into a restricted pool and dipping them out with a net made either by tightly interlacing foliage to a frame consisting of a bent green sapling, or by attaching some porous article of clothing to such a loop.

Make a net by tightly interlacing durable foliage and then secure it to a stick frame. Be sure your weave is consistent and tight, as a net made in this fashion can be ideal for capturing crayfish that school in shallow pools.

HOW TO RIG LIVE BAIT The following drawings illustrate how to attach live bait to a hook. These methods have proven to be very successful over the years.

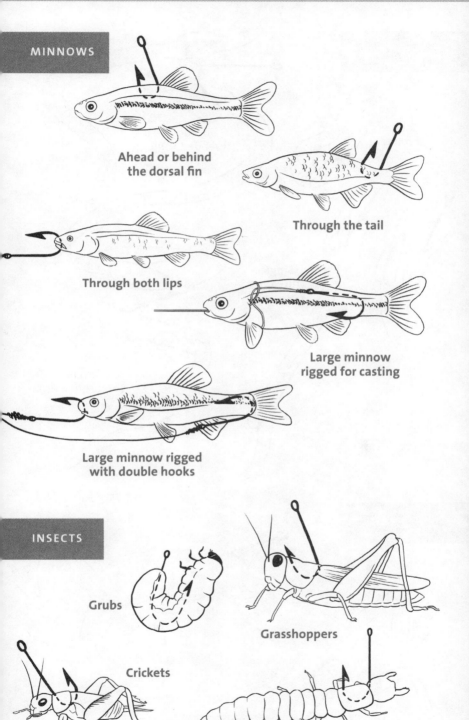

MINNOWS

Ahead or behind
the dorsal fin

Through the tail

Through both lips

Large minnow
rigged for casting

Large minnow rigged
with double hooks

INSECTS

Grubs

Grasshoppers

Crickets

Hellgrammites

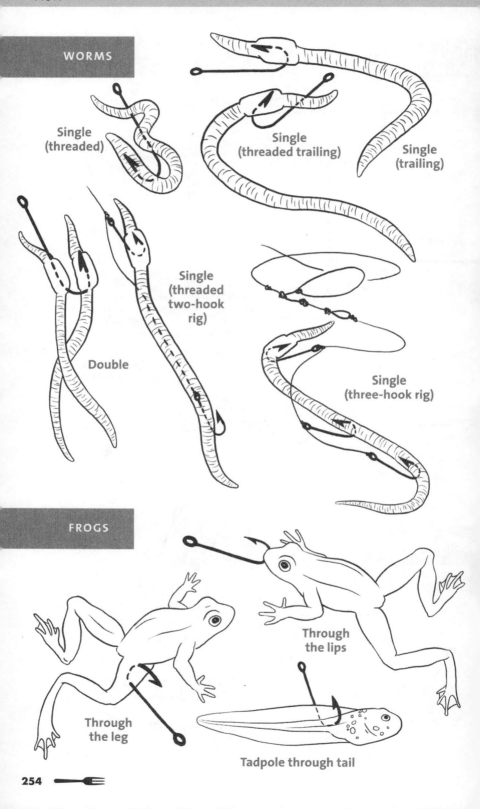

WORMS

Single
(threaded)

Single
(threaded trailing)

Single
(trailing)

Single
(threaded
two-hook
rig)

Double

Single
(three-hook rig)

FROGS

Through
the lips

Through
the leg

Tadpole through tail

In addition to baits such as minnows, worms, and so forth, leeches, suckers, and waterdogs can also be used as bait.

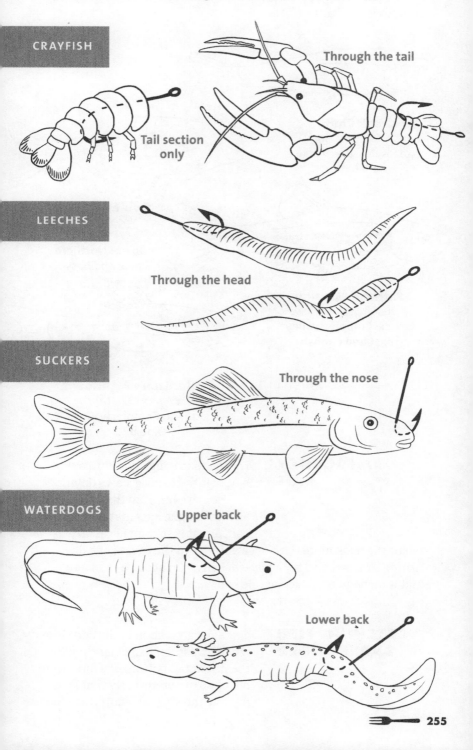

CRAYFISH

Through the tail

Tail section only

LEECHES

Through the head

SUCKERS

Through the nose

WATERDOGS

Upper back

Lower back

Minnow Selection

The following illustration shows just a few of the more common minnows used as live bait.

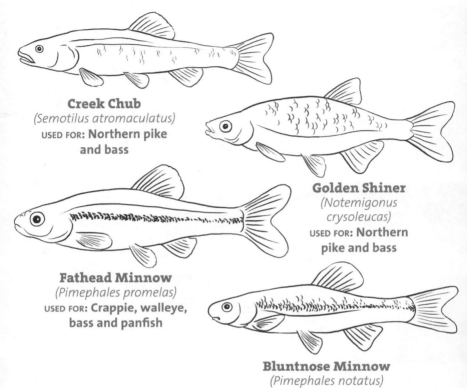

Creek Chub
(Semotilus atromaculatus)
USED FOR: **Northern pike and bass**

Golden Shiner
(Notemigonus crysoleucas)
USED FOR: **Northern pike and bass**

Fathead Minnow
(Pimephales promelas)
USED FOR: **Crappie, walleye, bass and panfish**

Bluntnose Minnow
(Pimephales notatus)
USED FOR: **Crappie, walleye and bass**

EMERGENCY BAIT

Try the following if you run out of bait or if the fishing slows down.

Use the eyes from the fish you already caught. Eyes make exceptional bait, and it is seldom necessary to rebait the hook more than once or twice in the course of a day's fishing. You can also try a piece of belly skin about ½ inch long and ⅛ inch wide, hooked at one end.

CATCHING FISH BAREHANDED

One spring vacation in the Berkshires when I wasn't much older than ten, the fish at the bottom of a dam were biting so disinterestedly that I hid my rod and started wading around the boulders of the fast little river. I sloshed back that evening with a pretty good string of perch and trout after all. I'd found them wedged among the rocks.

Another way to capture fish with bare hands, I discovered later that same week, is by feeling carefully among the nooks and cavities in stream banks. You can even catch fish, strange to say, by forming a sort of cave with your cupped hands held motionless against a bank. Trout in particular will investigate, whereupon by the acquired art of closing the hands quickly enough but not too hurriedly you'll have them.

Catching fish barehanded is best done in small streams with undercut banks. Place your hand into the water and slowly reach under the bank, moving it as close to the bottom as possible. Let your arm become one with the stream, moving it slightly with the current. Once contact with a fish is made, gently work the palm of your hand up its belly until you reach its gills. Grasp the fish firmly behind the gills, and scoop it out of the water.

WHOLESALE FISHING WITH BARE HANDS

Fish such as salmon and herring throng up streams in such numbers at certain times of the year that you can catch and throw ashore large numbers of them with your bare hands. It is also possible on occasion to secure by hand alone quantities of such fish as smelt, when schools come up on beaches to spawn in the surf. During spawning seasons, fish such as herring and salmon leap upstream in bountiful numbers. In such conditions, it is easy to amass a veritable cornucopia by catching great numbers in your bare hands while standing in the stream systematically tossing them to shore.

SPEARFISHING

Using a spear to procure fish is a time-consuming challenge, but under the right circumstances it can yield a tasty supper. You'll need to compensate for light refraction below the water's surface. To obtain proper alignment, place the spear tip into the water before aiming. If you are near shallow water (about waist deep) where the fish are large and plentiful, you can spear them. To make a spear, cut a long, straight sapling. Sharpen the end to a point or attach a knife, jagged piece of bone,

TYPES OF SPEAR POINTS

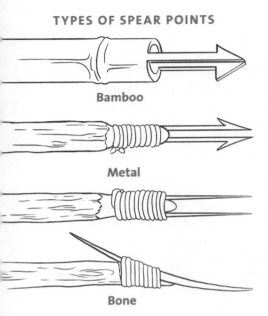

Bamboo

Metal

Bone

or sharpened metal. You can also make a spear by splitting the shaft a few inches down from the end and inserting a piece of wood to act as a spreader. You then sharpen the two separated halves to points.

To spear fish, find an area where fish either gather or where there is a fish run. Place the spear point into the water and slowly move it toward the fish. Then, with a sudden push, impale the fish on the stream bottom. Do not try to lift the fish with the spear, as it will probably slip off and you will lose it; hold the spear with one hand and grab and hold the fish with the other. Do not throw the spear, especially if the point is a knife. You cannot afford to lose a knife in a survival situation. Be alert to the problems caused by light refraction when looking at objects in the water. Moving the spear tip slowly will allow the fish to get accustomed to it until you are ready. Once the fish has been speared, hold it down against the bottom of the stream until you can get your hand between it and the tip of the spear.

GILL NET If you have the time and materials to construct a gill net, it is worth doing. A net hung vertically so that fish get trapped in it by their gills is a very effective method of procuring fish, requiring limited work once the construction is complete, and it will work for you while you attend to other needs. If you have parachute cord or similar material, its inner core provides an ideal material for making a net. Another option is braided cordage. In order for the net to stay clear of debris, it should be placed at a slight angle to the current using stones to anchor the bottom and wood to help the top float.

Follow these steps to make a gill net:

1. Tie a piece of line between two trees at eye height. The bigger the net you want, the further apart the trees should be.

2. Using a girth hitch, tie the center of your inner core line or other material to the upper cord. Continue to tie lines in this manner across the width of the upper cord, using an even number of lines. Space the lines apart at the width you desire for your net's mesh. For creeks and small rivers, 1 inch is about right.

3. Starting at either end, skipping the line closest to the tree, tie the second and third lines together with an overhand knot. Continue on down the line, tying the fourth and fifth, sixth and seventh, and so on. When you reach the end, there should be one line left. If you are concerned about the mesh size, first tie a guideline between the two trees. For a 1-inch mesh, tie this line 1 inch below the top line, and use it to determine where the overhand knots should be placed. Once a row of knots is completed, move this guideline down another inch.

4. Moving in the opposite direction, tie the first line to the second, third to the fourth, and so on. When you reach the end there shouldn't be any lines left.

5. Repeat the last two steps until done.

6. When done, run parachute line or other material along the net's sides and bottom to help stabilize it.

MAKING A GILL NET

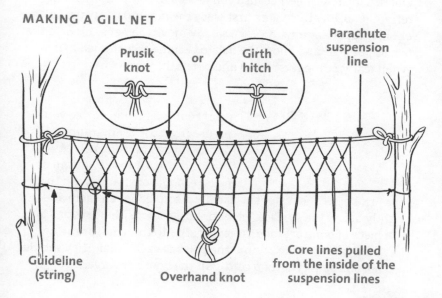

Prusik knot

or

Girth hitch

Parachute suspension line

Guideline (string)

Overhand knot

Core lines pulled from the inside of the suspension lines

Setting a gill net in the stream

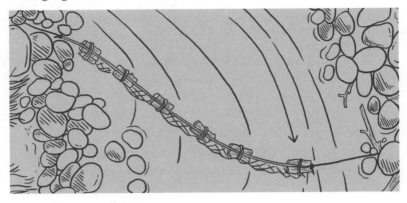

SCOOP NET   A scoop net can help secure a line-caught fish or can be used alone to scoop a fish out of the water. To make a scoop net, procure a 6-foot sapling or similar material and bend the two ends together to form a circle, allowing some extra length for a handle. You can also use a forked branch by forming a circle with the forked ends. Lash the ends together. The net's mesh can be made using the same method as described for building a gill net, tying the initial girth hitch to the sapling. Once the net is the appropriate size, tie all the lines together with an overhand knot and trim off any excess. A net should be used in shallow water or other areas where fish are visible. Because you'll need to compensate for light refraction below the water, first place the net into the water to obtain proper alignment. Next, slowly move the net as close to the fish as possible, and allow the fish to become accustomed to it. When ready, scoop the fish up and out of the water.

STAKEOUT   A stakeout is a fishing device you can use in a hostile environment. To construct a stakeout, drive two supple saplings into the bottom of the lake, pond, or stream with their tops just below the water surface. Tie a cord between them and slightly below the surface. Tie two short cords with hooks or a long thin piece of bone or stone, called a gorge, to this cord, ensuring that they cannot wrap around the poles or each other. They should also not slip along the long cord. Bait the hooks or gorges.

STAKEOUT

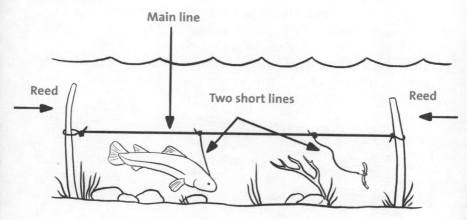

Main line

Reed → Two short lines ← Reed

MAKING A FISH TRAP

Fish can often be trapped with considerable success in cases of emergency. One such basic trap recommended by the Hudson's Bay Company can be made by driving sticks and branches into the bottom so that their tops protrude above the water. The trap, as the accompanying drawing shows, consists of a narrow-mouthed enclosure into which the fish are led by a wide funnel-like V.

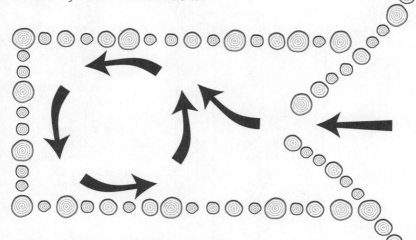

Be sure that the makeshift walls of stone or sturdy logs are consistently joined together and tall enough that they emerge above the water's surface, leaving as little room for escape as possible.

Attracted by some such bait as spoiled fish or decomposed meat, the fish guided into the pen through the slit at the apex are, in enough cases, unable to find their way out.

Materials used in making such a trap vary. Stretching a net around stakes will, if the former is available, conserve considerable energy. Stones can be utilized, perhaps leading into a natural freshwater or tidal pool.

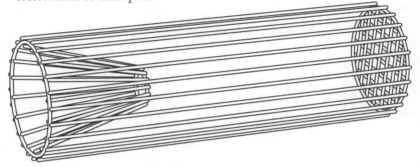

Wire or branches cut into uniform lengths can be used to contrive a funnel-mouthed fish trap. The most important and distinctive component of the design is the opening. Make sure the funnel is long and gradually-angled enough so that it will not seem too unnatural for a fish to glide right in. Conversely, make certain the opening is small enough that your intended prey will not easily find its way out.

Trapping a fish by sectioning off a space in the water uses the same principles of capture as the funnel-mouthed fish trap. Using logs or stones, create a V-shaped entryway. Once in, fish will be surrounded on all sides by the makeshift enclosure.

FISH CORRALS

Fish corrals aim to herd the fish into a fenced enclosure. The opening is designed like a funnel with the narrow end emptying into a cage.

When building these traps in ocean water, select your location during high tide and construct the trap during low tide. On rocky shores use natural rock pools; on coral islands use the natural pools that form on the reefs; and on sandy shores create a dam on the lee side of the offshore sandbar. If able, block all the openings before the tide recedes. Once the tide goes back out, you can use either a scoop net or spear to bring your dinner ashore. As always, the potential for poisonous fish must be considered.

In creeks and small rivers, use saplings to create the trap and its funnel. The opening should be on the upstream side so the current will aid in the funneling process. To herd the fish into your trap, start upstream and wade down toward your corral. Once there, close its opening and scoop net or spear the fish out.

FISH BASKETS

You may trap fish using several methods. Fish baskets are one method. These are constructed by lashing several sticks together with vines into a funnel shape. Close the top, leaving a hole large enough for the fish to swim through.

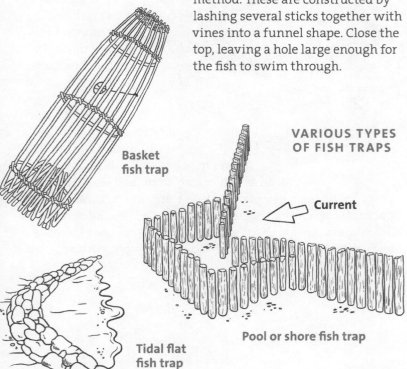

Basket fish trap

VARIOUS TYPES OF FISH TRAPS

Current

Pool or shore fish trap

Tidal flat fish trap

WHAT ABOUT TURTLES?

In the absence of conventional game meat, the slow-moving turtle may supply a wealth of energy and sustenance to yet another slow-moving and weary body, perhaps lost in the wilderness and dogged by fatigue. Boiling the turtle will help to remove its shell. The enormous nutritional value of turtle fat is guaranteed to renew strength.

Turtles are found throughout the temperate and tropic regions of the world almost anywhere there is water. Marine, freshwater, and land turtles are all edible.

A turtle can be killed by clubbing or by decapitation, and the smaller turtles can perhaps be caught with fishing line. Care should taken to avoid both jaws and claws, even after the turtle is dead.

To cook the turtle, you'll need to remove the shell. This can be done from its belly side. If it is convenient, the turtle can be scalded for several minutes by being dropped into boiling water. The undershell may then be quartered and the entrails removed, whereupon the meat can readily be simmered until it is free of the upper shell. Finish cooking in any fashion desired. Don't discard the shell, as it will be useful in improvising for many needs.

Turtle fat, which renders a clear, savory oil, is so nutritious that the reptile is an unusually valuable food source. Blood and juices are often used to relieve thirst. It is sometimes possible to trace the tracks of a female back to a fresh nest of eggs, generally buried in sand or mud not far from water. Although not greatly esteemed for taste by those more accustomed to hen's eggs, these are nourishing in all stages.

TURTLES TO AVOID The box turtle is a commonly encountered turtle that you should not eat. It feeds on poisonous mushrooms and may build up a highly toxic poison in its flesh. Cooking does not destroy this toxin. Avoid the hawksbill turtle, found in the Atlantic Ocean, because of its poisonous thorax gland. Poisonous snakes, alligators, crocodiles, and large sea turtles present obvious hazards, but it is unlikely that you will encounter these in the woods.

TRAPS FOR SNAPPING TURTLES When food was scarce, Indians hunted and trapped snapping turtles. Today, many people relish snapper cutlets and snapper soup. The common snapper sometimes weighs as much as 50 pounds. The alligator snapping turtle of the South often weighs as much as 100 pounds, and 200-pounders have been recorded. Both turtles have strong jaws, and their bites can sever fingers or even a wrist. The common snapping turtle can strike with the swiftness of a snake.

The Indians also hunted land tortoises and caught them in various simple traps and by hand. These land tortoises were often caught in the early morning when they came out of their burrows to drink the cool dew.

Shown in the accompanying drawing is a snapping-turtle trap that the author developed from Indian designs. This trap is built from modern materials, and several Indian groups now use this modernized version of ancient traps with great success.

An old but strong wooden box 3 or 4 feet square and 10 or more inches high, depending on the size of the turtles to be taken, is the basis of the trap. The wood should be about ¾ inch thick. Drill a number of 1-inch holes through the sides and bottom of the box to allow it to sink quickly and to let the water out of it when it is lifted.

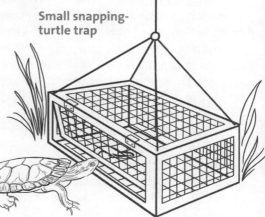
Small snapping-turtle trap

The trap may also be made by covering a strong wooden frame with 1½-inch heavy wire mesh, as is shown in the drawing. One end or side of the box or frame is hinged to form a door. The door should be made smaller than the frame so that the water will not swell the wood enough to jam it when closed. About 1 inch trimmed from one end and one side of a close-fitting door usually prevents jamming, but it is wise to soak the wood in water overnight before sawing the edges off to make sure that the door will not swell too much.

A block of hardwood nailed onto the frame of the floor of the trap at both corners or a narrow, thin strip of wood nailed across the bottom of the box on the outside prevents the door being pushed open from the inside by a trapped turtle. Once the doorstops are in place, hinge the door at the top with two strong oiled-leather hinges, since metal hinges deteriorate too quickly. The door must be centered in the opening with the same clearance all around or it will not open smoothly. A screw eye in each corner of the top of the box completes the trap. A short length of rope is tied to each screw eye, and the ends of these lines are tied to a metal ring. The main handling line is also fastened to this ring. The trap can be weighted down with a few stones to keep it from floating, but it's convenient to nail on some heavy metal if it is available.

Raw meat, fish heads, or whole fish are placed inside the trap as bait. The trap is lowered to the bottom where snappers have been seen or where they have been caught on the hooks of trotliners or rod-and-reel fishermen. The free end of the main handling line is tied to a float or an overhanging branch. When the trap is left overnight, the catch is often surprising and may even include big fish.

Snappers should be grasped firmly about halfway down the shell, a hand on each side. The jaws cannot reach your hands that way, but you have to be careful to make sure that your hands are also out of reach of the sharp claws. A snapper cannot withdraw its head inside its shell; so some trappers like to slip a wire noose fastened to a stout pole around the snapper's neck and handle it that way. Keep your legs clear of the turtle's jaws and claws too.

A big trap, often used to take snappers on a large scale, is also illustrated. The logs used in the frame are about 4 feet long and 8 inches in diameter. A wire basket about 2 feet deep made of old chicken wire hangs down from all four sides. The insides of the logs bordering the wire basket are covered with sheet metal to prevent the turtles crawling out of the trap.

The trap is set in water and anchored there. A wooden ramp leads from the water to the edge of the frame. The trap is baited with raw meat or fish. It is a good idea to wrap some of the bait in wire mesh so that the first snapper caught will not eat it all. Smelling the bait, snappers climb the ramp and drop into the trap. They cannot get out again because their claws cannot grip the sheet metal on the frame.

Remove the trapped snappers carefully by hand or with a strongly made scoop net or wire noose on the end of a pole. Don't try to handle any big alligator snapper alone. They are very strong.

This trap can take almost all turtles in the water where the trap is set. A sportsman keeps only the snappers. Most other freshwater turtles are poor table fare, and are not destructive to fish or waterfowl.

Large Snapping-Turtle Trap

WHAT ABOUT SNAKES?

All poisonous and nonpoisonous freshwater and land snakes are edible and can be located almost anywhere there is cover. For best results, hunt them in the early morning or evening hours. To catch or kill a snake, first stun it with a thrown rock or stick, and then use the forked end of a long stick to pin its head to the ground. Kill it with a rock, knife, or another stick. Be careful throughout this procedure, especially when dealing with poisonous snakes. Snakes can be cooked in any fashion, but all should be skinned and gutted. To skin a snake, sever its head (avoid accidental poisoning by burying the head), and peel back its skin until you can grab it and pull it down, inside out, the length of the snake. If you can't pull it free, make a cut down the length of the snake to help you free the skin. The entrails will usually come out during this process; if not, grab them at the top and pull them down to remove them.

WHAT ABOUT FROGS? Frog meat is one example of an often disdained food. Yet frog can be very expensive in the more fashionable restaurants of the world, though in nature it is free for the taking.

Frogs seldom move from the safety of the water's edge. At the first sign of danger, they plunge into the water and bury themselves in the mud and debris. Amphibians can be hooked with fishing tackle and a small fly. They can also be caught with string and a bit of cloth, the former being given a quick tug when the latter is taken experimentally into the mouth.

Frogs can be secured with spears of various types. A sharpened stick will do. At night, they can be so occupied by a light that you'll be able to net them and even, occasionally, to reach cautiously around and clamp a hand over one.

Most of the delicately flavored meat is on the hind legs, which can be cut off, skinned, and, in the absence of cooking utensils, extended over hot coals on a green stick for broiling. If rations are scant, you can use the entire skinned frog after removing or at least emptying and cleaning the entrails, perhaps boiling the meat briefly with some wild greens.

When you cannot see frogs, their presence is obvious by their easily distinguished croaking. In the absence of live bait, you may be able to capture a frog with a string and a bit of brightly colored cloth. Jerk the string so the cloth flutters. You may have luck with the chance that a frog will take it as food in its mouth. Then jerk the line and frog toward you to catch it.

TOADS Do not confuse toads with frogs. You normally find toads in drier environments. Several species of toads secrete a poisonous substance through their skin as a defense against attack. Therefore, to avoid poisoning, do not handle or eat toads. There are few poisonous species of frogs. Avoid any brightly colored frog or one that has a distinct X mark on its back.

SALAMANDERS Salamanders are nocturnal. The best time to catch them is at night using a light. They can range in size from a few inches to well over 2 feet in length. Look in water around rocks and mud banks for salamanders. Salamanders are easily found around bodies of fresh water.

MOLLUSKS This class includes octopuses and freshwater and saltwater shellfish such as snails, clams, mussels, bivalves, barnacles, periwinkles, chitons, and sea urchins. You find bivalves similar to our freshwater mussel and terrestrial and aquatic snails worldwide under all water conditions.

River snails or freshwater periwinkles are plentiful in rivers, streams, and lakes of northern coniferous forests. These snails may be pencil point or globular in shape.

In fresh water, look for mollusks in the shallows, especially in water with a sandy or muddy bottom. Look for the narrow trails they leave in the mud or for the dark elliptical slit of their open valves.

Mussels usually form dense colonies in rock pools, on logs, or at the base of boulders.

EMERGENCY MEASURES THAT PROCURE FISH When rations are short you can sometimes splash up shallow brooks, driving any fish ahead of you. When these are cornered in a pool, you can block their retreat with piled stones if necessary, then go in and kill them with a club. Small streams, too, can often be diverted so as to strand fish in pools.

If you are really up against it in beaver country, it is occasionally possible to strand a life-sustaining catch by prying an opening in a beaver dam. Another technique is to wade in riling with your feet the muck that amasses behind such a dam, and catch the temporarily mud-blinded fish with bare hands.

Primitive Fishing Device

One of the most primitive fishing devices, still used successfully if not sportingly, is made by tying the line to the middle of a short piece of bone or wood that has been sharpened at each end. Hidden in bait, this is swallowed by the fish, whereupon a jerk of the cord pulls it crossways.

An effective hook can be produced by sharpening the ends of a bone or a short, sturdy stick. Lash a line firmly to the middle of the straight, double-pointed hook, and then conceal it in bait. When a fish swallows the gambit, jerk the line with the intention to position the hook sideways in the fish's gullet so that it will not easily slip out of the mouth before it is pulled ashore.

Chop Fishing

Chop fishing is most often used to procure ocean fish at night and during low tide. Fish in shallow water are struck and stunned with the back of a machete or other solid handheld object. The stunned fish are then easily removed from the water. Fish are attracted to light, and shiny or reflecting objects may be used to lure them into shallower water.

Drugging Fish with Local Vegetation

"Certain Indian methods of fishing may prove life savers for the hungry wayfarer," as my wife and I noted in *How to Build Your Home in the Woods*. One procedure is to gather mullein or fish weed (*Croton setigerus*) and crush the leaves and stalks. These are dropped into a still pool or temporarily dammed brook. The fish therein, momentarily narcotized, will float to the surface, where they should be immediately secured.

The bulbous root of the so-called soap plant, *Chlorogalum pomdeidianum*, can be similarly used. So can the seeds of the southern buckeye, *Aesculus pavia*. Fish caught by these emergency means are as wholesome as if merely dazed by concussion.

Gigging, So Deadly It's Illegal

Gigging, which is illegal in many localities, is the practice of catching fish by hooking them anywhere in the body. An Eskimo method is to dangle a long smooth hook above which are suspended bits of bone that shine and flutter in the water. When a fish approaches to investigate, the line is suddenly jerked up 2 or 3 inches with a good chance of the hook being driven into the fish, which is at once hauled up before it has a chance to work loose. Gigging is often resorted to in waters where fish can be seen but not readily induced to bite.

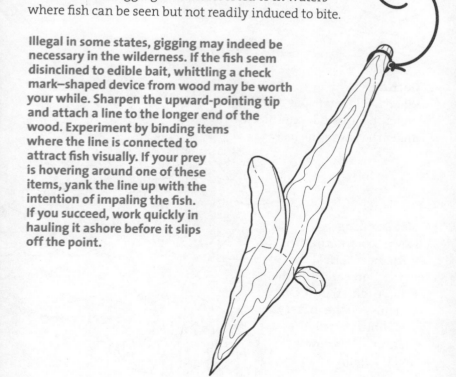

Illegal in some states, gigging may indeed be necessary in the wilderness. If the fish seem disinclined to edible bait, whittling a check mark–shaped device from wood may be worth your while. Sharpen the upward-pointing tip and attach a line to the longer end of the wood. Experiment by binding items where the line is connected to attract fish visually. If your prey is hovering around one of these items, yank the line up with the intention of impaling the fish. If you succeed, work quickly in hauling it ashore before it slips off the point.

LANDING YOUR CATCH

Here are a few tips on how to handle your catch after you've played it out. Don't try to land a fish until it's ready. Wait until all the flight is gone and the fish is wobbly and on its side.

Eye Pick-up

You can lift pike, muskie, and pickerel out of the water by putting your hand over the head and grasping the fish by the eye sockets.

Mouth Pick-up

Bass or fish with small teeth can be picked up by the lower lip. This hold will paralyze the fish as long as you hang on to it. When placing your thumb in the fish's mouth, make certain that you avoid the hooks on your lure or bait.

Gaffing

When using a gaff, put it in the water under the fish and come up either under the jaw or the belly.

Net Landing

Never scoop at the fish with the net. Hold the net in the water and lead the fish (headfirst) into it. If you miss on the first try, wait until the fish tires more or calms down, and try again.

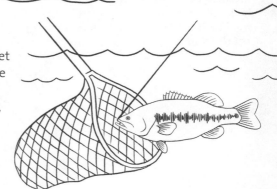

Chapter 4
Cleaning and Cooking Fish

TO PREVENT SPOILAGE, PREPARE THE FISH AS soon as possible. Gut the fish by cutting up its abdomen and then removing the intestines and large blood vessels (kidney) that lie next to the backbone. Remove the gills. When applicable, scale or skin the fish. With bigger fish you may want to fillet the meat. Be sure to prepare the fish well away from your shelter. Smoke, sun-dry, or cook in any fashion desirable.

CLEANING FISH

Fish can be slit from vent to throat and the viscera removed easily and cleanly, in the case of pan fish often with a single stroke of the thumb. Many like to scrape away the blood vessels and kidneys, which form dark lines next to the backbone. If the fish has scales, it can be held by the tail and these scraped off, working from tail toward head, with the back of a knife or something similar. You may not want to bother with head, tail, and fins of small fish except to eat around them, for the bones will then hold together better and will not be so much of a nuisance. Furthermore, a few choice tidbits will be thus saved which would otherwise probably be wasted. If you ever have a number of heads, you may care to find out, perhaps by making a chowder with them, why these are regarded by many as the most delicious part of the fish.

Fish Cleaning Tips

Generally, removing the head from smaller fish is needless and can in fact produce a greater hassle by loosening bones in the flesh.

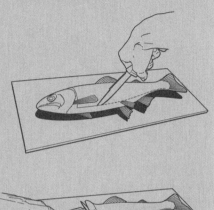

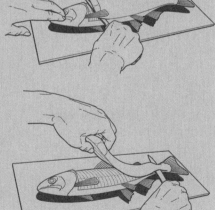

PANFISH

Most panfish are less than 12 inches long and are difficult to fillet. Unless you are experienced at filleting fish, use the following method to clean your catch.

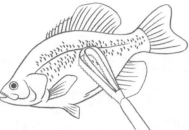

Step 1 Hold the fish by the tail and scrape from tail to head to loosen and remove the scales, using a dull knife or a fish scraper.

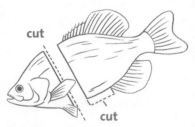

cut

cut

Step 2 Cut off the head behind the pectoral fin and cut open the belly cavity.

pull

clean out cavity

Step 3 Remove fins by cutting into flesh on both sides and then pulling them out.

FILLETING

Step 1
Cut deep on each
side of the dorsal fin.

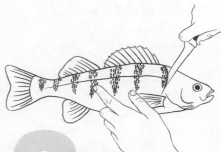

Step 2
Cut deep around the
head, gills,
and fins.

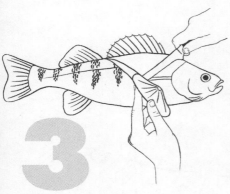

Step 3 Separate the
flesh from the rib cage.

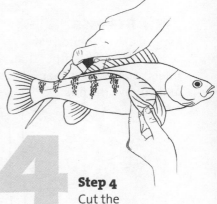

Step 4
Cut the
fillet loose.

Step 5 Repeat steps
1 through 5 on the
opposite side.

Step 6 Skin fillets by starting
at the tail end
and inserting blade
between skin and meat.

FISH CHEEKS

The cheeks are the filet mignon of the fish. When cleaning large fish, don't forget to remove these choice tidbits before you discard the head.

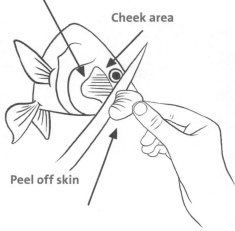

Slice into cheek and scoop out with blade

Cheek area

Peel off skin

FISH STEAKS

Large fish like salmon can be cut into steaks rather than fillets after you gut them and remove the fins.

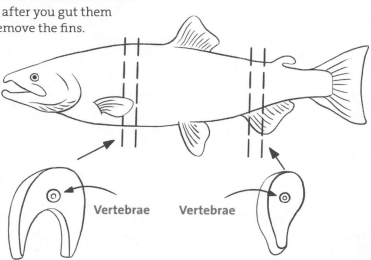

Vertebrae   Vertebrae

SKINNING CATFISH/BULLHEADS

Step 1
Cut through the skin, completely around the head.

Step 2
Nail the head to a board and peel the skin back with pliers.

Step 3
After the skin is peeled back, cut through the backbone behind the dorsal fin at an angle toward the head.

Step 4
Break the head downward from the body, removing the head and entrails at the same time.

CLEANING TOOLS

If you can't find your scraper or you forget to bring it with you, try using a teaspoon or a tablespoon as a scraper. The spoon will do an excellent job, and the dull edges won't cut the fish.

Homemade Fish Scaler

All you need to make a dandy scaler are two bottle caps from a soft drink or beer bottle, a couple of screws, and a piece of wood 1 inch wide and 6 inches long by ½ inch thick.

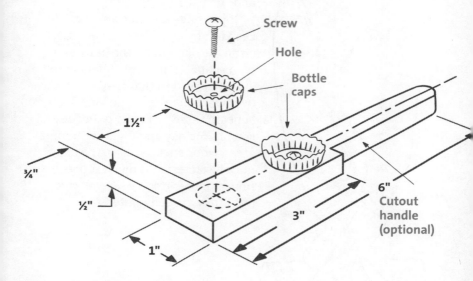

SPOILED ROTTEN

Do not eat fish that appears spoiled. Cooking does not ensure that spoiled fish will be edible. The following are signs of spoilage:

- Sunken eyes.

- Peculiar odor.

- Suspicious color. (Gills should be red to pink. Scales should be a pronounced shade of gray, not faded.)

- Dents that stay in the fish's flesh after pressing it with your thumb.

- Slimy, rather than moist or wet body.

- Sharp or peppery taste.

Eating spoiled or rotten fish may cause diarrhea, nausea, cramps, vomiting, itching, paralysis, or a metallic taste in the mouth. These symptoms appear suddenly, one to six hours after eating. Induce vomiting if symptoms appear.

Fish spoils quickly after death, especially on a hot day. Prepare fish for eating, as described above, as soon as possible after catching it.

PRESERVING FISH

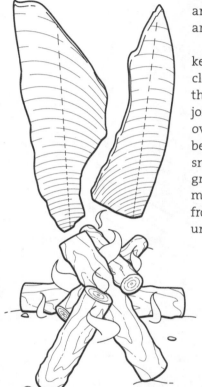

Fish can be preserved for a day or two and longer by immediately cleaning, cutting into thin strips, and hanging these strips in the wind and sun to dry.

If you have the time and want to keep fish for considerable periods, clean the fish, cut off the head, and then split each into two fillets so joined by the tail that they will hang over wooden racks. Build long fires beneath these racks. Keep the fires smoldering day and night with some green wood such as alder. The fish must be protected as much as possible from dampness for the several days until they are dehydrated.

Part IV

BASIC ESSENTIALS

Chapter 1

Water

OUR BODIES ARE COMPOSED OF APPROXIMATELY 60 percent water, and it plays a vital role in our ability to get through a day. About 70 percent of our brains, 82 percent of our blood, and 90 percent of our lungs are composed of water. In our bloodstream, water helps to metabolize and transport vital elements, carbohydrates, and proteins that are necessary to fuel our bodies. Water also helps us dispose of our bodily waste. In a survival situation water is more important than food. Food requires water for digestion, and is more essential to surviving.

The truth of the matter is, as we have learned, that a healthy human being can get along entirely without food for a month or two under favorable conditions. But anyone would do well to stay alive for much more than a week if he did not have water.

There fortunately need not be a shortage of drinking water, especially when we understand how to locate some of the more unusual sources recognized by only a very few. The much more common problem lies in making sure that the water found is fit for human use. With a minimum of fundamentals, this we can also solve with reassuring certainty, for it is only basic common sense never to take the slightest unnecessary risk with doubtful water.

Any of us can generally get along a while longer without a drink. Just moistening our lips in water one drop of which is contaminated can, on the other hand, so sicken us that if nothing worse we'll become too weak to travel.

NEED FOR WATER During a normal, non-strenuous day, a healthy individual will need 2 to 3 quarts of water. When physically active or in extreme hot or cold environments, that same person would need at least 4 to 6 quarts of water a day. Being properly hydrated is one of the various necessities that wards off dehydration and environmental injuries. Remember, thirst is not a reliable guide for your need for water, and even when water is plentiful, thirst should be satisfied in increments. Quickly drinking a large volume of water may result in severe cramping. A basic rule is to drink small amounts often.

A person who is mildly dehydrated may develop excessive thirst and become irritable, weak, and nauseated. As dehydration worsens, individuals will show a decrease in their mental capacity and coordination.

Caution

Quickly drinking a large volume of water may result in severe cramping.

At this point it will become difficult to accomplish even the simplest of tasks. The ideal situation would dictate that you don't ration your water. Instead, you should ration sweat. An often unbelievable amount of water is exuded through the pores of the skin, and the rate of perspiration is markedly increased both by heat and by exertion. The need of water intake can be lessened, therefore, by our keeping as quiet as possible and as comfortably cool as we can. If water is not available, don't eat.

NEVER DRINK URINE! By the time you think about drinking your urine, you are very dehydrated, and your urine would be full of salts and other waste products. For a hydrated person, urine is 95 percent water and 5 percent waste products like urea, uric acid, and salts. As you become dehydrated, the concentration of water decreases and the concentration of salts increases substantially. When you drink these salts, the body will draw upon its water reserves to help eliminate them, and you will actually lose more water than you might gain from your urine.

NEVER DRINK BLOOD!

Blood is composed of plasma, red blood cells, white blood cells, and platelets. Plasma, which composes about 55 percent of the blood's volume, is predominantly water and salts, but it also carries a large number of important proteins (albumin, gamma globulin, and clotting factors) and small molecules (vitamins, minerals, nutrients, and waste products). Waste products produced during metabolism, such as urea and uric acid, are carried by the blood to the kidneys, where they are transferred from the blood into urine and eliminated from the body. The kidneys carefully maintain the salt concentration in plasma. When you drink blood, you are basically ingesting salts and proteins, and the body will draw upon its water reserves to help eliminate them. You will actually lose more water than you might gain from drinking blood.

OTHER THINGS TO AVOID WHEN THIRSTY

When one becomes extremely thirsty, any liquid is a temptation. If you should ever be in such a plight, you'll want to warn any companions against drinking alcoholic beverages, which, aside from other possibly dangerous effects, will only further dehydrate the body.

Medicines, it will be realized, cannot be substituted for drinking water either. Most compass fluids are poisonous antifreezes. Body wastes contain harmful by-products and at best will only increase thirst. Smoking, incidentally, is dehydrating and heightens the need for fluid.

Sluggishness of the digestive system is a natural consequence of going without normal amounts of water and nourishment. This condition need not cause concern, as it will adjust itself when regular eating and drinking habits are returned. One should very definitely not take any laxatives under such conditions, as such medication depletes the system of moisture already in it.

FINDING WATER IN THE WILD Since your body needs a constant supply of water, you will eventually need to procure water from Mother Nature as you seek to find nourishment in the woods. Various sources include surface water, groundwater, precipitation, condensation, plant sources, and man-made options that transform unusable water sources.

If you do not have a canteen, a cup, a can, or other type of container, improvise one from plastic or water-resistant cloth. Shape the plastic or cloth into a bowl by pleating it. Use pins or other suitable items—even your hands—to hold the pleats. If you do not have a reliable source to replenish your water supply, stay alert for ways in which your environment can help you.

INSECTS If bees are present, water is usually within several miles of your location. Ants require water and will often place their nest close to a source. Swarms of mosquitoes and flies are a good indicator that water is close.

BIRDS Birds frequently fly toward water at dawn and dusk in a direct, low flight path. This is especially true of birds that feed on grain, such as pigeons and finches. Flesh-eating birds can also be seen exhibiting this flight pattern, but their need for water isn't as great, and they don't require as many trips to the water source. Birds observed circling high in the air during the day are often doing it over water, as well.

FROGS AND SALAMANDERS Most frogs and salamanders require water and if found are usually a good indicator that water is near.

MAMMALS Like birds, mammals will frequently visit watering holes at dawn and dusk. This is especially true of mammals that eat a grain or grassy-type diet. Watching their travel patterns or evaluating mammal trails may help you find a water source. Trails that merge into one are usually a good pointer and following the merged trail often leads to water.

LAND FEATURES THAT INDICATE WATER

Drainages and valleys are good water indicators, as are winding trails of deciduous trees. Green plush vegetation found at the base of a cliff or mountain may indicate a natural spring or underground source of water. Springs occur when the water table crosses the ground's surface, and are often dependent on rains. Likewise, the presence of

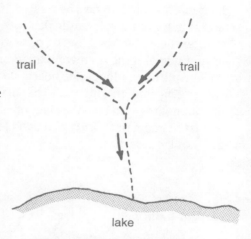

Two trails that merge together often point toward water.

basin lakes may depend on recent rainfall. These lakes occur where water is trapped without any means of escape, such as in low-lying areas where intermittent creeks or rivers flow into a place without an exit. Finally, if there has been a recent rain, water is often trapped in rock depressions. This water is often stagnant, and should be purified before it is consumed.

DOWSING

Dowsing, or witching, is a highly debated skill that some say helps them find water. Those who profess to have this skill use a forked stick (shaped like a Y) about 18 to 20 inches long and ⅛ to ¼ inch in diameter. The most common branch used comes from a willow tree. The two ends of the Y are held in the hands, which are positioned palms up, while the dowser walks forward. The free end of the stick is supposed to react when it passes over water. This reaction may be toward or away from the body.

SURFACE WATER Surface water may be obtained from rivers, ponds, lakes, or streams. It is usually easy to find and access, but because it is prone to contamination from protozoans, viruses, and bacteria, it should always be treated. If the water is difficult to access or has an unappealing flavor, consider using a seepage basin to filter the water. The filtering process is similar to what happens as groundwater moves toward an aquifer. To create a seepage basin well, dig a 3-foot-wide hole about 10 feet from your water source. Dig it down until water begins to seep in, and then dig about another foot. Line the sides of your hole with wood or rocks so that no more mud will fall in, and let it sit over night so the dirt and sand will settle.

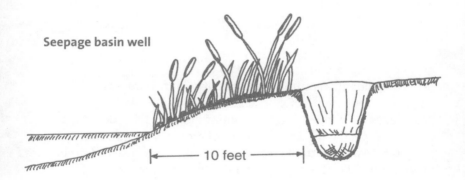

Seepage basin well

|← 10 feet →|

GROUNDWATER Groundwater is found under the earth's surface. This water is naturally filtered as it moves through the ground and into underground reservoirs called aquifers. Although treating this water may not be necessary, you should always err on the side of caution. Locating groundwater is probably the most difficult part of accessing it. Look for things that seem out of place, such as a small area of green plush vegetation at the base of a hill or a bend in a dry riverbed that is surrounded by vegetation. A marshy area with a fair amount of cattail or hemlock growth may provide a clue that groundwater is available. To easily access the water, dig a small well at the source (see direction for seepage basin above), line the well with wood or rocks, and let it sit overnight before using the water.

RAINWATER   When it rains, you should set out containers or dig a small hole and line it with plastic or any other nonporous material to catch the rainwater. After the rain has stopped, you may find water in crevasses, fissures, or low-lying areas.

DEW   Although dew does not provide a large volume of water, it should not be overlooked as a source of water. Dew accumulates on grass, leaves, rocks, and equipment at dawn and dusk and should be collected at those times before it freezes or evaporates. Any porous material will absorb the dew, and the moisture can be consumed by wringing it out of the cloth and into your mouth. Try tying rags or tufts of fine grass around your ankles and walking through dew-covered grass before sunrise. As the rags or grass tufts absorb the dew, wring the water into a container. Repeat the process until you have a supply of water or until the dew is gone.

SNOW   Should you find yourself in the woods in winter, you may find snow provides an excellent source of water—but it should not be eaten. The energy lost eating snow outweighs the benefit. Instead, melt it by suspending it over a fire or adding it to a partially full canteen and then shaking the container or placing it between the layers of your clothing and allowing your body's radiant heat to melt the snow. If the sun is out, you could melt the snow by digging a cone-shaped hole, lining it with a tarp or similar nonporous material, and placing snow on the material at the top of the cone. As the snow melts, water will collect at the bottom of the cone.

Chapter 2
Is Wild Water Safe?

THE WATER GUSHING OVER ROCKS, SHOOTING bubbly plumes into the air, forming blue pools, looks so clean, so inviting. Can you safely dip your cup into the clear blue pool and enjoy a refreshing drink?

Today, pollution from larger numbers of careless outdoorspeople and infected wildlife compel you to treat all of the water you drink, use to clean your teeth, and use to prepare your food. Never drink untreated water, no matter how "clean" it appears. Most of the surface water in the United States is contaminated with *Giardia lamblia* and *Cryptosporidium*. These disease-causing microorganisms are invisible to the naked eye. They can make you seriously ill, causing months of stomach cramps, diarrhea, nausea, dehydration, and fatigue. Cases of *Giardia*, the most common waterborne pathogen, have more than doubled in the United States during the past decade.

Giardia and *Cryptosporidium* are spread through fecal-oral transmission. They are passed from person to person and from domestic and wild animals to humans. You can avoid spreading these pathogens by using good field practices and common sense. Camp at least 200 feet from any water source. Properly bury your feces, pack out toilet paper, and always wash your hands thoroughly with soap and water after defecating or changing a diaper and before handling food. When scouting for a water source, use the best-looking one available. Avoid water that contains floating material or water with a dark color or an odor. Filter murky water through a clean cloth before treating it.

If possible, carry plenty of treated water from home in your vehicle and pack in as much as you can comfortably carry.

PURE OR NOT PURE? How can we tell then if water is pure? Short of laboratory tests we cannot, for even where a mountain rill bubbles through sheer mountain fastness, the putrefying carcass of a winter-killed animal may be lying a few yards upstream.

The folklore that any water a dog will drink is pure enough for his master is unfortunately as baseless as it is charming. The more reasonable assumption that anything your horse will drink is safe for humans is likewise at fault, inasmuch as pollution may be entirely odorless, and a horse's basis for rejection or acceptance is familiarity of smell.

The fact that natives may assert a water source is pure may mean, instead, either that they have built up a certain degree of immunity or that because of familiarity they cannot believe the water is tainted. A domestic water supply used by the inhabitants and guests of a Montana ranch for some twenty years was found to have been infecting not only present but previous users with tularemia, the germs of which can be carried to water by pets such as dogs and domestic animals like pigs even though they themselves may seem perfectly healthy.

Even the loneliest wild stream can be infected with so-called rabbit fever by such wild animals as muskrats and beavers. Yet taking a chance with drinking water in a well-settled community is in one sense a lot less dangerous than laying ourselves open to a small fraction of similar risk in wilderness where medical help may be hours and perhaps days away. The safest principle in any event is to assume all water is impure until it has been proved otherwise, positively and recently.

MAKING SURE IT IS PURE Water can be rid of germs by boiling. The exact time required to accomplish this depends on altitude, the nature of any impurity, and several other factors that altogether are so elastic that although a shorter time will often suffice, a safe general rule is to boil questionable water for at least five minutes.

If there is any reasonable doubt that water may be contaminated, it would be hard for the most hurried and harried of us not to agree that it should be purified before human consumption, although such a process may be expected to require both time and trouble.

A great deal more inconvenience and delay can result from drinking unknown water indiscriminately.

Nor does this apply only to water that is actually drunk. It is applicable with equal gravity to even a drop of any water that may enter the human body; examples being, as may be appreciated, water in which a toothbrush is dipped, water in which food utensils are washed, and water used in cooking except when kept at a high enough temperature for a sufficient time to ensure purity.

Boiled water, as everyone knows, tastes flat because air has been driven from it by heat. Air and therefore taste can be restored by pouring the cooled water back and forth between two utensils or by shaking it in a partially filled jar or canteen. Or if one is in a hurry and has salt, it is a common practice to add a pinch of that.

SIMPLE CHEMICAL PURIFICATION

If you think ahead, you can purchase halazone tablets at most sporting goods and drug stores. Since their purifying action depends upon the release of chlorine gas at the proper time, these should be fresh and the container kept tightly closed and its contents dry.

No purification of water by chemical means is as dependable as boiling, but two halazone pills will ordinarily make a quart of water safe for human consumption in half an hour. If the water is muddy or if its integrity seems particularly questionable, it is good insurance to double the amount of halazone, and preferably the purifying time as well.

Care should be taken with chemical purifiers so employed to disinfect all points of contact with the container, so that the water once sterilized will not be easily reinfected. If a jar or canteen is being used together with halazone, replace the cover loosely and wait two or three minutes so that the tablets can dissolve. Then shake the contents thoroughly, allowing some of the fluid to spill out over the top and lips of the holder. Tighten the cover then and leave it that way for the desired time before using any of the liquid.

CHLORIDE OF LIME Chlorine in some form is regarded as the most dependable disinfectant for drinking water. When introduced in proper quantities it destroys any existing organisms, and for as long as enough remains in the water it prevents recurring contamination. It is better to err moderately on the side of overdosage if at all, for waters of varying chemical and physical composition react differently to equal quantities of a given disinfectant, just as two individuals are to some degree affected differently by like doses of an antibiotic.

Emergency chlorination of drinking water may be accomplished in three steps:

1. Dissolving one heaping tablespoon of chloride of lime in eight quarts of water

2. Adding one part of this solution to one hundred parts of the water to be disinfected

3. Waiting at least thirty minutes before using.

The stock solution should be kept tightly corked in a cool, dark place, and even then it should be frequently renewed.

IODINE AS A GERMICIDE Tincture of iodine can be used as an emergency water purifier. A drop of this fresh antiseptic, mixed thoroughly with one quart of water in the same manner as halazone, will generally make the water fit for human consumption in thirty minutes. Both the amount and the time may be doubled if this precaution seems warranted.

HOW TO RECOGNIZE POISONOUS WATER HOLES A few water holes, like those in the southwestern deserts of this continent, contain dissolved poisons such as arsenic. One is usually able to recognize such a water hole easily, partly because bones of unwary animals may be scattered about, but mainly because green vegetation will be conspicuously absent. The safest general rule, therefore, is to avoid any water holes around which green plants are not thriving.

HARD WATER

If the area where you are traveling has hard water to which you are not accustomed, severe digestive upset may result if, while getting used to it, you sip more than small amounts at any one time. Boiling may be of some help, inasmuch as when magnesia and lime carbonates are held in solution by carbon dioxide, these hardening agents can be partially solidified by using heat to drive off the gas.

WATER FILTRATION DEVICES

If the water you find is also muddy, stagnant, and foul-smelling, you can clear the water either by placing it in a container and letting it stand for 12 hours, or by pouring it through a filtering system. Note that these procedures only clear the water and make it more palatable. You will still have to purify it.

To make a filtering system, place 2 or 3 inches or layers of filtering material such as sand, crushed rock, charcoal, or cloth in bamboo, a hollow log, or an article of clothing. Remove the odor from water by adding charcoal from your fire. Let the water stand for 45 minutes before drinking it.

A WAY TO SWEETEN WATER

One evening you may make camp in a swamp or by a pond that has an unpleasant odor. It will be handy in such a contingency to know how to sweeten and purify water in a single operation.

This can usually be accomplished by dropping several bits of charred hardwood from the campfire into the boiling pot; fifteen or twenty minutes of simmering will usually do the job. Then skim away most of the foreign matter and either strain the water by pouring it through a clean cloth or, if you've plenty of time and utensils, merely allow it to settle.

IF WE ARE TO SURVIVE Bark may be used to fashion numerous types of water-holding containers. To make a primitive basin, one handy way is to scoop a hole in soft ground and to line that with a piece of waterproof canvas, plastic, or something similar. Do you want hot water? Scatter a few clean pebbles along the bottom of the water-filled receptacle and place on these, perhaps with temporary tongs made by bending a green stick back upon itself, stones that have been heating in the campfire.

WHEN WATER IS REPLENISHED When inadequate water supplies are eventually replenished, it will be inadvisable to drink a great deal at once. If the satisfaction is extended over several hours, the body will utilize the intake to the fullest possible extent instead of sluicing it through the system and dissipating a considerable amount wastefully in rapid elimination. Even when there is suddenly all the water we can possibly want, partaking of it too rapidly and in too large amounts will cause nausea.

Chapter 3
Fire

FIRE IS THE THIRD LINE OF PERSONAL PROTECTION and in most cases will not be a necessary source of heat if you've adequately met your clothing and shelter needs. In addition to providing light, warmth, and comfort, fire can also provide a source of heat for cooking and purifying water. For the reader seeking to eat in the woods without access to a backpacking stove or sterno, the skills involved in building a fire may be helpful.

BUILDING A FIRE When man-made heat sources are not available or don't meet your needs, you may elect to build a fire. Always use a safe site, and put the fire completely out, so that it is cold to the touch, before you leave. Locate the fire in close proximity to fire materials and your shelter. It should be built on flat, level ground and have adequate protection from the elements. Before starting the fire, prepare the site by clearing a 3-foot fire circle, scraping away all leaves, brush, and debris down to bare ground, if possible. To successfully build a fire, you need to have all three elements of the fire triad present—oxygen, fuel, and heat.

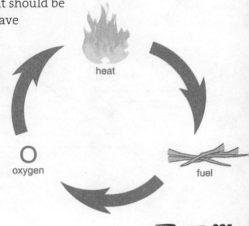

heat

oxygen

fuel

OXYGEN

Oxygen is necessary for the fuel to burn, and it needs to be present at all stages of a fire. To ensure this, you'll need a platform and brace. Gather or create a platform and brace before you start breaking your fuel down, and use it to keep smaller stages off the moist ground.

PLATFORM

A platform can be any dry material that protects your fuel from the ground, such as dry tree bark or dry nonporous rock. Waterlogged rocks may explode when heated; don't use them. In snow-covered areas, a snow platform may be necessary. To build this platform, use wrist-thick green logs and break or cut them into workable lengths (approximately 3 feet long). Construct a 3-foot-square platform by using two rows of the green logs. Place the top row perpendicular to the bottom row.

BRACE

A brace is vital. It ensures that the fire will get the oxygen it needs to exist. A 6-foot-long wrist-thick branch or a dry nonporous rock 2 to 3 inches high will suffice. (Again, don't use waterlogged rocks, as they may explode when heated.) Lay the brace on or next to the platform. Leaning the kindling against the brace, and over the tinder, allows oxygen to circulate within the fire.

Caution

Waterlogged rocks may explode when heated. Don't use them.

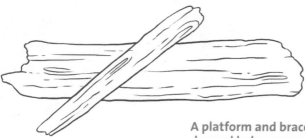

A platform and brace keep tinder dry and help ensure adequate oxygen flow to your fuel.

CATEGORIES OF FUEL

Fuel can be separated into three categories: tinder, kindling, and main fuel. Each builds upon the previous one. Before gathering the fuel, make sure to prepare your site and position the platform and brace in the center. Next, gather enough fuel to build three fires. This allows you to step back to a smaller fuel if your fire has problems igniting a larger stage. When breaking the fuel down, lay the smaller stages of kindling against the brace, keeping it off the ground and within reach of the fire you intend to build. The exact type of fuel used will vary depending on your location.

TINDER

Tinder is any material that will light from a spark. It's extremely valuable in getting the larger stages of fuel lit Tinder can be man-made or natural.

Man-Made Tinder

When venturing into the wilderness, always carry man-made tinder in your survival kit. If you should become stranded during harsh weather conditions, it may prove to be the key in having or not having a fire that first night. Since it is a one-time-use item, immediately start gathering natural tinder so that it can be dried out and prepared for use once your man-made tinder is used up. The most common man-made forms of tinder are petroleum-based compressed tinder tablets and solid compressed fuel tablets. Man-made tinder may need to be scraped or fluffed so it can catch a spark.

Natural Tinder

For natural tinder to work, it generally needs to be dry, have exposed edges, and allow oxygen to circulate within it. Gather natural materials for tinder before you need it so that you have time to dry it in the sun, between layers of your clothing, or by a fire. Remove any wet bark or pith before breaking the tinder down, and keep it off the damp ground during and after preparation. Some tinder will collect moisture from the air, so prepare it last and keep it dry until you're ready to use it. Natural tinder falls into three basic categories: bark; scrapings; and grass, ferns, and lichen. If you are uncertain if something will work for tinder, try it.

Bark

Prepare layered forms of tinder by working pieces of bark between your hands and fingers until they're light and airy. To do this, start by holding a long section of the bark with both hands, thumb to thumb. Use a back-and-forth twisting action, working the bark until it becomes fibrous. Next, place the fibrous bark between the palms of your hands and roll your hands back and forth until the bark becomes thin, light, and airy. At this point you should be able to light it from a spark. Prepare this tinder until you have enough to form a small bird's nest. Place any loose dust created from the process in the center of the nest. Many barks

Making wood shavings

will work as tinder, but birch is best because it will light even when wet, due to a highly flammable resin it contains.

Wood Scrapings

Wood scrapings or shavings are created by repeatedly running your knife blade at a 90-degree angle across a flat section of pitch wood, which is resinous pine, or heartwood, which is the nonliving, hard central wood of trees. To provide effective tinder, you'll need enough scrapings to fill the palm of your hand. Like birchbark, pitch wood will light even when wet. The high concentration of resin in the wood's fibers makes it highly flammable.

Breaking down bark

Grass, Ferns, Leaves, and Lichen

As with bark, fashion a bird's nest with these materials. You may need to break them down further, depending on the materials at hand. This form of tinder needs to be completely dry to work successfully.

KINDLING Kindling is usually comprised of twigs or wood shavings that range in diameter from a pencil lead to pencil thickness. It should easily light when placed on a small flame. Sources include small dead twigs found on the dead branches at the bottom of many trees; shavings from larger pieces of dry dead wood; small bundles of grass; heavy cardboard; and gasoline- or oil-soaked wood.

FUEL Fuel is any material that is thumb-size or bigger that will burn slowly and steadily once it is lit. Kinds of fuel include dry dead branches at the bottom of trees; heartwood (the dry inside portion of a dead standing tree, fallen tree, tree trunk, or large branch); green wood that is finely split; dry grasses twisted into bunches; and dry animal dung.

Dry, Dead Branches at the Bottom of Trees

This material is great during dry or very cold weather. It provides all of the various stages of fuel when broken down properly. To decrease the risk of injury, wear gloves to protect your hands, and protect your eyes by looking away when snapping the branch off the tree. If the branches are wet, you'll need to prepare them by scraping off all the wet bark and lichen. Run your knife across the wood's surface at a 90-degree angle. If it is still too wet, split the wood to expose its inner dry material.

Heartwood

Heartwood requires a lot more energy and time when used to build a fire. However, it is ideal during wet conditions when you need a dry surface that will easily ignite. The best source is a stump that has a sharp pointed top—in other words, a stump that wasn't created with a chainsaw. Stumps that have a flat surface can absorb massive amounts of moisture, especially when capped with snow. In addition, certain coniferous trees that die from natural causes will contain large amounts of pitch. This wood is commonly called pitch wood and is a great find when you are cold and in need of a quick fire, since it lights easily even under the worst conditions. To gather heartwood, pull, kick, or rip the pieces off of the stump. If unable to separate the wood from the stump, wedge a sturdy pole between the stump and a loose piece of wood, or use an ax or a large fixed-blade knife to help it along. A small-diameter standing dead tree can be knocked over and broken into workable sections by running it between two trees (a foot or so apart) and pulling one end back until the pole snaps in half. Once gathered, break the wood down from large to small. If using an ax or knife, follow basic safety rules.

Green Wood

If you have a hot fire, green wood that is finely split will burn. However, it should not be used in the early stages of your fire. To increase your odds of success, remove the outer bark and cambium layer.

Dry Grass Twisted into Bunches

Dry grass is not only great tinder, but also provides an excellent fuel when tied into bundles. If this is your only source of fuel, tie the grass into bundles that are 12 to 24 inches long with varying diameters, so that you can stage your fire up from small to big.

Animal Dung

Because herbivores eat grass and other plants, their dried dung makes excellent fuel. Break the dung into various sizes to create tinder, kindling, and fuel.

HEAT Heat is required to start a fire. Before applying heat to your fuel, however, make sure you have enough of each stage to light three fires. This allows you to step back to a smaller fuel when your fire has problems igniting a larger stage. Since matches and lighters often fail and will eventually run out, you must consider alternative sources of heat to start your fire. Options include both man-made (often spark-based) and primitive (friction-based) heat sources.

Man-Made and Spark-Based Heat Sources

Man-made heat sources include matches, lighters, artificial flint, flint and steel, pyrotechnics (flares), battery and steel wool, and convex glass. Most man-made heat sources are easy to use, and at least one should be part of your emergency survival kit.

Natural Friction-Based Heat Sources

Friction-based heat works through a process of pulverizing and heating appropriate woods until an ember is created. This ember can be used to ignite awaiting tinder. The biggest problems associated with these techniques are muscle fatigue, poor wood selection, and moisture that prevents the material from reaching a hot enough temperature.

Candles

Candles make a great heat and tinder source. Once lit, a candle can provide the heat needed to light tinder, or it can even serve as a fire's tinder. Stay-lit birthday candles are a good option, as are the eight- to ten-hour emergency-survival candles.

Once you have an ember, relax and take your time. Don't blow on it; the moisture from your mouth may put it out. If you feel it needs more oxygen, gently fan it with your hand. In most cases, however, simply waiting a few seconds will allow the ember to achieve its pleasant glow.

STEPS TO BUILDING A FIRE

When building a fire, it is important to gather enough fuel to build three knee-high fires. This allows you to go back to a previous stage if the fire starts to die and to keep the fire going while you get more material. Once the wood or other fuel is gathered, break it down from big to small, always preparing the smallest stages last. This will help decrease the amount of moisture your tinder and kindling collect during the preparation process. If conditions are wet, you'll need to strip off all lichen and bark, and for best results, split the branches in half to expose the inner dry wood. Construct a platform and brace (described earlier) and use the brace to keep the various stages of fuel off the ground while breaking it down.

Once all the stages are prepared, place the tinder on the platform next to the brace and light it. Use the brace to place your smaller kindling directly over the flame. Spread a handful of kindling over the flame all at once, instead of one stick at a time. Once the flames lick up through the kindling, place another handful perpendicularly across the first. When this stage is burning well, advance to the next size. Continue crisscrossing your fuel until the largest size is burning and the fire is self-supporting. If you have leftover material, set it aside in a dry place so that it can be used to start another fire later. If you have a problem building your fire, reevaluate your heat, oxygen, and fuel to determine which one is not present or is inadequate for success.

MAINTAINING A HEAT SOURCE

The best way to keep a flame is to provide an ongoing fuel source. The type of wood you use will directly impact this process. Softwoods such as cedar, pine, and fir provide an excellent light and heat source, but they burn up rather fast. Hardwoods such as maple, ash, oak, and hickory will burn longer and produce less smoke. These woods are ideal for use at night.

If you are staying in one place, bank the fire to preserve its embers for use at a later time. Once you have a good bed of coals, cover them with ashes and/or dry dirt. If done properly, the fire's embers will still be smoldering in the morning. To rekindle the fire, remove the dry dirt, lay tinder on the coals, and gently fan it until the tinder ignites.

COOKING ON FIRES

Campfires used to be a necessity in the backcountry; now they are usually a luxury. The growing number of backcountry travelers has resulted in the depletion of firewood in many areas, and the abuse of fire has caused everything from scarring to wildfires. Abuse is the key word here. Built properly, campfires can still be an enjoyable part of backcountry camping and cooking, but the decision to build one should never be made automatically or lightly. Regulations, ecological conditions, weather, skill, use level, and firewood availability should be considered when making the decision.

In a heavily used area, the best site for a fire is in an existing fire ring. In a pristine area, use Leave No Trace fire techniques. These techniques enable you to enjoy a fire without leaving any evidence. One quick minimum-impact method in sandy areas is a shallow pit fire. Scrape a depression several inches deep in a dry streambed, sandbar, or beach—any place with exposed soil that contains no decomposing organic material (mineral soil)—and build your fire in the depression. Never excavate a fire pit in vegetation. Research

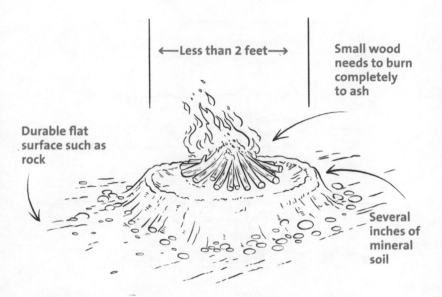

←—Less than 2 feet—→

Small wood needs to burn completely to ash

Durable flat surface such as rock

Several inches of mineral soil

has shown that fire pits dug in sod are still evident years later. Avoid environmental damage by using stoves and existing fire rings.

A platform or mound of mineral soil can also be used for a Leave No Trace fire. Simply pile up mineral soil into a flat-topped platform 6 to 8 inches thick and about 2 feet across and build your fire on top. The platform insulates the ground and prevents scarring. Where do you find mineral soil? Soil at the base of uprooted trees, sandy areas near streambeds, or exposed soil near boulder areas are all excellent sources. A tarp or fire cloth laid under the soil facilitates cleanup. Finally, portable fire pans, such as metal oil-drain pans or backyard barbecue grills, allow you to enjoy small fires with virtually no impact. The pan should be lined with mineral soil or propped up on small rocks to protect the surface underneath from heat.

The best firewood is small in diameter (1 to 2 inches), lying loose on the ground, and not attached to downed or standing timber. Small-diameter wood is easier to burn to ash and is less critical to the ecosystem. Gather wood from a wide area; do not denude the immediate surroundings. Collect only enough for a small fire.

Be sure to allow yourself enough time for thorough cleanup and camouflaging of the site. Regardless of whether you used an established fire ring or constructed a fire in a pristine area, burn all the wood down to cold ash. Crush any remaining charcoal. If the ash is cool enough to sift through your fingers, your fire is out. Scatter the remains and any leftover firewood far from the site.

If you constructed a mound fire, after scattering the leftover ash and small bits of charcoal, return the soil to where you found it.

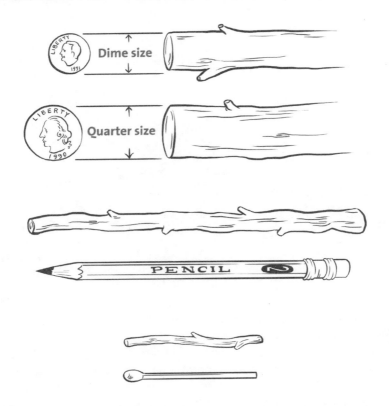

The best widths and lengths of wood to use for a cooking fire

If the mound was built on a rock, rinse the rock off. When using a shallow pit, disperse the ash and fill in the pit with the excavated soil. Finally, camouflage the area to match the surroundings. This allows others to enjoy the same site later. Leaving no trace means leaving your cook site as clean as you found it (or cleaner) for the benefit of future campers.

Chapter 4
Cooking in the Wild

EATING PLANTS   Although some plants or plant parts are edible raw, you must cook others to be edible or palatable. Section I provides details on how to best cook different plants.

EATING ANIMALS   If possible, keep all animals alive until ready to consume. This ensures that the meat stays fresh. A small rodent or rabbit may attract big game, so be sure to protect it from becoming a coyote's meal instead of yours. This doesn't apply, of course, if you are using the rodent for bait.

EATING FISH   You can impale a whole fish on a stick and cook it over an open fire. However, boiling the fish with the skin on is the best way to get the most food value. The fats and oil are under the skin, and, by boiling, you can save the juices for broth. Any of the methods used to cook plant food can also be used to cook fish. Or pack fish into a ball of clay and bury it in the coals of a fire until the clay hardens; break open the clay ball to get to the cooked fish. Fish is done when the meat flakes off. If you plan to keep the fish for later, smoke or fry it. To prepare fish for smoking, cut off the head and remove the backbone.

Fish can remain edible for considerable lengths of time when their heads have been removed and their individual flesh has been split into a pair of fillets. By keeping the meat over a smoldering fire for several days, the fillets will eventually become completely dehydrated, and you will have what can rightly be referred to as fish jerky.

RARE OR WELL DONE When food supplies are limited, nothing should be cooked longer than is considered necessary for palatability. The only exception is when there may be germs or parasites to be destroyed.

The more that food is subjected to heat, the greater are the losses of nutritive values. Even the practice of making toast diminishes both bread's proteins and its digestibility. The single greatest universal error made in preparing venison and similar game meat for the table is overcooking, which, in addition to drying it out, tends to make the meat tough and stringy. What this practice does to the flavor is a matter of opinion.

SCURVY EASILY PREVENTED AND CURED Scurvy, a disease caused by lack of vitamin C in the diet, is initially characterized by fatigue, bleeding gums and mucous membranes, and spots on the skin; if not treated, it can eventually lead to tooth loss, open wounds, fever, and even death. Scurvy is a very definite risk when fresh food is habitually overcooked, especially under survival conditions, as oxidation destroys the inherent vitamin C. It is, however, easily prevented or cured by eating fresh foods either raw or minimally cooked.

IMPROVISED COOKING AND EATING UTENSILS Even if you don't have a frying pan when on your own in the woods, the oversight need not be fatal. Just a few cooking utensils will make the job of preparing meals easier. Yet the more often you feast on such repasts as fat red sirloin that has been cooked on a forked green stick, the more pleasure you'll find in such primitively cooked foods.

Tidbits of meat skewered on a green wand thrust briefly into flames to seal in the juices, and then cooked not too near the steady heat of glowing coals, are one of life's great pleasures. You may like to gnaw each bite-size morsel off the stick as wanted, returning the spit to the warmth in between times so as to keep the remaining kabobs sizzling.

Many materials may be used to make equipment for the cooking, eating, and storing of food. Suppose you are without cooking implements and want to heat a liquid. Some large shells may be lying about, or perhaps you can find a stone with a hollow in it. If the stone is small enough, build a fire around it. If it is too ponderous for that, then why not preheat it by lighting the conflagration in the cavity itself?

You can fold a large rectangle of moist birchbark inward at each of its four corners and hold the resulting receptacle together with wooden skewers. A long wide strip of bark can also be folded in at the two ends to make a container shaped outwardly like a split log. A round piece of bark, first soaked if necessary to render it sufficiently pliable, can be tucked in at one end to make a conical cup.

It is usually a matter of some wonderment, when you first try it, to find that water can actually be boiled in something as unpretentious as birchbark if flames are kept from touching this above the water level. It is also easy enough to drop some clean pebbles into a large inflammable container and then add hot stones from a campfire, handling them with tongs made by bending a limber green stick.

Bowls and Pots

Use wood, bone, horn, , bark, large shells, or other similar material to make bowls.

To make wooden pots, use a hollowed-out piece of wood that will hold your food and enough water to cook it in. Bamboo is the best wood for making cooking containers, if you cut out a section between two sealed joints. *Caution:* Trapped air and water will cause a sealed section of bamboo to explode if heated.

Caution

A sealed section of bamboo will explode if heated because of trapped air and water in the section.

If you have a cord or wire to fashion a handle, hang the wooden container over the fire and add hot rocks to the water and food. Remove the rocks as they cool and add more hot rocks until your food is cooked. *Caution:* Do not use rocks with air pockets, such as limestone or sandstone. They may explode while heating in the fire.

You can also use this method with containers made of bark or leaves. However, these containers will burn above the waterline unless you keep them moist or keep the fire low.

Turtle shells make excellent pots. First thoroughly boil the upper portion of the shell, then use it to heat food and water over a flame.

Forks, Knives, and Spoons

Carve forks, knives, and spoons from nonresinous woods so that you do not do not taint the food or get a wood resin aftertaste. Nonresinous woods include oak, birch, and other hardwood trees. *Caution:* Do not use wood from trees that secrete a syrup or resin-like liquid on the bark or when cut.

Water Bottles

Make water bottles from the stomachs of larger animals. Thoroughly flush the stomach out with water, then tie off the bottom. Leave the top open, with some means of fastening it closed.

Caution

Do not use rocks with air pockets, such as limestone and sandstone. They may explode while heating in the fire.

Caution

Do not use wood from trees that secrete a syrup or resin-like liquid on the bark or when cut.

COOKING TECHNIQUES

In addition to killing parasites and bacteria, cooking your food can make it more palatable. There are many different ways to prepare game, and some are better than others from a nutritional standpoint. Boiling is best, but only if you drink the broth, which contains many of the nutrients that are cooked out of the food. Fried foods taste great, but frying is probably the worst way to cook something, as a lot of nutrients are lost during the process.

Boiling

Boiling is the best cooking method. If a container is not available, it may be necessary to improvise one. As described above, you might use a rock with a bowl-shaped center, but avoid rocks with high moisture content, as they may explode. A thick, hollowed-out piece of wood that can be suspended over the fire may also serve as a container. If your container cannot be suspended over the fire, stone boiling is another option. Use a hot bed of coals to heat up numerous stones. Get them really hot. Set your container of food and water close to your bed of hot stones, and add rocks to it until the water begins to boil. To keep the water boiling, cover the top of the container with bark or another improvised lid, and keep it covered except when removing or adding stones. Don't expect a rolling rapid boil with this process, but a steady slow bubbling should occur.

Broiling on a Stick

A fish, bird, or small animal may be cleaned and then impaled on a green hardwood stick. The top of the stick itself can be split and reinforced if necessary at either or both ends of the cleft by its own twisted and tied bark, clamped over the food. Many of us find it preferable to sear meat by shoving it momentarily into the blaze and then holding it over a bed of embers, scraping a few to one side of the fire if the flames are still blazing ardently. The prime secret of such campfire cookery, if it is to be most successful, is to cook unhurriedly with the uniform hotness of hardwood coals.

If we have other matters to attend to before eating, we can lay the spit between two crotched uprights, prop it over a stone, or merely push one end into the ground, thereafter pausing only to examine and occasionally to turn the meat until the meal is ready.

Baking on a Stick

Baking on a stick is so handy, especially when you are preparing small amounts to be eaten hot. You can prepare bannock, aka pan bread, in this fashion while kabobs are sputtering, having carried the dry ingredients ready-mixed so that nothing remains but to add enough water to make a stiff dough.

The basic recipe for this backwoods bread consists of a cup of flour, a teaspoon of baking powder, and ¼ teaspoon of salt. To this may be added, depending on taste and availability, a variety of spices and fruits as well as sugar and shortening or other fat.

Select a peeled green stick as thick as the forearm of a rifle. Quickly, so as not to release the carbon dioxide gas that is created and which makes the bread rise, twist the dough and the stick in a spiral ribbon. Secure the ends with plugs of dough to help keep the soft mass in place during baking. Rotate over a low bed of hot coals (not an open flame).

Baking on a Wooden Slab

Fish can be pegged on preheated, presoaked, green, hardwood slabs and leaned over a bank of glowing coals. If after they are opened and cleaned there is any difficulty in making them lie reasonably flat with their skin against the wood, the backbone may be removed. Rotating the slab a time or two will give the flesh a better opportunity to become flaky throughout.

The reason for using hardwood will be well understood by those who have learned from experience how pines and other evergreens can flavor food strongly enough to create an unpleasant taste. The wet green hardwood that grows beside streams is in general a particularly good choice, as it is even less prone to burning. Birch does burn readily when green, although it is worth using with a slight amount of extra care, as it imparts a delicately sweet smoky aroma. Birch or dry hardwoods may be soaked in water for at least 30 minutes before use to help prevent them from burning.

Such a slab, and a flat rock as well, can also be heated and used like a hot plate.

Steaming in a Hole

A hole for steaming is most easily scooped out of sand. A fire should already be blazing nearby, and in it a few stones should be heating. Be sure, however, that the stones are not porous, such as limestone or sandstone, and are not taken from a stream bed, as these may contain water and when heated may crack or even explode.

Place the hot stones in the hole, press a thick layer of wet green growth such as seaweed or damp grass over them, lay on the food, add an upper sheathing of similar damp vegetation, and then fill in the rest of the cavity with sand or loam. Using a stick, open enough of an inlet to allow some additional water to be poured on the rocks, and then stamp the topping down to compact it.

The food can then be safely left to steam until you're ready for it. As might be expected, the length of the cooking process depends on a number of variables, but usually requires at least several hours.

Baking in Mud

What amounts to small individual ovens can be provided by covering a fish, bird, or small animal with stiff, moist mud that has a clay texture to it, about an inch thick. This clay may be worked into a sheet on the ground and then shaped around the food like dough, or the article may be dipped and re-dipped as often as necessary in a thinner mixture. Tightly seal the fish or bird within the clay.

You may want to remove entrails from your meal before covering it, but no scaling, plucking, or skinning should be done, for this will be accomplished in a single operation when we break open and strip off the hard adobe made by laying the whole thing in hot ashes, above which a fire is burning. The tighter the seal, the better it will hold the juices and prevent the meat from drying out. A medium-size bird or trout will usually cook in about fifteen to twenty minutes, depending on the temperature of your coals.

Baking with a Campfire

You can use coals from your campfire to create a backcountry Dutch oven for baking. Set a flat-lidded pan with no plastic parts on a flat bed of coals, and shovel coals onto the lid in an even layer for even cooking. The coals should feel very hot but not quite burn when you hold your hand 6 inches away for 8 seconds. They can be cooled by spreading them out or sprinkling them with sand. The coals on the top should be hotter than those on the bottom. Replenish coals as they go dead.

Another great way to create a makeshift stove is to use a low flame under the baking pan (again, one that has no plastic parts) and build a small fire with twigs on the lid. This is called a "twiggy" fire and demands a level of care similar to that of a larger fire (regulations, wind, wood replenishment, and so forth). Bake slowly over a very low flame, offsetting the pan so that more than just the center gets heat and rotating it every few minutes to cook evenly. You can balance the pan on a flat rock and spread burning twigs around the sides to cook the outside edges.

Be careful when you check the progress of your baked goods. It's safest to scrape all the coals or twigs off the lid before you peek.

Don't peek too often (unless you smell burning), because the escaped heat cuts efficiency. Always wear an expendable pair of gloves— or better yet, a pair of oven mitts—when baking over an open fire.

Another technique is to flip bake. This method works best with stiff breads and cakes and when you have a fairly heavy-gauge lid for the baking pan. Make sure you grease and flour the pan thoroughly, including the inside of the lid. When the dough is firm and cooked most of the way through, loosen the edges with a spatula and then flip the bread or cake onto the lid. Place the lid directly on the heat to finish cooking the top. You can also flip the entire baked good in the pan to cook both sides. This works especially well with biscuits, bread, or brownies.

Use a rock to balance your pan in order to cook around the edges.

Other baking tips:

- Choose backcountry baking pans that are lightweight, have nonstick surfaces, and are of a relatively heavy gauge to distribute the often intense heat of fires and portable stoves.

- Fill the pan only half full, since baked goods rise.

- Never fill the pan to the point that ingredients touch the lid, or they'll burn.

- Rotate the pan every few minutes to ensure even baking. This is called the "round the clock" method.

- Use a frying pan turned upside down for rolling dough. Take a clean plastic bag, split it in half the long way, and cover the pan with it, dusting with flour to prevent sticking. Improvise a rolling pin from a water bottle or a fishing rod case wrapped in clean plastic bags and dusted with flour.

Oven in a Clay Bank

If the chances are that you will be in one place long enough to make the effort, you may elect to make an oven in a clay slope or bank. One way to commence this is by hammering a sharpened pole about as thick as your forearm straight down into the bank about 3 feet back from the edge.

Then, a foot or so down the side of the bank—far enough to allow a sturdy ceiling—scoop out an oven the size that you want. A usual procedure is to shape it like a beehive, with a narrow entrance. Dig back a little beyond the pole, which you'll then pull out to form the chimney. You can give the interior a hard coating by smoothing and re-smoothing it with wet hands. A small blaze may then be kindled within to harden this lining.

It is very possible that you will be able to find an old burrow to serve as the basis for such a contrivance. Or, at the other extreme, you can do as I have in New Mexico: construct a rough form of arched green sticks, and daub wet clay in thick layers over this. These successive layers may be allowed to dry in the sun, or each succeeding process can be quickened by small fires lit within.

Baking in such an oven is simplicity itself. Preheat the oven with a fire kindled inside, then scrape out the fire and ashes. Lay the food within on stones or nonpoisonous green leaves, or whatever may be handy. Tightly close both flue and front opening. Then go about your business while the meal cooks without further attention.

Cooking in Ashes

Many of us have at one time or another roasted vegetables in the ashes of a campfire, perhaps merely dropping or shoving them out of sight or, more scientifically, baring a heated bit of ground where the vegetables could be deposited and warm ashes and embers pushed over them. As with most such cooking, timing is a matter of some experimentation.

A few have even baked bread in this fashion. When we remember that the white of hardwood ashes can be substituted in equal parts for baking soda, this practice may not seem so unusual after all.

Leaf Baking

Wrapping your meat in a nonpoisonous green leaf and placing it on a hot bed of coals will protect, season, and cook the meat. When baking mussels and clams, seaweed is often used; when the shells open, they're done. Avoid using plants that have a bitter taste.

Underground Baking

Underground baking is very similar to underground steaming and is a good method of cooking larger meals, since the dirt will hold the oven's heat. Dig a hole slightly larger than the meal you intend to cook; it needs to be big enough for your food, the base of rocks, and the covering. Line the bottom and sides with rocks, avoiding rocks with high moisture content, which may explode. Start a fire over them. To heat rocks that will be used on top of your food, place enough green branches over the hole to support another layer of rocks, leaving a space to add fuel to the fire. Once the green branches burn through and a hot bed of coals is present, remove the fallen rocks. Place green twigs onto the coals, followed by a layer of wetted green grass or nonpoisonous leaves. Add your meat and vegetables, and cover them with more wet grass or leaves, a thin layer of soil, and the extra hot rocks. Then cover the hole with dirt. Small meals will cook in 1 to 2 hours; large meals in 5 to 6 hours or perhaps days.

Making a Soup Hole

You've just killed a moose. Hungry, you've a hankering for nothing quite as much as some hot soup, flavored perhaps with wild leeks whose flat leaves you see wavering nearby. Why not take the sharp end of a dead limb and scoop a small hole in the ground? Why not line this concavity with a piece of fresh hide? Then after adding the water and other ingredients, why not let a few hot clean stones do your cooking while you finish dressing out the animal?

Frying

Place a flat rock on or next to the fire. Again, avoid rocks with high moisture content, as they may explode. Let the rock get hot, and cook directly on it as you would a frying pan.

Broiling

Broiling is ideal for cooking small game over hot coals. Before cooking the animal, sear its flesh in the flames from the fire. This will help keep the juices, containing vital nutrients, inside the animal. Next, run a nonpoisonous skewer—a branch that is small, straight, and strong—along the underside of the animal's backbone. Suspend the skewered animal over the coals, laying the skewer across two forked sticks positioned upright on either side of the fire, or using any means available.

Barbeque

If you have enough fat meat to warrant the sacrifice of some nutriment in exchange for the psychological stimulus of a barbeque, you may want to allow a hardwood blaze to crumble to embers in a pit, over which green poles can then be spread and slabs of meat lain.

These chunks should be turned after a minute or two to sear in the juices, which will be further guarded if during subsequent handling the meat is not cut or pierced. The flavor will be better if any flames that lick up from time to time, particularly when grease begins to drop, are immediately quelled.

BUTCHERING

Butchering offers no particular problem for anyone with a sharp knife. If you are without a knife, as sometimes happens, you can improvise as well as possible with a thin-edged rock or the jagged end of a dead limb, puncturing and tearing more than cutting.

Birds can be dressed in a few moments with bare hands alone. The feathers can be plucked out with the least damage to the succulent skin when the fowl is still warm. If you have more birds than time, you may strip off the skin and feathers in one smooth operation.

If you see a small pouch near where the neck disappears into the body, pull that off and perhaps examine it to see what the species is eating, for it is the crop, which should be removed. Then pull the bird open, grasping it above and below the ribs. When you take out the viscera thus revealed, save the heart and liver. The gizzard is good, too, once it has been opened and emptied.

Animals are often most easily skinned when hung by the separated hind legs. Cut around each ankle, then slit up the inside of the leg to join a long cut made from the vent up the abdomen of the animal to the throat. Do the same with each foreleg. Then pull down the skin, using the cutting edge whenever it becomes necessary to free the hide from the body.

Carefully open an animal from the vent (anus) up through the ribs and pull out all the innards with as little cutting and puncturing as possible. Liver, kidneys, and heart are the parts most often saved. The flavor of small creatures such as muskrats is improved when care is taken to cut out the stringy white scent glands from the insides of the forelegs and thighs.

Blood Sausage

After an animal has been killed, slit its neck and collect the blood in a container. Mix all of the scrap meat with the blood and cook it slowly over a warm fire. Once it has become similar to hamburger in consistency, it is ready for the next step. The intestines from medium to large game animals provide a perfect skin for your blood sausage. You will need to clean them thoroughly inside and out in hot water before using. Cut the intestine into 6- to 8-inch sections and use line to tie off one end of each. Next, pack the cooked blood and meat into skin so that it is tight—but not so tight as to tear it—and tie off the open end. Finally, smoke the sausage in the same fashion as described on page 318. The smoking time will depend on many factors, but it usually ranges between 6 and 12 hours. You'll know the sausage is done when it has the consistency of store-bought sausage and is no longer moist.

How to Best Blowflies

If blowflies lay their eggs on meat, maggots will hatch within a few hours or days. Meat can be protected from blowflies by keeping it in a dark cold place such as a dry cave, by hanging it clear of foliage at least 4 yards above the ground, or to some extent by suspending fresh chunks in the smoke of a small fire until a protective casing hardens around them.

PRESERVING MEAT BY DRYING

One of the easiest primitive ways to preserve meat is by drying it to make jerky. This can be done by cutting it into long thin strips and hanging them apart in the sun, whereupon they will eventually lose most of their water content and become dry, hard, black, and, incidentally, both sustaining and delicious.

The strips can be soaked first, if one desires, either in brine or sea water. One method is to boil down ocean water until it becomes extremely salty, then simmer and dip the strips in this. If there is no place handy to hang the meat, it can be laid on sun-heated rocks and turned every hour or so.

The process that Colonel Townsend Whelen describes may become your favorite as it has mine:

Jerky is lean meat cut in strips and dried over a fire or in the sun. Cut the lean, fresh red meat in long wide strips about half an inch thick. Hang these on a wood framework about four to six feet off the ground. Under the rack, build a small, slow, smoky fire of any nonresinous wood. Let the meat dry in the sun and wind. Cover it at night or in rain. It should dry in several days.

The fire should not be hot enough to cook the meat at all, its chief use being in keeping flies away from it. When jerked, the meat will be hard and more or less black outside, and will keep almost indefinitely away from damp and flies.

It is best eaten just as it is; just bite off a chunk and chew. Eaten thus, it is quite tasty. It may also be cooked in stews. It is very concentrated and nourishing, and a little goes a long way as an emergency ration, but alone it is not a good food for long-continued consumption, as it lacks the necessary fat.

The fat, which would turn rancid, should be trimmed off before the drying operation is commenced. The fat may be rendered for later use as a food supplement or for more immediate employment in the manufacture of pemmican, a paste of dried meat pounded to shreds or powder and mixed with melted fat.

Sun-Drying

To sun-dry meat, hang long, thin strips in the sun. To keep it out of other animals' reach, run snare wire or line between two trees. If using snare wire, skewer the line through the top of each piece of meat before attaching it to the second tree. If using other line, hang it first and then drape the strips of meat over it. For best results, the meat should not touch its other side or another piece. It may take one to multiple days to dry, depending on the humidity and temperature. You'll know the meat is done when it is dark and brittle.

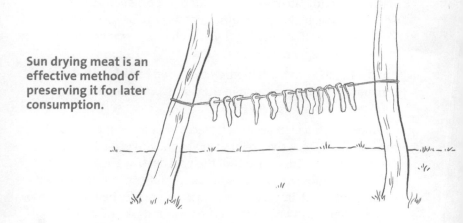

Sun drying meat is an effective method of preserving it for later consumption.

Smoking

Smoke long, thin strips of meat in a smoker constructed using the following guidelines.

A smoker is a quick, efficient method of meat preservation.

1. Build a 6-foot-tall tripod from three poles lashed together.

2. Attach snare wire or line around the three poles in a tiered fashion so that the lowest point is at least 2 feet above the ground.

3. If using snare wire, skewer it through the top of each slice of meat before extending it around the inside of the next pole. If using other line, hang it first and then drape the strips of meat over it. For best results, the meat should not touch its other side or another piece.

4. Cover the outer aspect of the tripod with any available material, such as a poncho. Avoid contact between the outer covering and the meat. For proper ventilation, leave a small opening at the top of the tripod.

5. Gather an armload of green deciduous wood, such as alder, willow, aspen, hickory, mesquite, or fruitwoods like apple. Prepare it by either breaking the branches into smaller pieces or cutting the bigger pieces into chips.

6. Build a fire next to the tripod. Once a good bed of coals develops, transfer them to the ground in the center of the smoker. Continue transferring coals as needed.

7. To smoke the meat, place small pieces or chips of green wood on the hot coals. Once the green wood begins to heat up, it should create a smoke. Since an actual fire will destroy the smoking process, monitor the wood to ensure that it doesn't flame up. If it does, put it out, but try to avoid disturbing the bed of coals too much. Keep adding chips until the meat is dark and brittle, about 24 to 48 hours. At this point it is done.

Pemmican

Made from dehydrated meat, dried berries, and suet tallow (rendered animal fat most often taken from the loin and kidney area), pemmican creates an excellent meal for later use.

Noted outdoorsman Colonel Townsend Whelen recommends the following procedure:

> To make pemmican you start with jerky and shred it by pounding. Then take a lot of raw animal fat, cut it into small pieces about the size of walnuts, and dry these out in a pan over a slow fire, not letting the grease boil up. When the grease is all out of the lumps, discard these and pour the hot fat over the shredded jerky, mixing the two together until you have about the consistency of ordinary sausage. Then pack the pemmican in waterproof bags. The Indians used skin bags.

The ideal proportion of lean and fat in pemmican by weight is approximately one-half well-dried lean meat and one-half rendered fat. It takes about five pounds of fresh lean meat to make one pound of dried meat suitable for pemmican. Add about ¾ cup dried berries for every one cup of meat in the recipe.

Such true pemmican, extremely seldom obtainable commercially, will afford practically every necessary food element.